"Dealing with inequality and maximising chances for all children requires the best education can muster. However, in practice we see an enormous amount of time and talent of both teachers and students wasted. Taking a Lean perspective helps to empower teachers and improve educational outcomes. Close to a thousand schools, supported by the leerKRACHT-foundation, experience this power of Lean every day. This book adds a valuable new perspective on Lean and education, and how to make most of the talents of students and teachers!"

Jaap Versfelt
founder of leerKRACHT and former
senior-partner at McKinsey & Company

"Professor Wiegel's workshops provided inspiration and plenty of lightbulb moments on how to transform university education to meet the challenges and opportunities of the 21st Century."

Dr. Lizann Bonnar
Vice Dean (Academic), Faculty of Humanities
and Social Sciences, University of Strathclyde
Senior Teaching Fellow, School of Psychological
Sciences and Health, University of Strathclyde

"The application of Lean in education has historically focused on nonacademic and academic support processes. Wiegel provides the first insightful, comprehensive, and practical approach integrating Lean in the core academic processes of teaching, learning, and curriculum development. This book provides a framework, based on research and practice, which demonstrates how faculty, academic programs, and educational institutions can apply Lean as a strategy to the mutual benefit of students, teachers, and the educational process."

William K. Balzer, Ph.D.
Professor of Industrial – Organizational Psychology
Vice President, Faculty Affairs and Strategic Initiatives
Bowling Green State University

"Workshops delivered by Professor Wiegel quickly clarify how powerful the use of Lean management philosophy is in the context of Education. His expertise and enthusiasm is inspiring."

Professor Debbie Willison, Ph.D. CChem FRSC PFHEA
Vice Dean (Academic), Faculty of Science
University of Strathclyde, Glasgow, Scotland

"As the Chair of Lean HE and as a lean practitioner here in Edinburgh Napier University I am so excited about Vincent's new book. We know how Lean can unlock many benefits for universities and I have seen real improvements with applying Lean approaches in universities. Many Lean practitioners focus on the office operational and service processes upon which universities, their students, teachers, and researchers rely. Vincent's work cuts to the heart of education however, focusing on the learning process itself. As a leader in designing innovative educational processes, Vincent is in a unique position to tell this story, which has the real potential to transform how we educate our people at every stage and critical to how we approach the challenges ahead of us."

Steve Yorkstone
Chair for the Lean Higher Education
Global Committee, Business Improvement
Consultant, Edinburgh Napier University

Lean in the Classroom

The Powerful Strategy for Improving Student Performance and Developing Efficient Processes

Vincent Wiegel

A PRODUCTIVITY PRESS BOOK

Dealing with inequality and maximising chances for all children requires the best education can muster. However, in practice we see an enormous amount of time and talent of both teachers and students wasted. Taking a Lean perspective helps to empower teachers and improve educational outcomes. Close to a thousand schools, supported by the leerKRACHT-foundation, experience this power of Lean every day. This book adds a valuable new perspective on Lean and education, and how to make most of the talents of students and teachers!

Jaap Versfelt, founder of leerKRACHT and former senior-partner at McKinsey & Company

First edition published in 2020
by Routledge/Productivity Press
52 Vanderbilt Avenue, 11th Floor New York, NY 10017
2 Park Square, Milton Park, Abingdon, Oxon OX14 4RN, UK

Routledge/Productivity Press is an imprint of Taylor & Francis Group, an Informa business

No claim to original U.S. Government works

Printed on acid-free paper

International Standard Book Number-13: 978-1-138-32313-1 (Hardback)
International Standard Book Number-13: 978-0-429-83701-2 (eBook)

Library of Congress Cataloging-in-Publication Data

Names: Wiegel, Vincent, author.
Title: Lean in the classroom : the powerful strategy for improving student performance and developing efficient processes / Vincent Wiegel.
Description: New York : Taylor & Francis, 2020.
Identifiers: LCCN 2019016904 (print) | LCCN 2019981295 (ebook) | ISBN 9781138323131
Subjects: LCSH: Effective teaching. | Education--Philosophy. | Educational change. | Academic achievement.
Classification: LCC LB1025.3 .W454 2020 (print) | LCC LB1025.3 (ebook) | DDC 371.102--dc23
LC record available at https://lccn.loc.gov/2019016904
LC ebook record available at https://lccn.loc.gov/2019981295

Visit the Taylor & Francis Web site at
http://www.taylorandfrancis.com

and the CRC Press Web site at
http://www.crcpress.com

Dedicated to Giel

Contents

SECTION II   Lean in the Classroom

SECTION III   In Support of Lean Education

Preface

On April 3rd and 4th, 2018, a special classroom event took place. The classroom was the production facility of a prefab concrete factory. The pupils were high school students, high school teachers, university undergraduates, lecturers from the university, workers from the shop floor, and shift supervisors. The subject matter was industrial robotics. They all learned from each other and together as one group of students. There were three subject matter experts to guide the group. Their assignment: finding applications for industrial robots in a company that deployed none, and they had 2 days.

This special occasion was the culmination of several years of increasingly experimental forms of education. None had been so complex, so diverse, nor so satisfactory. The banner was crossing educational borders, it's intent, the exploration of the learning process and concepts like learner agency. It was made possible through an educational innovation award that was awarded for a previous initiative: New Engineers. New Engineers is a post-bachelor education initiative that some colleagues, Lejla Brouwer-Hadzialic, Hide van der Geld, Nienke Vos, Carina Pullens and I started. In this study we work with industry some educational pioneers come together to increase the relevance and impact of technical education. New Engineers mixes freshly graduated engineers and experienced staff from the industry to learn and develop knowledge, attitude, and skills. The topics covered have a broad range. The teaching formats are experimental and innovative.

These events grew out of my increasing discomfort with the way we organize our education. As a professor for 10 years at the HAN University of applied sciences, I had come to realize we needed to go about teaching in a different way. Bottom line: we waste too much of our students' talent. Lean is quintessentially about adding more value through the reduction of waste. We do so by looking at processes and organizations through the eyes of the person for whom we deliver our services and products. As a Lean practitioner and theorist, I have been applying and teaching Lean to others for many years. Around 2010, we gradually started applying the Lean philosophy to our own school. The application was limited to support processes like scheduling, administration, etc. It was successful. We reduced lead times for scheduling, increased room occupancy rates, streamlined enrollments processes, etc. It became increasingly clear that we ought to start somewhere else: the primary process. The primary process, the most important process of education, is the process of learning. Anyone who skips the primary process runs the risk of barking up the wrong tree. We might be streamlining something we ought not do at all. As we started applying Lean to our own teaching processes, we learned a lot. The knowledge we gained we used to help other schools. As it turned out, we weren't the only ones experimenting this way, though we were, and still are a clear minority. Several primary schools had preceded us in applying Lean to learning and teaching.

This book grew out of my personal frustration as a professor, my experiments, the joy of learning as an educator, and the wonderful interactions with students, teachers, administrators, and industry experts. All who are passionate about their work, care for our children, and are eager to pass on their knowledge, know-how, scars, and pride. But who are also eager to keep learning. We need much more of that. We are working in an educational system that despite best intentions wastes talent of students and teachers on a grand scale. With Lean Education, we have an approach that supports those who want to improve education in a way that is not done unto the teachers, but driven by teachers. By eliminating wasteful activities, we free up time for teachers to do what they are good at and passionate about.

With this book, I intend to provide much more than a personal story. It is based on extensive scientific and practical research over many years. The book is, however, above all, meant as an inspiration with practical guidelines for all those who are eager to move things in education. This book defines a young and new field of theory and practice: Lean Education. The scope is therefore wide: ranging from the primary processes of education to strategy, from the need for change to professional services. The reader will find ample footnotes with references to sources to deepen a topic. As a new field there is much to do, to investigate, and to learn. It builds upon valuable work already done by others. I hope it will give rise to many more publications that will improve on the basic ideas expounded in this book. The book will also be of interest to readers that are more action oriented through concrete case studies and practical action schemes.

There is some irony in writing a book about Lean Education. One of the core tenets and ideals of Lean Education is that you meet the student where they are at and provide them with what they need in the form they need it. For you as reader, I ought to provide what you need in the form you need it. A book by its very nature excludes the direct interaction and feedback required to tune the offering. It also is just one form. I tried to remedy some of these inherent shortcomings by partitioning the book to fit different reader groups. I also included four different formats: infographics, cases, hands-on guidelines, and close argued texts. Finally, I added ample references that will enable the reader to follow-up.

The book is structured around three sections. Section I, the backdrop against which the need for change in education arises is described in Chapters 1 through 3. It describes the "why" of Lean Education. By understanding the drivers for change and the challenges they pose, it will be easier to determine the changes that are needed. Section II, in which the approach to develop and provide education is detailed in Chapters 4 through 7. It focuses on the "what and how" of Lean Education. It addresses how to apply Lean Education. It explains how Lean in the classroom works in an everyday way. It addresses both teaching classes, but also the development of new classes and courses. It does so in a way that is pedagogically sound, building upon recent insights from educational research. Section III, Chapters 8 and 9, address what is required to make learning and teaching a success. Success in education requires not just good teaching and good classes, teaching is facilitated through professional services and guided through strategy. These are essential in directing the innovation and the underlying support for the actual teaching.

Readers can get a quick overview of the book by checking out the infographics and the introduction at the beginning of Chapters 1 through 9, plus the case and "HANDS-ON!" guidelines sections at the end. The cases and guidelines are recognizable by their different typographical mark-up. The core of each chapter expands the main focus of that chapter and provides argumentation and references. Readers that are primarily interested in the educational aspects are advised to read the introduction, but can skip Chapters 1 through 3.

The book is closed by an extensive case description of New Engineers case in which I am involved. With help of many people, I decided to put the ideas expounded in this book to the test and set up a new school by way of experiment. As a good friend of mine, John Maes, likes to say, "talking about bulls is something entirely different from standing in the arena." So, I know from firsthand experience that the ideas are sound, some were adjusted based on the experience. I also know that it is not easy, there are no free lunches. But more than anything I can ensure the reader that is a joyful experience! With the end in mind, readers might start with chapter 10 to get a picture of what the book is leading up to.

It is empathically a book about Lean in education and not about Lean in general. I tried to reduce management speak to a minimum and always relate it to the educational practice. At some places in the book, Lean terms will feature more prominently to explain what Lean in "Lean Education" is. In most parts, experienced Lean practitioners will have to make the connection with education themselves. I'm confident that the book has been written in such a way that they will easily recognize what Lean concepts are being used. I hope they will find the clarification on the link between education and Lean useful to embark on Lean initiatives in education. Administrators and policymakers will be familiar with both the educational and managerial aspects that are addressed in this book. To them, the book will hopefully make a clear case for Lean Education and provide them with a frame of reference for their work in leading schools. Teachers will find inspiration and practical help to put learning and their professionalism first.

In this book, I will refer to teachers, lecturers, and professors interchangeably. In various cultures and languages, as well as in different schooling systems, job titles vary. In some systems, "professor" refers to academics with a so-called full professorship at a university, whereas in others, it designates both these, but also teachers at high schools. My reference is to all staff involved in the process of learning and in the acquisition of knowledge and skills. "Educator" is the common signifier I will use to refer to this staff in the educational sector. Likewise, the reference to people who are learning varies. Sometimes they are referred to as students and sometimes as pupils. Again, I will use these terms interchangeably. Our pupils are educated first at kindergarten, then at primary school, high school, and then often at vocational and university college and/or university. These different levels and educational institutions have different ways of being referenced across various countries and systems. I will refer to all these different institutions as schools and as educational institutions.

I am passionate about education. The book is intended as a help for everyone who shares this passion and has a drive to improve the way we work at schools. Everyone who feels we are not making the most of the talents of our pupils (or our own)! It has been written with pupils in minds for teachers, lecturers, administrators, staff, and policymakers engaged in teaching, the development of new classes, and organizing our schools.

Acknowledgements

This book is a broad reflection of my experiences over many years as well as those of many others that I had the pleasure of working with, visiting, and observing. It is a tribute to all teachers, administrators, and professional services staff working hard every day to help our children, colleagues, and workers to keep learning and developing their talents.

In writing this book, I've received support and encouragement from many people for which I am very grateful. My university, the HAN University of Applied Sciences, gave me time to run this research. Thank you: Janneke Hoekstra.

The initial work and projects from which my ideas and this book have sprouted were done as part of the work at our professorship Lean and World Class Performance, which I have the pleasure to co-chair with my colleague and friend Jannes Slomp. So, thank you dear colleagues: Arian Hofland, Cees Vermeulen, Gerlinde Oversluizen, Jannes Slomp, and Stef Tiggeloven.

Various pedagogical experts inspired me through their work and sometimes through their time. I owe an intellectual debt to: Simon Kavanagh, Philip Dochy, Manon Ruijters, and many of the education thinkers I have not yet had the pleasure of meeting.

Roel Venderbosch design the infographics and illustrations at the start of the chapters. He gave a visual expression to my ideas. Thank you Roel.

The fellows from the Lean Higher Education (HE) network gave me ample opportunity to test some of my ideas, hosted me at various conferences, and inspired me. Thanks to the Lean HE global and continental steering committees. So thank you: Christine Stewart, Dave Speake, Fin Miller, John Hogg, Marilyn Thompson, Mark Robinson, Mick Gash, Pat Browne, Rachel McAssey, Stephen Yorkstone, Sue Jennings, Susanne Clarke, Tammi Sinha, Svein Are Tjeldnes, Valerie Runyan.

Several universities hosted me and provided generous access and insights into their workings. It inspired me and provided the necessary input and time to work on this book. Thank you: Edinburgh Napier University, Strathclyde University in Glasgow, Macquarie University in Sydney, University of Waterloo, and the Artic University in Tromsø.

I ran the Crossing Educational Borders experiment with the help of colleague educational designers, experts, and financiers who need to be noted. So, thank you: EBM Bruil Beton, FieldLab Industrial Robotics, Aimée Hoeve, Instituut Gak, Luc Dorenbosch, Nathalie de Zoete, NSvP, Rik Grasmeijer, and Sonia Sjollema. With special thanks to José Cuperus for the close cooperation on this project and all the pedagogical insights you shared, plus the rigorous feedback on the draft of this book!

I had the pleasure of visiting various schools and working with teachers and administrators. Thank you: Anne Frank School Arnhem, school federation Gelderse Onderwijsgroep and Overbetuwe college (OBC Bemmel, OBC Elst), HAN University of Applied Sciences, Stichting Leerkracht, New Engineers, and school federation Quadraam (Scholengemeenschap Quadraam).

Much of the thinking in this book has been tested on New Engineers and enriched. Thanks to my colleagues at New Engineers: Jan-Willem de Blok, Hilde van der Geld, Carina Pullens, and Nienke Vos. A special thanks to my partner in crime and co-founder at New Engineers and fellow traveler in Lean Education. This experiment and our joint working and writing have given me so many learnings that I would not have been able to write this book without them. Thank you: Lejla Brouwer-Hadzialic.

I've been away from home often and working odd hours on this book. Without support from my wife that would not have been possible. So thank you: Carina Pullens.

Author

Dr. Vincent Wiegel, Lean Professor, Co-chair Lean and World Class Performance research group at the HAN University of Applied Science, the Netherlands, and Co-founder of New Engineers School.

Discovering new ideas and applying them to make a difference in the lives of people is what drives me. What is it that communities need to thrive? How can improvements in processes and new technologies help employees, citizens, students, patients, etc. grow and prosper?

Our task at the HAN and New Engineers is finding out how we can educate people to realize this growth. As there are no clear-cut answers, we need to experiment and research. In my view, this requires an open mind and a willingness to both confess to one's ignorance and act boldly.

Of the hundreds of Lean projects I've been involved in, one that stands out was for primary schools in Flanders, Belgium. A drive to do well for their pupils encouraged participants to look for ways to improve their schools using Lean.

In 2013, my bestselling management book *Successful Lean* was published. Based on the Lean thinking I founded a new private engineering school, New Engineers, because I felt the need to improve the way we educate beyond what is possible within our formal institutions. I hope it will serve as a lab for others to learn from and with Lean facilitators and processes.

Dr. Wiegel received his master's degrees in economics and in philosophy from the Erasmus University Rotterdam, the Netherlands. He earned a PhD from Delft University of Technology, the Netherlands. He worked in academia and industry before being appointed to the HAN University of Applied Sciences, where he founded the research group on Lean and World Class Performance. He has published extensively, is a regular sp‑‑‑ international conferences, and advises industry leaders ‑

Introduction

...the fundamental constraints on teacher development are surely those set by our own limited capacity to envisage alternatives to what is taken for granted. Those who support teachers as well as teachers themselves seek the freed imagination, to see alternatives to conventional assumptions.

Macleod and Golby[1]

Technology is fast changing society and the economy. Information technology changes the way we retrieve and process information; 3D printing is on the brink of changing production processes; big data and artificial intelligence have a huge impact on the way we work, robotics introduces artificial colleagues on the shop floor, new materials heal themselves, and so on. These changes in turn force education to change and ensure these developments are captured.

These same changes also have an impact on teaching itself as the means of teaching change. Digital devices are becoming ubiquitous in schools, smart programs detect plagiarism, and massive open online courses bring high quality teaching to thousands of students at the same moment and on demand. We have to teach students and the people currently working at higher levels to keep up with all the changes.

Pedagogical research has seen lots of new insights in how the brain works while learning, how students learn, and what effective teaching methods are. Some of these imply deviations from current teaching methods. A focus on learner agency is key. By learner agency I mean roughly the freedom and ability on part of the student to co-own and co-direct her learning. This is critically important in light of the need to keep learning during everyone's lifetime.

Addressing these changes in combination with day to day teaching obligations is a humongous task that is putting a lot of pressure on teaching staff and administrators. This pressure is further increased by budget pressures and aging teaching staff.

---

[1] Flora Macleod and Michael Golby, "Theories of Learning and Pedagogy: Issues for Teacher Development," *Teacher Development* 7, no. 3 (2003): 360. doi:10.1080/13664530300200204.

In short, there is a huge drive for education to improve the important work that is being done. The current way of organizing education is not tenable in the coming decade. The changes are on how we teach, how we organize schools, how we increase the effectiveness of learning, how we construct classrooms, and how we deploy new technologies.

Lean Education brings all these elements together in a coherent framework that will allow schools to bring all these changes into one concerted effort. Teaching, professional support, managing the day to day work, and changing the way schools work are all brought together in Lean Education as a schoolwide strategy to organize learning in a way that serves our students by making the most of their talents.

WHY LEAN EDUCATION?

As a teacher or a school administrator, you are preparing your next day of work. Your daily routines require you to prepare classes, grade work by your pupils, make sure everyone is safe and sound, decide on staffing allocation, assign budget for renovations, and so on. The day to day work is substantial. The impact you have on (young and old) people is the reason why you do it, the joy of seeing people grow, their engagement in creating projects in which new insights are gained, the sheer pleasure of learning! But of course, it is not all joy and plain water sailing. The daily routines can be a bore, bureaucracy is always looming, and a lot of things distract from the actual teaching.

There are three major developments around the globe that put pressure on all people involved in education: one, socio-economic changes that make new demands on the way we educate and the knowledge and skills our pupils acquire while at school; two, fast developments in technology, information technology in particular, that impact both the way people work and the way we learn and teach; and three, cumulative new insights in pedagogy that affect the way we think about learning and how we should be facilitating that learning. These developments affect teachers, administrators, as well professional services staff. They apply also regardless of the level of education. Primary schools are affected as much as high schools, colleges, and universities.

So, you have the day to day routines to keep you busy. In addition, you need to keep up-to-date on your fields of expertise, assessing new text books and methods. On top of these activities, new major developments will change the way we think about education in a radical and fundamental way. This is a lot to take on!

PARADOX OF EDUCATION

Education is one of those parts of society that impacts the whole of society in a fundamental and lasting way. From a young age when children enter the educational system throughout their formative years, they are formed in schools as much as at home and on the street. Since we are striving for universal schooling around the globe, education affects everyone.[2] What students learn affects the way companies can compete, the way we partake in society, the way we organize our government, etc. Education is a part of, and a carrier of, our culture. Yet, the esteem we give the people at the core of our educational systems is eroding over the years.[3] And so are the budgets we provide for education.[4] This is the paradox of education!

---

[2] It is noted that there is a strong correlation between the state of education in a country and the happiness of its people. Michael Brooks and Bob Holmes, "Equinox Blueprint," April (2014): 11.

[3] This is a generalization. Some countries, notably Finland, and communities make substantial demands on and investments in the quality of their teachers and bestow esteem accordingly. These, however, are the exception. Esteem is a much broader concept than salary, though an honest salary certainly features in the appreciation felt. In the US, teachers' salaries have typically not kept up with the rise of living expenses.

[4] "The global economic crisis that began in 2008 had major adverse effects on various sectors of the economy. Data from 2008 to 2014 show clearly the impact of the crisis on the funding of educational institutions..." OECD, *Education at a Glance 2017: OECD Indicators* (OECD Publsiher, 2017), 186, doi:10.1787/eag-2017-en. See also Christine Redecker et al., *The Future of Learning: Preparing for Change—Publication, Publications Office of the European Union*, 2011, 39, doi:10.2791/64117.

THE TRAGEDY OF EDUCATION

The tragedy of education is that while the majority of the people involved in education are working very hard (sometimes even getting a burn out), the education that is provided to our students is often substandard. The quality levels vary greatly across countries, across individual schools, and within schools.[5] This is an indicator that many pupils are not receiving education according to the best practices available. In addition, however good a pedagogical approach may be, it never fits everyone to the same degree. Our students are different, have diverse ambitions and backgrounds, and have different needs when it comes to learning. Yet, we mostly provide one, single way of learning.[6] This single way often differs per teacher or school. It is exceptional to have a mix of more than two modalities of teaching, e.g., plenary classroom teaching mixed with some project work, mixed small group, large group, and individual activities. Mostly, it is still plenary classroom teaching with a cognitive focus that dominates education. This means, as a simple exercise in stochastics, that the chance we deliver the students the proper, fitting education is small. As a consequence, we waste a lot of talent.

Our teachers struggle to keep up-to-date on fast changing technologies, methods, and theories. As a former student of mine expressed it when he left my school with a bachelor's degree to go to one of the top-ranking technological universities to pursue a master's degree in Innovation Management: "I'm actually studying the history of innovation management." The curriculum was outdated and had not kept pace with the innovations in industry. There is now a widespread, shared understanding that education as a sector needs to change the way we educate our students. There are vocal proponents of change around the globe. Many of them passionate, well-meaning, and very articulate.[7]

This has given rise to a whole host of new pedagogies, teaching methods, etc. without real change. In the words of Ben Levin, "…most schools have been inundated with change. The problem is that many of the changes

---

[5] John Hattie, *Visible Learning for Teachers: Maximizing Impact on Learning* (New York: Taylor & Francis Group, 2012), 25–26.
[6] Of course, there are schools that are actively addressing these differences and providing different methods of learning to fit each student. These, however, are still the exception.
[7] Prof. Ken Robinson is a well-known proponent of change in education. He is one of many.

have not brought the desired positive effects or have not been sustained. Despite all the interventions [...] most of the basic features of schooling remain largely unaltered even over a century. [...] buildings, full of classes of children, organized by age with a subject-based curriculum."[8]

Of course it is not all bad. Quite to the contrary! Overall, both quality and quantity of education are improving. The value of education is recognized and most children around the globe can now expect to at least complete a primary education and a growing number secondary and higher education.[9] But the growth is not as fast as it could and should be. The growth and nature of new technologies makes the need for education only more important. Various reports outlining technological developments emphasize the need to transfer not only knowledge, but also focus on the development of a new skill set.[10] The tragedy of education is the well-intended and hard-working efforts of so many dedicated professionals resulting in education that falls short of what is needed.

Lean Education does not introduce a new pedagogy. What is needed is an approach that increases the effectiveness of all the energy that is spent on education. It builds on all the research and insights that have been generated over the past decades on effective teaching and learning. It combines these with proven, practical organizational insights to form a workable framework that offer schools a concrete way forward, a unified approach to address the overwhelming amount of change.

THE ROLE OF TECHNOLOGY

Because of fast changing technologies and thereby the changing nature of work, the demands on the skills and knowledge our students acquire are changing, resulting generally speaking, in a greater need for higher education. This trend is magnified by fast growth in some economic sectors that requires many more new employees. These are in themselves good and

---

[8] Benjamin Levin, *How to Change 5000 Schools: A Practical and Positive Approach for Leading Change at Every Level* (Cambridge, MA: Harvard Education Press, 2008), 64.

[9] Brooks and Holmes, "Equinox Blueprint," 11; OECD, *Education at a Glance 2017: OECD Indicators*, 11.

[10] Redecker et al., *The Future of Learning: Preparing for Change—Publication*; Brooks and Holmes, "Equinox Blueprint"; OECD, *Education at a Glance 2017: OECD Indicators*; Partnership for 21st Century Learning, "P21 Partnership for 21st Century Learning," *Partnership for 21st Century Learning*, 2015, 9.

welcome trends. They put pressure, though, on our schools throughout the educational chain to offer more places and prepare our children better for a fast-changing future.

One of the core drivers for all this change are the developments in new technologies. In particular, information technology and its associated branches. In their book, Race Against the Machine, Brynjolfsson and McAfee document wonderfully concisely and convincingly the advent of digital technologies and the impact they have on our economy.[11] They describe the growing impact of general-purpose technologies such as computing. These technologies, electricity is an example, have the power to "interrupt and accelerate the normal march of economic progress," leading to "a cascade of benefits that is both broad and deep." This leads to what economists call a "skill-biased technical change." The impact of skill-biased technical changes is profound. "The most productive forms reinvented and reorganized decision rights, incentives systems, information flows, hiring systems, and other aspects of organization capital to get most from the technology. This, in turn, required radically different and, generally, higher skill levels in the workforce."[12]

How these macro-trends translate to individual organizations and the networks they form has been described brilliantly by Dave Gray and Vander Wal in *The Connected Company*.[13] Here arises the image of companies organized on platforms in which they share services. The frontline in which they communicate with customers is expanding. There is much more customer interaction than in the last century. Innovation is driven by continuous experimentation which feeds on customer interaction. The upshot, again, is that employees will need new and different skill sets. Organizations become "podular," that is, made up of many "small, autonomous units of staff that are enabled and empowered to deliver things that customers value."[14] Managers in this system become coaches and teachers. That is also something most managers have not learned. Teaching our students some of these skills will help them as they grow into managerial roles.

---

[11] Erik Brynjolfsson and Andrew McAfee, *Race Against the Machine: How the Digital Revolution Is Accelerating Innovation, Driving Productivity, and Irreversibly Transforming Employment and the Economy* (Lexington, KY: Digital Frontier Press, 2012).

[12] Brynjolfsson and McAfee, 41–42.

[13] Dave Gray and Thomas Vander Wal, *The Connected Company*, Oreilly and Associate Series (Sebastopol, CA: O'Reilly Media, Incorporated, 2012).

[14] Gray and Vander Wal, 148.

THE CHALLENGES FACING EDUCATION AND THE PEOPLE WORKING IN EDUCATION

The myriad of socio-economic and technological developments described above pose tremendous challenges for people working in education. Goodyear, Resnick, Levin, Brynjolfsson and McAfee,[15] and many others have described part of these challenges quite succinctly. We can now attempt to bring them together and group these challenges together for a good overview. These analyses lead to three groups of challenges that need to be addressed: socio-economic change, technological change, and pedagogical change.

One, demands from society including the economy for new, more diverse knowledge and skill sets to be taught with fewer public resources. "Employers and their representatives are continuing to criticize universities for failing to produce work-ready graduates. Students themselves are questioning whether they are getting a fair return on the time and fees they are investing."[16] This applies not just to higher education, but trickles down to all levels of education, with universities complaining about the entry level of their students, for example. Across the whole sector, schools are facing budget pressure. "Dwindling public funding of teaching, as well as competing demands on time—for research, service, entrepreneurial activities, etc.—are intensifying the pressures on teaching staff."[17]

Two, technological developments that change the way we work and teach at an ever faster pace. This relates to the workforce of the future that is being educated, as well as the employees that need to remain up to speed. "…the demand for skilled labor is closely correlated with advances in technology, in particular digital technologies."[18] Education itself is affected just as much. "The technologies being used in knowledge work—for research and teaching and in other areas of intellectual life—are changing rapidly.

---

[15] Peter Goodyear, "Teaching as Design," *HERDSA Review of Higher Education,* 2, no. 2 (2015): 27–50; Mitchel Resnick, *Lifelong Kindergarten: Cultivating Creativity Through Projects, Passion, Peers, and Play,* (Cambridge, MA: MIT Press, 2017); Brynjolfsson and McAfee, *Race Against the Machine: How the Digital Revolution Is Accelerating Innovation, Driving Productivity, and Irreversibly Transforming Employment and the Economy;* Levin, *How to Change 5000 Schools: A Practical and Positive Approach for Leading Change at Every Level.* All subsequent references in this section will be to these works, unless stated otherwise.

[16] Goodyear ibid.

[17] Goodyear ibid.

[18] Brynjolfsson and McAfee ibid.

New knowledge practices are emerging, such as those involving data analytics, visualization, and very complex forms of computational modelling. The pace of technological innovation is accelerating. This creates risk and uncertainty for university managers, especially with respect to campus planning, IT, and educational strategies in the longer term."[19]

Three, pedagogical innovations that impact the way we teach and organize education, "Too often, schools focus on delivering instruction and information rather than supporting students in creative learning processes."[20] We need to adopt new ways of learning and teaching that support changing subject-matters fast and are capable of including the development of skills and attitudes of and in our students. "Making real gains across a range of outcomes means that daily teaching and learning practices have to change across many, if not most, classrooms and schools."[21] What is needed is transformational learning experiences in which students learn in authentic, real live situations, and where they co-design and co-own the learning process. This in turn requires a substantial transformation of the way we run our schools.

It is important to understand these challenges first. They can be daunting, but certainly surmountable if approached right. These challenges will be discussed in detail in the first part of this book, Chapters 1 through 3, respectively.

TEACHERS AS PROFESSIONALS

The above section described the underlying trends of what we witness now and the unprecedented rise of familiar companies like Uber and Airbnb. Whole economic sectors are changing fundamentally, and with them the role of the professionals working in these sectors. Law practice is currently on the advent of a huge shift in which lots of (para)legal work will be automated, and done more reliably, by artificial intelligence. This affects many professions. Susskind and Susskind argue that the whole phenomenon of professions is changing.[22] Professions are institutionalized ways

[19] Goodyear ibid.
[20] Resnick ibid.
[21] Levin ibid.
[22] Richard Susskind and Daniel Susskind, *The Future of the Professions: How Technology Will Transform the Work of Human Experts* (Oxford, UK: OUP, 2015).

of solving a problem: the problem of making specialized knowledge and expertise available and accessible. Physicians and lawyers are two examples of professions. These professionals are granted a special status because they know things and know how to do things that most of us do not. But as technology is changing the way we store and operationalize knowledge, this special status is put into question. "We contend that professions are on the brink of transformation. As currently constituted, they face problems that they seem unable to solve."[23] They are failing, for example, to make the same high quality available to all who need them, they are expensive and rarely world-class. The dismantling of professions they predict, is driven by technological change.

This has two main impacts on education. One, the profession of teacher will be affected. Two, knowledge, skills, and attitudes our pupils learn and acquire will be different, and keep on changing, from what we currently include in our curricula. As teachers, we will need to reevaluate the way we teach and what we teach. As services like fielding helpdesk queries can be provided by artificial agents, it is not evident a priori that some classes cannot be taught be artificial agents as well. Today, in a more basic, human form, we see lectures provided through, for example, the Khan Academy. This is not to say that all work teachers do will disappear. But neither is it self-evident "…that all the work that our professionals currently do can *only* be undertaken by licensed experts."[24] I will argue that the key elements in teaching are determining together with our students where each of them wants to go, where they currently are, and devising a strategy to acquire the necessary knowledge, skills, and attitudes. Rather than relaying knowledge as we teachers currently often do, we will be guides and mentors. Very knowledgeable guides at that! Again, I'm not advocating the demise of expertise, rather the supplementing of knowledge with other skills such as mentoring and coaching. Though the profession of teacher is one that is expected to be among the most difficult to automate, it is clear that technological developments will have a huge impact. And beware, practitioners from every profession say that they understand how others can be automated, but that they are the exception. This is a self-delusional attitude coined by Susskind and Susskind the "status quo bias."

---

[23] Susskind and Susskind ibid.
[24] Susskind and Susskind ibid.

DOOMSDAY COMING?

Confronted with these developments, some thinkers are predicting "the end of the educational world as we know it." Christensen predicts that not half of all US colleges and universities will survive the coming decade. In *An Avalanche Is Coming*,[25] an urgent picture of changes in higher education is painted. In Bavaria, Germany, unions of teachers sounded the alarm over the lack of teachers that threatens to disrupt substantial amounts of classes at primary and secondary schools. They demanded more teachers (budget is not the problem here). The list of doomsday messages, cries of dissatisfaction, and rallies for change is overwhelming and seemingly endless. Others are jubilant of the technologies like big data and the Internet that will change education for the better and solve all problems. Learning with big data is such an approach in which the use of big data technologies is used to tailor for each student her learning materials.[26] They point to the use of massive open online courses, online universities, open educational resources that offer reuse of materials, easy access for all to course work, and so on.

Though many of the analyses have it right (some of), they offer scant solutions. The techno-optimists reliance on new technologies requires a grasp of, and investment in, these technologies that is beyond most schools. Nonetheless, these views are valuable. They point to potential that is often missed in a strongly status quo oriented sector. Other approaches demanding more money and/or more staff rely too much on the current ways of education. These ways are not sustainable. Even if teachers or money were to appear miraculously, they would not be able to keep pace with the changes in society, economy, and technology. The pace of change is much faster than budget and staff increases can keep up with. Nor do they address the issue of wasted talent that results from uniform ways of teaching.

We must acknowledge that fundamental changes are coming. What education needs are creditable approaches founded in everyday experience; a willingness to try new approaches in ways that are within reach of all teachers and schools; solutions that are daring without disheartening the already fully loaded staff. So, what is a creditable approach?

---

[25] Saad (IPPR) Rizvi, Katelyn (IPPR) Donnelly, and Michael (IPPR) Barber, "An Avalanche Is Coming," 2013, https://www.ippr.org/files/images/media/files/publication/2013/04/avalanche-is-coming_Mar2013_10432.pdf.

[26] Viktor Mayer-Schönberger and Kenneth. Cukier, *Lernen Mit Big Data: Die Zukunft Der Bildung* (REDLINE-Verl, 2014).

THE HALLMARKS FOR A NEW FRAMEWORK FOR EDUCATION

To rise to the challenges of this age, schools need a framework that will allow them to keep going while innovating at a faster pace. And that is no mean challenge! Moreover, as education is a very heterogenous undertaking, needs will vary across communities, cultures, and countries. Therefore, any creditable approach must cater to these differences. Any creditable approach toward education needs to meet seven hallmarks.

1. *Address the individual needs of its pupils*: As the recipients of education differ in their capabilities, the prior knowledge and skills, their attitudes, the ambitions, and so on, it is obvious that no one form of learning and teaching will fit all. Hence, we need to break radically with the uniformity of education[27]
2. *Meet ever faster changing needs of society and economy*: Our students grow up in a world different from our own. They will become full citizens of a different world. As such, society will have certain needs. The organizations where they will, or already are working do have requirements for the skills and knowledge they acquire. These needs will change at an ever-faster pace and will not be easily predictable
3. *Integrate insights from recent and different pedagogies*: Research into neurophysiology has yielded insights that drive new ways of teaching. Pedagogical research and experiments have shown many ways to foster learning effectively. Any framework of education must be able to incorporate different pedagogies and quite possibly multiple pedagogies at once
4. *Integrate new technologies at the core of education*: Information technology is one of the shaping forces of this age, sometimes phrased as "IT is eating the world." Related technologies such as artificial intelligence, machine learning, as well as other innovative technologies such as 3D printing, are together changing the way we organize ourselves, interact, and work. Of course, this will have an impact on education as well. Both as subject matters that are developing at an ever-faster pace as well as tools for education

---

[27] Let me state very clearly that I do not mean that education should be a solitary activity! I do empathically think that at least some part, and often a very substantial part of education should be a social activity. Partly because learning benefits from peer interaction, partly because some of the knowledge, skills, and attitudes to be learned are social. This does, however, not imply that it should thus be uniform.

5. *Operational feasibility: Nothing "just" works.* Whatever we change in the way we organize education, it must be done in a way that allows both staff and students to stay on board. Schools have everyday jobs that need to be done. Classrooms need cleaning, lessons need preparing, and schedules must be laid. Any approach must allow for these activities and not just heap new innovations on already overburdened staff without acknowledging and addressing the existing workload. It must offer a view of operational execution that reduces the work load

6. *Self-sustaining ability of continuous improvement and continuous innovation*: Since there is no magic wand, every school will have to find ways to experiment with new ways of learning and teaching. Given the pace and diversity of developments in society, economy, and technology, we cannot rely solely on *a* new pedagogy or *a* new technology that will at best solve issues for a short while. Sustained continuous improvement to ease the workload and free up capacity for change is a key element. The complementary element is continuous innovation. Innovations need not always be mind boggling and world shattering. Small innovations have together the potential for order of magnitude change. The prerequisite for this is a structure of goal setting, evaluation, and learning plus a mindset that is open to change

7. *Integrality*: Each of the previous elements could be attempted to implement on its own. Such a piecemeal approach is easier to oversee, but will deliver fewer results. Results that will moreover be harder to sustain. Each of the elements should reinforce the others. The result is a stable yet adaptive school.

THE "WHY" OF LEAN EDUCATION

Sometimes we can make a clean break with the past and start anew. Olin college did so. But there are not that many schools that bring a multi-million-dollar endowment along to get started. iFoundry of the University of Illinois showed that that is not necessary.[28] But in their case, there was an extraordinary show of leadership which cannot be reasonably expected

---

[28] These fascinating and insightful cases are described in D E Goldberg, M Somerville, and C Whitney, *A Whole New Engineer: The Coming Revolution in Engineering Education* (ThreeJoy Associates, Incorporated, 2014).

of everyone. What most schools will need is a framework that meets the hallmarks mentioned above.

Lean Education as presented in this book offers such a framework. To be of use it needs to be conceptually strong, but also offer an actionable account of the organization of education. Lean Education offers this by integrating technological developments with pedagogical insights and the Lean management philosophy. Lean thinking has transformed many sectors already. Though originally conceived in the automobile industry, its principles and techniques have been shown to be generic. They have been applied successfully in healthcare, financial services, government, and construction, to name just a few sectors. It has been successful in the transfer to different sectors by relying on two factors: one, by having very generic principles and techniques and two, by adapting to the sector specific characteristics and incorporating technologies, institutional arrangements, laws, and regulations that are unique to the sector.[29] In the case of education, pedagogy is such a "technology." Lean Education combines the common sense and action focused approach of Lean with pedagogies and techniques unique to education. The core idea is to turn education into a continuously improving and continuously innovating sector. By freeing up scarce time and intellectual resources through streamlining day to day processes, it generates the mental and physical spaces to incorporate new technologies and pedagogies that have the potential for full blown innovation.

WHAT IS LEAN EDUCATION?

Lean Education is an organization-wide strategy that aims at generating value for students, and supports schools' chosen pedagogical philosophy through:

1. Alignment of the whole organization, its processes, and technology to create an effective learning environment
2. Short cyclic continuous improvement and innovation of the learning environment and the elimination of waste.[30]

---

[29] Vincent Wiegel and L Brouwer Hadzialic, "Lessons from Higher Education: Adapting Lean Six Sigma to Account for Structural Differences in Application Domains," *International Journal of Six Sigma and Competitive Advantage* 9, no. 1 (2015): 72, doi:10.1504/IJSSCA.2015.070104.

[30] Slightly adopted from Vincent Wiegel and Lejla Brouwer-Hadzialic, "Lean Education," in *The Routledge Companion to Lean Management*, ed. T H Netland and D J Powell, Routledge Companions in Business, Management and Accounting (New York: Routledge, 2017), 422–434.

Lean Education is primarily focused at the school level. All elements in the school need to be aligned to create an effective learning space. The learning space is both the physical and digital space in which learning is supported and takes place. In this learning space, the chosen pedagogy is key in the support of the learning. It is supported by professional services that focus on non-teaching processes and the physical and digital infrastructure. All functions in the schools are working toward sustained continuous improvement and innovation of that learning space. This means, for example, that teachers measure and evaluate the impact of their teaching on the learning of their pupils. This is more than the collection of grades which, at best, reflects only partially the learning that is taking place. Based on the evaluation, they will try to improve their interventions in the students' learning. They are working together with professional services staff to effect this. Activities, systems, etc. that do not contribute to the learning are waste and will be eliminated.

Throughout the book, all these elements of Lean Education will be discussed and illustrated.

HOUSE OF LEAN LEARNING AND EDUCATION

Lean Education: House of Lean Learning & Education — "Everybody Learns!"

In Lean, we use the metaphor of a house to describe all elements that together constitute the Lean philosophy. The Lean house shows which elements make up the philosophy and how they relate to one another. It is an apt metaphor in the context of education. A house is a physical manifestation of a group of people that belong together, who form a community. It is an open structure, not a gated community. The house shows its fundaments, the pillars that hold the roof, and the space encompassed by all.

HOUSE OF LEAN LEARNING AND EDUCATION (Continued)

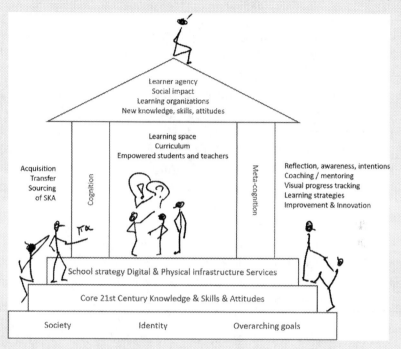

The foundation of the House of Lean Education is formed by society, the identity of a school, and the overarching goals that arise from our civic and social views. These are the core and most lasting parts of a school. Based on broader socio-economic and technological developments, we can identify sets of knowledge, skills, and attitudes that are relevant for all schools. They are reflections of the times we live in. Given these two fundamental layers, a school formulates its strategy. It builds its physical, digital, and service infrastructure that match the needs of the school as defined in its strategy. Thus, the House of Lean Education has three solid fundaments on which rests the core of schools: the learning space. This learning space is contained by two pillars: one, cognition, skills, and attitudes and two, meta-cognition. They form a pair that constitutes learning: *what* on the one hand (cognition) and the *why* and the *how* on the other (meta-cognition). Cognition refers here to

HOUSE OF LEAN LEARNING AND EDUCATION (Continued)

the process of the acquisition and formation of knowledge through (sub)conscious thought, experiencing and sensing. Meta-cognition refers to the awareness of learning and includes thinking about the goals of the learning and how best to learn. Every curriculum, all learning and teaching will encompass these elements. They address skills, knowledge, and attitudes, and also the formation of learning strategies, the expression of learning intentions, and the tracking of progress of the learning. All these elements together ultimately lead to students that direct their learning, i.e., learner agency, who have impact on society at large as citizens and members of learning organizations. The student is the most tangible and direct result of schools. It is primarily, though not exclusively, through the students that schools have impact on society and organizations. That is why learner agency is the key aim of a twenty-first century school. Learner agency means that student exhibits some degree of self-management, reflection both when acting and after the action,[31] and self-efficacy.[32] Another way in which schools have impact is through the creation of new knowledge, skills, and attitudes. As I will argue in Chapter 3, we cannot educate the future, but we can educate *for* the future by engaging in its invention.

Every metaphor has limitations and misses some points. In the case of a house, the dynamics, and sequential dependencies get less attention. One might get the idea that the whole construct is fixed. Which in the case of a real house is exactly the purpose. But houses do get extended, refurbished, enlarged, sub-divided, redecorated over time, and sometimes demolished. The same goes for schools. There is a lasting element that defines the identity and sets it apart from other schools, and, generally speaking, other organizations. Yet, at the same time, it must be open to change. One of the key points in this book is that schools need to be more adaptive to

---

[31] Filip Dochy and Mien Segers, *Creating Impact Through Future Learning: The High Impact Learning That Lasts (HILL) Model* (London, UK: Taylor & Francis Group, 2018), 36–37.

[32] John Hattie, *Visible Learning for Teachers: Maximizing Impact on Learning* (New York: Taylor & Francis Group, 2012), 46.

HOUSE OF LEAN LEARNING AND EDUCATION (Continued)

the fast changes in technology and economy. The House of Lean Education has to be understood as the Greek agora, the Chinese Confucianism teachers in the woods, and the African sage's dwellings. They are delineated, structured spaces that are open to other, new influences. And just as the learning space is an open and not a confined space, the learning is open to all. Teachers, experts, society at large, and student are all learning. The learning is not fixed, noone is done learning.

The Lean contribution to education is the focus on what we have just informally defined as value. Given this value, the question is how to organize education. Lean thinking starts at the end: the value as it is delivered. We then reason backward to see what is being done to deliver that value. As we take a critical look, we will notice that many activities we undertake are actually not contributing to the delivery of that value. Quite to the contrary, they deflect from the value. We call this waste. Examples of waste are a digital board that is not working and hampers a lesson, bureaucratic forms that duplicate information, overloaded lessons with so many slides that the students can never retain all the information, students learning to pass the exam and then forgetting all they have learned, searching for information on the school's learning management system, classroom that are used only part of the time, and so on. Though there are no hard data yet, based on experiences in other sectors, we can estimate that these wasteful activities easily make up 40% and more of all the time spent! Some of these activities cannot be avoided (in the short-term), but are nonetheless not helping the learning. By way of exercise, the reader can actively track a day's activities and ask with every activity: "Does this activity actually, tangibly contribute to my students' learning?" Be critical, do not make excuses. Facts are what they are. And waste means that there is an opportunity for improvement which is good news. We do not blame people for wasteful activities. We try to improve the process so that the waste is eliminated. Continuous improvements, small steps at a time, are another hallmark of Lean thinking. Lean offers a well-filled toolbox with proven, easy to use methods and techniques that let you identify and remove waste. The concept

HOUSE OF LEAN LEARNING AND EDUCATION (Continued)

of flow, known from both psychology and process management is a powerful concept aimed at letting value flow. In the case of education, this means offering students what they need, in formats that fit them at times which match their studying needs. To teachers, it means supporting them in what they as professionals need. Providing support for effortless generation and sharing of materials, providing them with the physical and digital means when they need it, how they need, and where the need it.

We reason from the student's learning needs backward to the teacher, then to the professionals services, and finally to the organization rather than the other way around. Simple as it may sound, it is a revolutionary way of looking at education.

Section I

Why Lean Education

1

Economics and Education: Scarce Talent, Abundant Educational Resources

INTRODUCTION

The economy and education are deeply intertwined. Technological innovations drive the economy and the demand for new skill sets and knowledge. Changing economic conditions together with politics drive the budgets for education. Education also has its own economics. Old economics with its focus on cost cutting and economies of scale falls short in this age of new technologies, cheap capital, and scarcity of talent. To understand where the educational sector is headed, we have to understand the economic backdrop and the logic of scarcity and abundance. We are wasting both the talents of our students and our educators. On the other hand, we fail to capitalize on abundantly available resources. The way we organize education today makes it hard to scale up and hampers growth.

TECHNOLOGICAL DEVELOPMENTS

Technological developments shape the economy to a substantial degree. In order to understand how the economy impacts education, we first look at some crucial technological developments. The well-known law of Moore on the growth of computing capacity of computer chips states roughly that every 1.5 years that capacity doubles. Consequently, computers become faster and can handle more complex calculations. Next, the bandwidth of the connections between our computers, mobile devices, and other equipment grows exponentially allowing more data to be exchanged faster. Last, the law of Metcalfe on networks indicates that the value of a network grows as the number of nodes in the network grows.[1] As people, computers, and machines are evermore connected, with faster connections and more powerful processors the capacity for complex, innovative products and services grows. These three laws together help drive the ever faster increase of innovations, ideas, products, and knowledge. Processors, networks, and

---

[1] Metcalfe's law actually refers to the number of connections possible in a network. Connections obviously do not equate value automatically. Whatever the mathematical relationship is, n^2 or $n \log_n$, the key message here holds, namely, that there is a substantial increase as networks expand.

software protocols are general purpose technologies (GPT) that can be applied across a very broad range of products and services, across a broad range of economic sectors, and across a broad range of professions.

> …computers and networks bring an *ever-expanding* set of opportunities to companies. Digitization, in other words, is not a single project providing one-time benefits. Instead, it's an ongoing process of creative destruction; innovators use both new and established technologies to make deep changes at the level of the task, the job, the process, even the organization itself. And these changes build and feed on each other so that the possibilities offered really are constantly expanding.[2]

But technological developments are not limited to digitization. We also witness fast paced developments in biotech, medicine, materials, nanotech, and 3D printing. Even these are to some extent enabled by IT and require strong IT capabilities. The common thread is that the people working in these fields need strong analytical skills. This is one of the red threads throughout this book in the case for change in education.

GROWING DEMAND FOR TALENT

We witness two simultaneous developments regarding organizations and personnel. One, a growing demand for skill-based talent: For people that know how to do things, construct things, and fix them when they are broken, people with the manual dexterity whether in the care of these things or the industry producing them. These tend to be jobs that require vocational training, make more practical demands rather than cognitive. Two, a growing demand for knowledge-based talent. People with strong cognitive abilities in particular in the fields of science, technology, engineering, and mathematics (STEM). These are analytical jobs across a wide range of economic sectors. At the same time, we see an eroding job base in the middle category. Knowledge workers, people in offices and services

---

[2] Erik Brynjolfsson and Andrew McAfee, *Race Against the Machine: How the Digital Revolution Is Accelerating Innovation, Driving Productivity, and Irreversibly Transforming Employment and the Economy* (Lexington, KY: Digital Frontier Press, 2012), p. 21.

that have a mid-level education. These jobs are increasingly automated. And the people that lose those jobs find it increasingly difficult to find other jobs.[3]

This is nicely illustrated by the growing number of virtual assistants that replace customer service personnel and paralegal workers that are replaced by smart algorithms that scan and analyze legal documents. Mid-level jobs are being made redundant, whereas the demands for the people that know how to build these assistants and algorithms are in high demand. Brynjolfsson and McAfee citing work by Tyler Owen, David Autor, and their own research, describe two important developments that follow.[4] One, median income is steadily declining. This means that workers in the middle of the income spectrum have seen little or even negative growth of their salary. Two, the relationship between skills and wages is U-shaped. This means that demand for people with mid-level skills is lagging behind the demand for people with cognitive skills and those with manual, practical skills. This can be understood intuitively as dressing hair or fixing plumbing is more difficult to automate or robotize than the job of checking people in at the airport. The design itself of systems that allow people to check-in without human aid is again much harder to delegate to computers. We leave that job to IT and data science specialists.

Brynjolfsson and McAfee conclude: "The stagnation in median income is not because of a lack of technological progress. On the contrary, the problem is that our skills and institutions have not kept up with the rapid changes in technology." Herein lays one of the main challenges for education: to increase the pace at which new skills, such as boundary crossing and IT literacy, are integrated into curricula and to be more responsive to the changes in technology.

This has implications for companies as well. The increasingly complicated, high skills jobs that drive the economy require people with these skills who are in short supply. Organizations that are able to attract talent, know how to keep, and develop them fare better than the ones that do not. One recent study shows that companies that run structural and strategic HR development programs are running operating margins that are 30%–50% higher than industry average.

---

[3] Banking personnel laid off in and after the 2008 financial crisis in the Netherlands, for example, are among the job seekers with the lowest success rate in finding new jobs.

[4] Erik Brynjolfsson and Andrew McAfee, *Race Against the Machine: How the Digital Revolution Is Accelerating Innovation, Driving Productivity, and Irreversibly Transforming Employment and the Economy*, (Lexington, KY: Digital Frontier Press, 2011), pp. 28–52.

...companies that apply real discipline in their management of human capital are on average 40% more productive than the rest. These companies lose far less to organizational drag. They attract, deploy, and lead talent more effectively—taking full advantage of the unique skills and capabilities their people bring to the workplace. Finally, they unleash far more of their employees' discretionary energy through inspirational leadership and a mission-led culture. The resulting productivity difference is a huge advantage for the best companies, producing operating margins that are 30%–50% higher than industry averages. And every year, as this difference is compounded, the gap in value between the best and the rest grows bigger.[5]

WHAT JOB?

As jobs are disappearing and new ones are created, the educational system is challenged to stay relevant, that is not educating for the disappearing ones and preparing for the newly created ones. The jobs that people work in are changing in the wake of the technological advances. Though not for everyone equally fast, but changing they are. Think of driverless trains, virtual assistants, the gig economy, the gradual, but fast disappearance of cash, etc. These are just a few developments, enabled through technological changes, that impact many different jobs in sectors from transport to services, from banking to food. It is not just our students entering the labor market, but also everyone else in the workforce that is affected by the loss of certain jobs and the creation of new ones yet unknown. The question is for what job are we educating?

The answer is that more and more we do not know. People are expected to change jobs and to craft their own jobs. This requires lifelong learning skills. And exactly here we witness two shortcomings of the current educational system. One, our students hardly ever really learn how to learn. Knowing what different learning strategies a student has, knowing what fits her best, when she best learns, how she learns best, is something that is not structurally addressed in our education. It is, however, in this

---

[5] Michael Mankins, Karen Harris, and David Harding, Strategy in the age of superabundant capital, *Harvard Business Review*, 2017 (2017): 66–75.

changing environment an essential skill and knowledge set. Two, most of our formalized, state sponsored education has a strong focus on young students. Even though we acknowledge that there are many functionally illiterate people, that not all adults have the needed digital proficiency, education for these groups are outside the main stream education, almost as an afterthought. Given the need for continuous learning as part of job crafting, and the demographic developments, in which the proportion of young people is declining, it is an omission that needs redressing fast. At several places in this book, I will also argue that there are huge pedagogical gains by sometimes mixing different age groups in one learning environment.

CHANGING DEMANDS ON PUPILS

The implications for education are manifold. But before we address these implications, let us also be clear that there are some things that do not change (as fast). The basic laws of physics do not change. Mathematics in the basics stay the same as does the grammar of languages, and our history. Though even these domains do not go untouched by the technological developments. This being said, we can still expect to see major changes to what and how we learn.

> ... technology does not only affect what we will need to learn, but also how we will learn in the future. A range of (foresight) studies underline the impact of technological change on education and training. According to the European Internet Foundation, for example, the key to adequately preparing learners for life in a digital world is to 'redesign education itself around participative, digitally-enabled collaboration within and beyond the individual educational institution'.[6]

To the core components of the curriculum at primary and secondary schools are now added a new skill set, generally referred to as the twenty-first century skills. These are essential to prepare our students for later vocational and academic training. These 13 skills[7] are grouped

---

[6] Christine Redecker et al., *The Future of Learning: Preparing for Change—Publication, Publications Office of the European Union*, 2011, doi:10.2791/64117.

[7] Critical thinking, Creativity, Collaboration, Communication, Information literacy, Media literacy, Technology, Literacy, Flexibility, Leadership, Initiative, Productivity, and Social skills.

in three categories: learning skills, literacy skills, and life skills. Now the suggestion is sometimes being made that these skills should replace the current knowledge-based curriculum. That, however, is a false hope and misleading claim. We need knowledge as much as ever. And, these skills on top! You must know things in order to ask meaningful questions. Assessing whether a source found on the Internet is correct requires, among other things, knowledge to assess the information found.

ECONOMICS OF SCARCITY AND ABUNDANCE

There is a need to update what and how we support our students' learning. We need to do so fast, especially in the face of scarcity in teachers and budget pressure that pose a conundrum. Interestingly, the technological changes that drive the need for change in education also come to the aid of education through the economics of abundance.

Economics is traditionally the science of scarcity. It addresses how and when we use resources to produce goods and services, and how and when we will buy them. This is a gross oversimplification that surely does not do justice to a whole field of economics, but it serves our purposes. The basic idea is that our days are limited, the number of hours in a day is limited, the number of teachers and administrators is limited, budgets are limited. Given these limitations, how and where do we spend these limited resources? The traditional answer is that this is determined through prices established in the market. Traditionally, we have not left education to market forces. Though this is different in various countries and throughout history, education has been, for the last hundred or so years, predominantly government dominated. There is, however, a change setting in, where commercial parties offer education. Whether education is offered through the market or via governmental intervention, the scarcity remains as a driving force. Qualified teachers by and large are the scarcest resource in education in the last decades. They are almost exclusively the source of knowledge transfer to and instruction of our pupils. The profession of teacher, lecturer, and professor has been heavily regulated through a system of accreditations, diplomas, etc. This creates a bottleneck. This bottleneck is further increased through pedagogies and educational philosophies that form the way we educate. These pedagogies and educational philosophies often favor classroom teaching. They determine, mostly limit, the size of classrooms and the number of students. Lifelong learning combined with a drive for more and higher levels of education increases the demand for education. A growing demand met by supply that is set by a combined fixture of classroom teaching, limitations in classroom size, and restricted access to the profession means we have a real problem.

Over the last decade, education budgets have increased little at best, more often remained constant, or even decreased.[8] That is not enough to provide for the growing need for education. At least not in the way we currently organize education. In the current situation we are stuck. The government controls budgets, while job opportunities are organized through the market luring talented youngsters away from a career in education. Throwing more money at education helps in some circumstances where education is underfunded. Confronted with the demographics of an aging lecturer population, more money is not necessarily sufficient to solve the problem. Unattractive career perspectives for lecturers and restrictive regulations will have to be changed in order to attract more teachers. I do not envision a fundamental change in the near future. This means that schools, organizations, and industries have to get together and be smarter in educating.

We will have to go about organizing education in a radically different way. A point, in case, is the fact that there are marked differences across countries in educational achievements, in PISA scores,[9] for example, and the money that is spent on education as a percentage of gross domestic product.[10] There are also very interesting other telling differences in the educational systems. Pupils in Japan, for example, spend roughly half the time at school compared to their peers in most developed countries. Japan spends less than the Organisation for Economic Co-operation and Development (OECD) average on education. Yet, their achievements at school are generally better. These numbers must be interpreted with care. They can be notoriously hard to compare. School achievements are also only a part of the broader picture of life and learning. Nonetheless, it tells us that there is something to be learned. Some countries or systems

[8] OECD, *Education at a Glance 2017: OECD Indicators* (OECD Publsiher, 2017), doi:10.1787/eag-2017-en.
[9] PISA (Programme for International Student Assessment), "Pisa 2015," 2015, 2015–2016.
[10] OECD, *Education at a Glance 2017: OECD Indicators*.

do perform better. Copying them is not a good idea generally speaking. Learning from them, however, is. This requires schools to become continuously improving and innovating organizations. This will be addressed in Chapter 8 more extensively.

Old economic thinking with government intervention is not going to provide us with the solutions we need. We need an approach in which schools look at their institutions and consider the cost and price of talent and the learning opportunities provided with the budget available. One line of improvement will be looking at the deployment of other educational resources. In economics of abundance resources are not necessarily free. They can, however, be made available and reproduced at little or no marginal cost. Digital materials, for example, are almost limitlessly reproducible at no cost. An instructional video on the Khan Academy can be viewed, once, a hundred, or a thousand times, each costing marginally more in terms of bandwidth, computing power, and Internet connection. This does not mean less work for a teacher, but different work: selecting, editing, curating, and configuring these other resources. But once that is done, it can be scaled easily and time is freed-up to do other value adding activities, such as individual coaching, small group learning activities, etc. The key idea is to make easily scalable, limitless resources work for the critical, scarce resources so that the overall impact grows. This will require some upfront investments. That is why formulating a clear, coherent strategy that can be shared with all staff is so important (more on this in Chapter 8). Lean Education can play an important role in reducing waste and thus freeing up the scarce resources to invest in these new development activities. Schools should also seriously consider working together even more at local, regional, and national levels to share and curate resources.

WASTED TALENT

Given that some resources are scarce, we have a reason to be careful in their use. The scarcest resource in society, in general, and in education in particular, is talent. We want everyone, young and old, to count and make the most of her and his talents. As far as education is concerned, this means that we must not waste the talents of our students and teachers.

We know that there are differences in the ways people process information, differences in ambition, prior knowledge, preferred learning styles, times during the day when cognitive performances are better, and so on. All these differences impact the way we learn. This argument has been made many times already. Watch, for example, Ken Robinson's brilliant video on educational paradigms.[11] Still, we provide mostly one uniform way of learning to our students: classroom teaching to more or less fixed size groups, at fixed times, for fixed age groups of similar cognitive abilities. Statistically speaking, the chance that this format works for any arbitrary student is rather slim. For some it will be too much, for others too little, yet others will struggle with the format of textual instruction and would rather observe. As a consequence, we are wasting the talents of our students at a grand scale! Of course, there are experiments with different formats, there is project-based learning, students get iPads to work at their own pace. These activities, valuable as they are, are an add-on, an extra. They are not at the core of our approach to education. Sometimes there are schools based on an entirely new approach toward learning.[12] They are brilliant, but small initiatives with little systemic impact. The goal should be to provide every student with what she needs to learn, when she best learns, in formats that are most conducive to her learning. The key argument is that we have an ideal of learning and teaching tuned to the individual needs. And a culture of trying and experimenting to find the best ways to do so.

The proviso in all the above is of course that some guidance is required, and sometimes a lot. Not every student is "just" able to articulate her needs. It is a careful path with lots of guidance at the beginning, in which students mature at their own pace toward self-efficacy and become owners of their learning. It is a delicate balance between structure and freedom that comes with ownership. This also does empathically not mean that all learning should be individual. Learning is an inherently social activity. The key here is to devise formats in which groups of pupils learn together, but each potentially something different. This is a tall order, but also a fun challenge for teachers.

---

[11] https://youtu.be/zDZFcDGpL4U accessed November 9, 2018.
[12] Agora schools and Democratic schools in the Netherlands provide inspiring examples of schools that are undertaking a school wide change.

WHERE DO TEACHERS ADD VALUE?

Not only do we waste the talent of our students, a lot of the scarce time and energy of teachers is wasted as well: fixing the connection to a digital board, writing reports that are never read, searching for email, etc.[13] Such waste is endemic in most organizations, not only in schools. It is pervasive and substantial in education.[14] This does not add value and distracts teachers from adding value for the students. Adding value is helping students master the knowledge, skills, and attitudes they need in life. This points to another category of waste: teaching that misses the goal of adding value. This could be teaching students more than they can process, teaching in formats that are not conducive to their learning. It is the waste of talent that was referred to in the previous section. The key aim of a teacher is to set goals with and for his students, determine where they are in their learning and develop strategies together to reach those goals, and keep monitoring the progress and adjusting the strategies accordingly. Hattie phrases it well:

> A typical lesson never goes as planned. Expert teachers are skilled at monitoring the current status of student understanding and the progress of learning towards the success criteria, and they seek and provide feedback geared to the current understanding of the students [...]. Through selective information gathering and responsiveness to students, they can anticipate when the interest is waning, know who is not understanding, and develop and test hypotheses about the effect of their teaching on all of the students.[15] Wiliam makes the point even more forceful.
>
> The teacher's job is not to transmit knowledge, nor to facilitate the learning. It is to engineer effective learning environments for the students. The key features of effective learning environments are that they create

---

[13] An extensive overview of waste is contained in Vincent Wiegel and Lejla Brouwer-Hadzialic, "Lean Education," in *The Routledge Companion to Lean Management*, ed. T H Netland and D J Powell, Routledge Companions in Business, Management and Accounting (New York: Routledge, 2017), pp. 422–434.

[14] M L Emiliani, "Improving business school courses by applying lean principles and practices," *Quality Assurance in Education* 12, no. 4 (2004): 175–187, doi:10.1108/09684880410561596; M L Emiliani, Special issue: Lean six sigma for higher education evolution in lean teaching, (2016): 1–17.

[15] John Hattie, *Visible Learning for Teachers: Maximizing Impact on Learning* (Abingdon, UK: Taylor & Francis Group, 2012), 30.

student engagement and allow teachers, learners, and their peers to ensure that the learning is proceeding in the intended direction.[16]

One does not necessarily have to agree with these views, but take away a very important point. The key focus is learning and not teaching. We teachers all know this, but often enough we find ourselves teaching in a specific way that has grown over the years, that fits the infrastructure where we work, the institutional setting within which we work. Then we suddenly realize, "I'm not having the impact I want to. The students are missing the point, hence I'm not making it well." This is waste that is even bigger than all the needless reports. So, if we want to improve education, the starting point is the process of learning and how we add the most value for our students and society at large. And from that starting point with new technologies and the Lean Education philosophy rethink the way we best support that learning.

BACK TO ECONOMICS

Economics is the field of scarcity and value. In the limited time available, with limited resources, we work to provide as much value as we can. In usual economic analyses, value is equated with price. That does not necessarily work in education. Value for students is something that society at large determines. As in regular economic practices, we need to start our analysis and our organization from a clear view on value. In the next chapters, I will look into value for students in all its facets. It is clear that the core process in which value is created is in learning. Deriving from the definition of value and the needs of the learning process, we must organize our teaching and the support for the teaching process. The main scarce resource in teaching is the talent of teachers. To enrich the learning environment, reducing the waste of teachers time and energy must be the driving economic principle in organizing our schools, and not the focus on economies of scale and misguided standardization. The learning can be further supported through abundant educational

---

[16] Dylan Wiliam, *Embedded Formative Assessment* (Bloomington, IN: Solution Tree Press, 2011), p. 50.

resources. The (almost) freely scalable resources free up time of teachers to focus on the value adding activities. The logic of abundance requires schools to make an upfront investment in the curation of the resources. By teaming up, schools have the opportunity to create a rich and wide pallet of resources that will allow them to cater to the variation in the classroom.

MY U-TURN IN AUTOMOTIVE LECTURING

Saskia Monsma

We want our students to have a self-directed, critical way of learning focused on understanding. This showed to be more wishful thinking than reality. When, in addition, the efforts to improve traditional lecturing proved to have the opposite effect, Saskia Monsma, senior lecturer Automotive at HAN University of Applied Sciences made a U-turn in her lecturing. About the Just in Time Teaching (JiTT) and Process Improvement (PI) principle, quizzes and "convince your neighbor" discussions.

WHY A NEW TEACHING METHOD?

Being part of a university of applied sciences, we focus in our education on making the students put theory into practice by giving them assignments, lab work, modeling and simulation exercises, and real-life projects to work on. The theoretical topics are typically taught by traditional lecturing, predominantly based on one-way communication. Although students are told to study the material before class, they generally do not do so. Therefore, students have to absorb a lot of new information in a relative short time, and this allows little or no room for the needed critical reflection on the content nor for meaningful discussions. Questions posed during lectures to engage students are typically answered by a small group of students only—if at all. Most students remain passive, listening and taking notes, not showing, or perhaps not even knowing, if they really understand the topic. This all results in little variation and

MY U-TURN IN AUTOMOTIVE LECTURING (Continued)

interaction during lectures, which also makes it hard for students to keep their attention level up during the often-long hours of lecturing.

The lecture notes provided by the lecturer once the class is over are, in general, an excellent summary of the theory and therefore also do not encourage students to study the material themselves. The subsequent lack of reading skills poses problems for students, for example, during project research. For their project work, they need to study the literature and abstract relevant knowledge from the literature. The habit to improve your own lectures and lecture notes after each term, unintendedly reinforces this undesirable passive student behavior.

Problem-solving skills are, in general, well practiced by the students during the exercises, but the results drop as soon as the problem deviates from the learned approaches. This suggests that students learn "recipes for solutions" instead of truly understanding a problem and based on this, derive a solution. The practice to provide more similar exercises, often at the request of students, works counter-productively in the end. This could also explain the apparent contradiction we often find: students being able to solve difficult problems, but who cannot answer a relatively simple conceptual question about that same topic.

Exam results regularly showed that students have difficulties with properly answering a question, like giving to-the-point answers in clear sentences without irrelevant information. They often want to show their knowledge by extensively describing everything they know about every topic mentioned in the question, irrespective of the question itself. Regularly emphasizing this to students and even providing previous exams including correct answers did not prove to be an effective remedy.

This all made me realize that telling students how they should study and what we expect of them just did not work. They should be given several opportunities to practice, to make mistakes, and to learn from them. The exams at the end of the term should not be the first and final moment for this. This implied that my traditional

MY U-TURN IN AUTOMOTIVE LECTURING (Continued)

way of theory lecturing had to be reconsidered. Combined with an already existent desire of having more variation during classes and the need to cut down on class hours, this made me dive into the literature of student engagement methods, flipping the classroom and interactive teaching. As expected, my problems were not new, literature offers many solutions. The author that appealed to me the most was Mazur, a physics professor at Harvard University, who described in a compelling way how my problems were also his problems. Apparently, his were solved by radically changing his teaching method. He improved this method over the years guided by thorough research, and it is now known as "Just in Time Teaching" and "Peer Instruction." Inspired by his work, especially his results, I decided to follow in his footsteps. The results surpassed my expectations.

The method is based on the "flipped classroom" concept, where students study the theory before class, so that in class the precious contact time can be spend on clarifying difficulties students encountered, going more in-depth for important topics, and giving examples. This should also save class time, as it is not needed to explain everything in class anymore. To study the content before class is not new, to my knowledge this is what we have been telling students for years and years. The problem is: how do you make them study? They are not unwilling, but most of the times the good intentions drown in other important matters in the life of a student. I took the short-cut: I asked my students. The answer was strikingly simple: reward us for our work. In education this means: give us points for it.

Just in Time Teaching

So, this leads me to the first part: "Just in Time Teaching." At the start of the term, I provide students with the so-called "Pre-Class Study Assignments" which is a list with all the topics the students must study before coming to each class, like a chapter in a book, perhaps some videos or other theoretical material. Nothing new here, but now the students must show that they studied the material by

MY U-TURN IN AUTOMOTIVE LECTURING (Continued)

making a WarmUp Test before class starts. This is a test which contains relatively simple conceptual questions about the materials they studied. Questions that are not obvious from the material, so cannot be answered by copying or learning by heart, but require understanding of the material.

I have implemented the WarmUp Test in two different ways: an online quiz that is available a few days before class and closes the night before class and a test at the first 10 minutes at the start of class. The advantage of the online quiz is that the students are able to work and discuss together in the days before class. They can use all available sources and are working actively with the material provided. The last question is always what they found difficult and/or interesting about the material. Having the students answers available at the morning before class gives me the opportunity to go through their answers and select my lecture topics. This means I do not teach "everything" in my lecture anymore, but only the parts that student find difficult, which I can derive from their answers. This makes the lectures much more effective, addressing specific topics that need further explanation, and efficient, not wasting time by explaining things students already understand. To me, it was quite shocking how this content sometimes deviated from my perception of "easy" and "difficult" topics for students. In hindsight, this explained a lot of the mistakes made by students on exams. It also benefits my teaching a lot, I continue to learn more about students (mis)understandings after each WarmUp Test.

This is not only Just in Time Teaching, but also Just in Time Learning. This is apparent from the fact that almost all students finished the online quiz in the evening before class. This is good, as the topics are on top of their mind when they come to class the next day. The disadvantage of the online WarmUp Test was that students study only the parts of the Pre-Class Study Assignments that are needed to answer the questions. This forced me to make good conceptual questions about all parts of the material, which of course takes considerable time. A solution was again provided by my students: give the

MY U-TURN IN AUTOMOTIVE LECTURING (Continued)

WarmUp Test at the start of class. In this way, students do not know which topics will be tested, so studying all material is stimulated. In addition, this does not require me to make questions about all topics, which reduces the workload. Of course, the difficult topics are not available for me as lecturer before class, but these become clear during review of the WarmUp Test immediately following the test. This in-class WarmUp Test can be done on paper or with software where students fill them in by smartphone or laptop.

After the WarmUp Test, the start of my lecture is always the review of the questions. I have the answers of the students available, either through the online quiz or the test done in class. As they just finished the test, students are really "full on the topic" and start discussing with each other immediately after the test is done. I show student answers anonymously to the class and ask them what they consider good and bad answers and why. This always results in intense discussions, by also questioning their explanations, it covers much more than the topic of the question. This helps a lot: it gives students the possibility to explain their reasoning and it gives me much insight in their perception and understanding. It allows me to "lecture on the fly" on certain topics brought up by students, to discuss in class good and bad answers, proper understanding of concepts and relationships to other topics. As this is all related to their WarmUp Test results, students are engaged, especially because it is not rare that in these discussions students show that more than one answer is a good answer. This review of the WarmUp Test covers, in general, the first hour of my class and is a crucial part of my lectures. Spending time on making proper WarmUp Test questions that allow a good review, therefore pays off in class.

Peer Instruction

After a break, the lecture continues with the "Peer Instruction" part. Based on the input from the WarmUp Test, I select the difficult topics. In the case of the in-class WarmUp Test, I have some "likely candidate topics" prepared based on experience of previous classes. During the review of the WarmUp Test, I select materials from the set of

MY U-TURN IN AUTOMOTIVE LECTURING (Continued)

prepared topics. For a topic I give a few minutes lecture. Since the students studied the material, I can explain the main topic and then focus on the difficult or misunderstood aspects. I then end with a so-called ConcepTest, which is a conceptual question about the just lectured topic, which requires real understanding to be answered properly. This ConcepTest is given online and students are given some time, around 2 minutes, to answer it by themselves. Then I show the results anonymously to students on the beamer. Depending on the question, this can be a histogram for a multiple choice question or for a short answer question the actual answers are given. There are three possibilities for continuation then. If most of the students got it wrong, the topic is not properly understood and is explained again, clarifying difficulties. If most students answered correctly, the topic is shortly summarized, and we move on to the next topic. The third possibility is when the answers are spread. If the percentage of the good answers is between 30% and 70%, then a "convince your neighbor" peer discussion is started. I tell students to find another student that has a different answer than they have and then try to convince that student of their answer. Small groups are mostly formed and students are, often passionately, convincing their fellow students. This seems like chaos in class: a lot of students making a lot of noise. But it is not, they are actively involved in the topic, using books, Internet, and their social skills to emphasize their arguments. After the peak of noise drops, I end the discussion by opening again the same ConcepTest and asking students to put in their possibly revised answer. Almost all cases in the past years of lecturing showed that the vast majority of students now fill in the correct answer. Apparently, students can instruct their peers very well. A student with the correct answer is, in general, more convinced about his or her answer. In addition, she apparently also has a good way of explaining it to another student. Being a student herself new to the subject makes it easier to grasp what makes the subject difficult for other students. In my course evaluations many students mention these "convince your neighbor" discussions as one of things where they learned the most.

MY U-TURN IN AUTOMOTIVE LECTURING (Continued)

The exam results show that the method works: in general, students understand the theory better, formulate better answers, and receive higher scores. Student evaluations show that students state it was hard work, but that they learned a lot and enjoyed it much more than traditional lecturing. Often they suggest to use this method for other lectures.

So, is it all roses here? No, it is not. First of all, the method should be explained properly to students, and even more importantly, explain why you use this method. Then follows the hard part: stick to it! Students have to work hard before every class to get proper results for their WarmUp Test. They don't like that and they will complain about it. Every trick in the book will be used: that it absorbs all their time and they do not have time for other courses, that they pay for "proper lecturing," and that they were not able to study because of this or that. Often, I explain again why I use this method and that it will benefit them in the end. Also, the fact that student evaluations show that they do not have to study much before the actual final term exam helps a lot. Leaving out the lowest WarmUp mark of the term resolves the issue of not being always able to study. Be clear about the fact that this method is not open for discussion and follow it through consistently. As soon as you fall back to "lecturing every-thing," students will fall back in to passive absorbing.

Also from the lecturer perspective there are points to consider. Even good policies travel badly. This means that the method by itself does not do the job, the lecturer is the most important part. He or she must be enthusiastic about it, willing to invest time in WarmUp Tests and ConcepTest, and extracting relevant information from these. As a lecturer you must have a good overview of the theory so you can leave behind the fixed content of your lecture. You must be able to pick and relate relevant topics for your lecture based on students feedback from the questions. You must be able to deal with the "chaos" in class and discussions with students.

For me, it brought me much more than I had hoped for. Not only better student results in less class time, but also my lecturing is so

MY U-TURN IN AUTOMOTIVE LECTURING (Continued)

much more fulfilling for students and for myself. Thanks to this way of lecturing, I get to know my students better: how they learn, where their problems are, but also as individuals. Through the class and peer discussions, I get to know them as individuals instead as one class. This holds both ways. Every lecture is different, determined together with the students. Also, I learn from every review of a WarmUp Test, from every Peer Instruction, how to stay close to the students (mis)understanding. This gives me the feeling during lecturing of working together with our future automotive engineers and makes me confident I have "U-turned" the right way.

Short Reflection

This case by Saskia Monsma shows clearly the elements and power of Lean Education. It is about the learning as the core process and teaching as a supporting process. The key is finding out where the students are, and meeting them there. Just in time delivery is a corner stone of Lean thinking. Just in time-teaching shows it translates well to education. Provide the students with what they need, when they need it. The case shows also the importance of continuous improvement and innovation. Trying out new ways of teaching, allowing for short cycled feedback, and feed forward, are all crucial in learning. The impact of Saskia's teaching has grown, while ultimately even saving some time. I would argue the former is more important than the latter. However that may be it frees up time to do further experiments for improvement. Thus it initiates a culture of continuous improvement in which teaching is more fulfilling.

Vincent Wiegel

2

Educational Technology

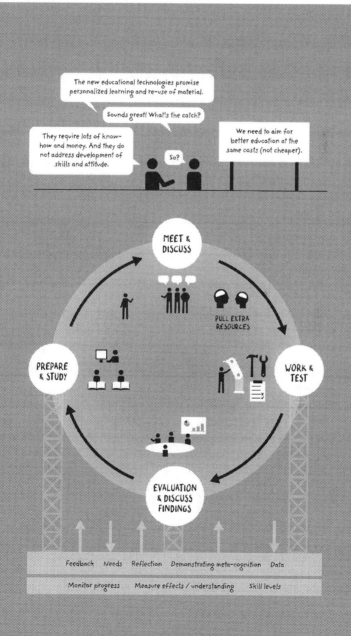

INTRODUCTION

The rise of information technology has only just begun to impact education. The replacement of chalk boards by digital boards has not fundamentally altered teaching. Communicating online with students and parents on schedules, grades, etc. is surely more effective. But it does not really change education.

Arguably, the biggest change is the availability of online resources such as the Khan Academy offers and such as can be found in massive open online courses (MOOCs). The application of these resources in main stream education remains limited though.

Educational technologies hold a huge promise. Tools that facilitate the interaction in the classroom offer a huge potential to activate students, to increase participation, and tune teaching to the actual needs and understanding of students. Likewise, educational analytics offer the potential for better tuning of teaching to the needs of individual students.

For all these technologies and tools, the key questions are how to harness their potential and how to integrate them into the educational system. As much as they promise improvements, they also lay huge claims on resources. They require financial investments and education of teachers and administrators who are already often overburdened, teachers and administrators who might not have the necessary skills and knowledge to deploy these tools and technologies.

One thing should also be made clear at the outset. Technology in and by itself will not bring the required change and not have the impact that is required. What does help is powering teaching innovations with technology.

A WAY THROUGH THE SWAMP

The last decade has seen a host of new digital applications focusing on education. The numbers are huge, the quality levels vary dramatically, and the impact is very uncertain. The situation has been likened to a swamp in an insightful study by Michael Fullan and Katelyn Donnelly.[1] They note that despite the overwhelming number of innovations, there is scant evidence

---

[1] Michael Fullan and Katelyn Donnelly, "Alive in the Swamp: Assessing Digital Innovations in Education," Institute for Public Policy Research 2013.

that they contribute to better learning. "…there is in general a lack of strong efficacy evidence demonstrating the impact of the digital innovations on student learning. Robust academic meta–analysis research, such as that by Steven Higgins et al., shows a current lack of causal links between the use of technology and student attainment."[2] This lack of impact is attributed to:

- A weak link of technology to pedagogy,
- Pedagogy that needs further development and understanding of how to harness the potential technology, and
- A lack of focus on the change management side of technology.

The efforts to introduce digital technologies "have put the technology above teaching and excitement above evidence."[3]

Yet, there is a generally felt notion that digital technology is bound to have a big impact on education as it has had, and still has, on other parts of society. Navigating uncertainty is at the core of some Lean concepts. The Lean Kata and Kaizen tools for continuous improvement start with a picture of an ideal state plus a mechanism to navigate from the current state to that ideal state through a series of small, controlled steps—experiments. The plan-do-study-act cycle of testing out new ideas to bring one closer to better understanding and performance is the scientific way of thinking. The idea of scientific thinking brought to the classroom is something that should come naturally. It does where the subject matter of classes is concerned. But interestingly enough, it is not always the natural way when it comes to the practice of teaching and learning itself. This is where Lean Education has a big contribution to make. Lean Education has an organization wide scope. This scope helps schools to synchronize content and pedagogy, teaching and support, and learning and technology. Using the same mode of scientific thinking across all domains, it both unifies and helps dealing with the inherent uncertainty, and in particular, with the application of educational technologies.

There is another role Lean Education has to play. Fullan and Donnelly note that efforts to improve education through the deployment of digital innovations have been disappointing. They distinguish between two types: school-based and technology-enabled innovations. The former are often wholesale change driven by a concerted effort of a small

---

[2] Fullan and Donnelly, 11.
[3] R Luckin et al., "Decoding Learning," *The Proof, Promise and Potential of Digital Education*, (London, UK: NESTA, 2012), p. 63.

team. It has genuine impact, however, "...the problem is scale. Schools are accountable for student outcomes; they can often control the basic infrastructure and the professional development of their teachers. However, systemic change is a big challenge. How does one school scale to five schools and, most importantly, how does it scale to 500 or 5,000?"[4] The latter, technology-enabled innovations, are weak on pedagogy. They scale well, but offer little, if any, improvements to teaching and learning practices. They "...use basic pedagogy—most often in the form of introducing concepts by video instruction and following up with a series of progression exercises and tests. Other digital innovations are simply tools that allow teachers to do the same age-old practices but in a digital format."[5] Lean thinking has proven over decades that it scales well. It has transformed whole organizations and even sectors of the economy. It has done so in industry, healthcare, and services to name just a few. Since the basic outlook of Lean thinking and innovative pedagogies are well aligned, we have a fit on the material aspect: the pedagogy, the teaching, and learning. This point is made in Chapters 3 through 6, plus the various in-sets with cases.

FOUR CATEGORIES OF EDUCATIONAL TECHNOLOGIES

How can we deploy digital technologies to make meaningful changes to the way our students learn and we teach, and to find ourselves a way through the swamp? A first step is to take a closer look at these technologies and better understand what they do. The various digital technologies serve different purposes and have their specific strengths and weaknesses.

The different applications span a wide range of technologies and applications. We distinguish four categories to facilitate the discussion of educational technology, its uses, and impact.[6] One, administrative platforms

---

[4] *Fullan and Donnelly, "Alive in the Swamp: Assessing Digital Innovations in Education,"* (London, UK: Nesta, 2013), p. 25.

[5] Ibid.

[6] Of course, these categories are coarse. There will be applications that do not fit them exactly, that cross boundaries. One could devise other categories as well. The main purpose of these categories is to facilitate the discussion of the impact of educational technology on education.

where teachers, educators, students, and parents can access material, information, and interact. They are also called Learning management systems or online learning platforms. Their prime focus is facilitating education and its support processes. It is not primarily focused on the very acts of learning and teaching. Information on schedules, holidays, grades, etc. is shared, teaching content can be stored on the platform, and accessed online. A student might access course materials online as much as she would reach for a book. It is not the presentation of the content itself that is the key focus. The scope of functionality of these platforms is wide. The various functions are integrated. Often these platforms support some standards that make the exchange of data easier, examples are Blackboard and Moodle. Two, educational applications (apps), these are relatively small, narrowly scoped applications that run on mobile devices and laptops. They serve a single purpose, run stand alone, and at best are weakly integrated with other applications or platforms, examples are EdPuzzle and Kahoot!. Three, content-oriented platforms, these platforms offer both content and a pedagogical approach that integrates and presents the content. The aim is the supplement and sometimes even supplant the traditional process of teaching, examples are Udacity, Coursera, and Khan Academy. Four, learning analytics, technologies aimed at gathering and analyzing data about the learning process. Based on the data, content or advice can be provided to facilitate the learning of individuals and groups of individuals. Attempts can be made to predict study results based on learning behavior. Ultimately, the aim is to develop evidence-informed teaching practices. It is based on big data and machine learning technologies. Learning analytics algorithms can run stand alone and integrated into one of the above types of platforms. The applications range from the analysis of student behavior in the content-oriented platforms to predict their grades to text analysis of email exchanges to improve MOOCs.[7] Each of these four categories has its own appeal and potential, but also drawbacks and different impacts on the schools in terms of required know-how, money, and time.

---

[7] Viktor Mayer-Schoönberger and Kenneth. Cukier, *Lernen Mit Big Data: Die Zukunft Der Bildung* (Munich, Germany: REDLINE-Verl, 2014); Miguel Conde and Ángel Hernández-García, "Learning Analytics: Expanding the Frontier," in *Proceedings of the 5th International Conference on Technological Ecosystems for Enhancing Multiculturality*, TEEM 2017 (New York: ACM, 2017), Vol. 36, pp. 1–36:5, doi:10.1145/3144826.3145386.

POTENTIAL FOR DEPLOYING EDUCATIONAL TECHNOLOGIES

Each of these categories has a different impact on learning and teaching. Some of these technologies make existing processes more efficient. The category of administrative platforms makes it easier to update students and their parents on changes in the schedule, inform them on events, etc. These are basically efficiency enhancers and do not impact the learning and teaching that take place. They have, for example, little ability to personalize the teaching. They claim to provide personalized information. It is personal only in the sense that a student does not have to filter out the information relevant to her. The information itself, however, is still impersonal.

The second category of educational apps increases efficiency of teaching. It enables, for example, running informal formative assessments fast and easy.[8] Questions still have to be formulated, but through the apps the answers are processed and visualized fast. This allows the teacher to adjust the teaching plan by offering (sub)groups or even individuals different, additional material. So, the app itself does not support the personalization of learning and teaching, but it is instrumental toward personalization. They can be used to offer the additional materials and exercise opportunities.

The third category of content platforms offers both a potential for time saving and personalization. The materials themselves are already available and can save a teacher the development time and effort. Teachers will have to spend considerable time on the other hand on familiarizing themselves with the materials and tuning them to fit their teaching plans. Given the breadth of materials available, they offer the potential for pupils to pull the materials they need at high quality levels. It is important that teachers, "…realize that they can save time and money and they can also get the best professors from all over the world if they are working with open educational resources."[9] Some of these resources will fit their needs better than others both in content and format. This is a passive form of personalization. Teacher and pupil still are active in the search for what is needed and what is available.

---

[8] By informal formative assessment, I mean mostly small assessments that are used to inform students and teacher on the progress that students are making. They allow the teacher and students to tweak the learning strategies and teaching. They do not have a formal status in the grading and assessment processes.

[9] Nina Hood and Allison Littlejohn, "Knowledge typologies for professional learning: Educators' (Re)Generation of knowledge when learning open educational practice," *Educational Technology Research and Development* 65, no. 6 (2017): 1591, doi:10.1007/s11423-017-9536-z.

The last category is both a potential time saver and an active form of personalization. Through gathering data of the pupil's behavior while, for example, reading an online text the learning analytics system can assess the pupils progress, pace, stumbling blocks, etc. By asking some questions it can analyze the pupils understanding. By combining all the information, it can generate advice on what to study next, revisit particular topics, and offer additional materials. In this case, the efficiency gains are in the assessment which is carried out by the system.

DRAWBACKS AND LIMITATIONS OF EDUCATIONAL TECHNOLOGIES

Each of the technologies has potential as highlighted above. Their use is, however, not a simple endeavor. They have generic drawbacks and concerns, in addition to ones that are specific to an individual technology. All face, to some degree, the following drawbacks and limitations.

Information retention: Information that is offered as digital text is less easily retained than paper-based versions. Though many technologies offer a combination of graphic, oral, and textual information, all rely in substantial degree on textual information. As digital information is presented in applications and on digital platforms, such as Android or iOs, that offer more information than just the educational content, there is diversion that hampers the processing of information. Features that are considered useful, such as hyperlinks to related sources providing additional explanation, form distractions that interfere with the learning process and leave it less effective.

Cost: Schools with tight budgets, which are most schools, will find even minor investments in apps a challenge, let alone investments in platforms, which can easily cost many thousands of dollars. These investments can be prohibitive. Schools will probably have to syndicate to negotiate for better, affordable prices. At the same time, there are many good sources that are free. The already mentioned Khan Academy is just one of these. Many apps are free of charge, and some content platforms offer free access and demand payment only for certificates and diplomas.

Integration: With a myriad of free or cheap applications, another challenge will be the integration. Many apps can be used as standalone and require little configuration or administration. But given concerns over privacy and security, this may not last. In addition, learning analytics require data in order to be effective. Data that are generated across many different applications. If these are not stored and somehow related to student characteristics, they will be of little use.

Required know-how: Finally, each of these technologies requires some know-how. Teaching is not necessarily known as the most tech-savvy profession, and the openness and proficiency with new technologies varies greatly across the profession. Schools will need to decide whether to train all or some of its staff, and to what level. The same question applies to students. Though they are often considered digital natives, they have not necessarily mastered the required digital skills to work with these technologies. Whatever the choice, schools are in for some substantial investment in training.

Each of these categories of technologies has also its own, specific limitations. Administrative platforms have the big advantage of integrating various separate systems and even manual processes, e.g., student communication, resource administration, and enrollment. They do so on a proprietary platform, built specifically by the company that develops the platform. This ensures seamless integration of different tools and functionalities. The drawback is that it is much more burdensome to integrate external tools such as data and file storage platforms, e.g., Dropbox, and 3rd party apps. This drawback has two causes. The first cause concerns for standards and the adherence to them. There are some IT standards that detail the educational domain: how, for example, is a student defined? This sounds trivial, but is already challenging. How is a student ID formatted and stored, and does the information include race, gender, etc.? If a provider choose to implement its platform in line with a standard, the next question is which standard. Currently, there are multiple standards: SCORM, AICC, Common Cartridge, and xAPI,[10] to name some of most prominent. The second cause of difficulties in integrating different tools relates to the ownership of data. Data exchange from one app to another, from platform

---

[10] SCORM stands for Sharable Content Object Reference Model. AICC refers to Aviation Industry Computer-Based Training Committee. xAPI stands for experience API. Reinhold Behringer, "Interoperability Standards for MicroLearning," *MicroLearning Conference 7.0*, no. January (2013): 10, provides a good introduction to these various standards.

to app, and from platform to platform is far from common. A key question is "Who owns the data?" User information provided in one app cannot just be exchanged with another. There are both legal limitations driven by privacy considerations, as well as commercial restrictions. Drawing users to an app involves a lot of effort. Facilitating access to other apps is not commercially attractive after one has invested a lot of effort and money attracting users. Often, apps do not allow users of a platform to access the app through the platform even if they have a separate account with the app. Since not one platform or app does everything, students and teacher need they rely on multiple platforms and apps that are not well integrated. In short, it can be cumbersome.

Content platforms offer 3rd party content. The challenge is to integrate the external party's content with its specific pedagogy into the school's own curriculum and pedagogy. Broadly speaking, consistency is the key challenge here: consistency in terminology and definitions, and consistency in pedagogy, format, and size. It can be done, but it requires substantial work. Probably less than developing your own materials, but not as much less as one would hope. Luckily, most content offered is packaged in small sizes[11] that can be configured more easily than large, say, semester-sized courses. On the positive side, it requires teachers to re-engage with the topics and reflect on why they prefer one or the other. Hearing several providers cover their subjects stimulates self-reflection and enhances his own view on how to best present the topics. The final drawback is the formal recognition. Courses that are offered outside the school's jurisdiction, in another country, for example, are not necessarily officially recognized. This might mean that at least the grading has to be redone to ensure conformity with the national standards. At worst, the school has to provide additional reporting and explanation to justify its use of the content platform and its recognition within the national system as a fully accredited institution.

The latest of the main trends is learning analytics. Most of the promises of learning analytics will probably materialize somewhere down the line, but are many years yet to maturity. It is currently strongly technology driven with weaker links to pedagogy and the actual learning process, a point made by Conde and others.[12] One key question is, for example,

---

[11] Micro-learning is a trend (yet another one) in education that is of interest, especially in this respect. It refers to small units of learning content that are often though not necessarily accessed through mobile devices.

[12] Conde and Hernández-García, "Learning Analytics: Expanding the Frontier."

what measures and indicators are good proxies of actual learning? Clicks on videos or texts are not learning. So, what does a fast forward click on a video tell us about the learning of a pupil? Learning analytics requires by its very nature large amounts of data. Smaller institutions might need to syndicate in order to obtain sufficient data or share the content platforms.

ALIGNMENT OF TECHNOLOGY AND PEDAGOGY

In contemplating technology, schools have to consider how to integrate technology into the school's pedagogical philosophy. It is all too easy to be beguiled by all the options an app offers, the ease of a platform. Often it becomes technology for the sake of technology thinly veiled behind a pedagogical phrase or an argument of efficiency. Just as teaching gets in the way of learning if it becomes unreflective, a particular technology becomes ingrained in the institution regardless of what it was once meant to achieve.

Regardless of the specific pedagogy a school adopts, each kind of pedagogy will contain the steps of: (1) establishing where the students want and need to go, (2) assessing where the students are in their learning journey, (3) determining what materials to offer and at which pace, and (4) providing feedback on their achievements to help them in their learning. This is an admittedly very minimalist version. One that allows for many different ways to actually perform these steps. That is exactly the purpose here. Taking each step in turn, a school can determine how it wants to execute it. Based on that view, requirements for different apps and/or platforms can be defined. Using EdTech it should be easier for lecturers to execute these steps.

Let us look at each of the four steps in turn.

Step 1: Establishing where the students want and need to go, is one that is all too often not taken at all. The biggest challenge is therefore not how to support digitally, but what it means and how it is done. It concerns establishing the target condition: what is the student able to do, what does she know, and which skills does he possess?[13] It requires input from the student and not just the teacher. The student has ambitions and desires that she wants to realize. They are key in motivating and directing the

---

[13] Target condition is a Lean concept that describes a situation one wants to achieve. It is much more than numbers, like output or profit margins or quality. It also describes how a process functions, how people interact, and how they monitor progress. M Rother, *Toyota Kata: Managing People for Improvement, Adaptiveness and Superior Results* (Maidenhead, UK: McGraw-Hill Education, 2009).

study. Others might contribute to the discussion as well, for example, companies in the case of traineeships. Of course, the regional, national, sectoral norms for specific qualifications and diplomas still apply. When the notion of a joint established and adopted target condition has been accepted, we can focus on how to implement it. Defining the target condition and sharing with potentially multiple parties implies more work. And, in effect, it will be. Discussing the target condition is something different from telling students what the target is. And even that is something we often do not do. It will be worth the effort, though, because it will increase engagement on the part of the students. It can be made easier by deploying tools that structure the process of defining the target condition and facilitate the communication. A tool like Trakstar, which was originally developed to support HR departments to track the development and performance of personnel, can be used to define targets, define desired attitudes, and skills. Students can suggest their goals. In discussions with the teacher, more and other goals can be added. The school as a whole might set targets regarding desired skills and attitudes. Using rubrics,[14] a school can define the development over the entire school career of its students, and within a grade or cohort. People outside of the school are invited electronically to provide input.

The target condition is not passing an exam and getting a diploma. These are the measures, hopefully, that indicate the target condition has been reached. A target condition describes the future situation in terms of the new normal, the new norms, and conditions for success. These are the stepping stones toward a vision the student has. Depending on the age and maturity of the student, these can be smaller or bigger "dreams," e.g., being able to read Harry Potter, playing soccer, saving animals, becoming a physician, building a robot, or giving a presentation. These dreams are detailed by attaching adjectives, like convincingly, fluently, and concrete goals. The joint discussion on the target condition involves the skills, knowledge, and attitudes that are required to achieve the goals. Consider this example. Shirley, 12 years,

---

[14] A rubric is a tool for defining mastery or performance of a person's skill, knowledge, attitude, work, etc. It defines the criteria by which it is assessed and describes the various levels for each of the criteria. See, for example, Maria Langworthy and Michael Fullan, *A Rich Seam: How New Pedagogies Find Deep Learning* (Paerson, 2014), doi:10.1016/j.jbmt.2011.01.017. One should be careful of the limitations, as with any method. See, for example, H Ito, "Is a Rubric Worth the Time and Effort? Conditions for Its Success," *International Journal of Learning* 10, no. 2 (2015): 32–45.

is fascinated by robots. Her ideal is to build robots that can help elderly people. Her target condition for the coming year is to build a robot that can find Easter eggs in the classroom (the goal). In order to achieve this, she must know how to install sensors that guide the robot (knowledge). Since the goal is too big for her to achieve on her own, she must be able to enlist the help of others (skill). The goal is a rather ambitious one, so she is likely to experience setbacks which she must be able to overcome (attitude, perseverance) and learn from these setbacks (skill). To operate the robot she will need to know a programming language and some math to guide the robots trajectory (knowledge). These goals, skills, knowledge, and attitudes are described in a tracking tool in which she and the teacher work together.

Step 2: Assessing where the students are in their learning journey is much more than checking which materials the students have read, listened to, etc. It is about what they have actually understood. This is about executing small informal formative assessments as mentioned above. In a basic form, this can be quizzes using Mentimeter, Kahoot!, and several others. Student scores can be used to identify trends and performance of both the group and individual students. Are there specific areas that the class grapples with and that need more attention? Are there individual students that score persistently lower on the quizzes or show an upward or downward trend? Based on this input, a teacher can modify his teaching plan. He can also offer individual students other sources to study a topic in a different way. A more advanced format uses peer reviews of work produced by the student. Lecturer and students share some work that has been graded. By sharing both the grading guidelines, the actual work, and the peer reviews prior to getting together in the classroom, the discussion in the classroom can be focused on deepening the understanding. The sharing is done via an administrative platform. This approach is particularly powerful if students grade themselves prior to receiving the peer reviews and lecturer feedback. After receiving the feedback and the discussions, students can be asked to grade themselves again. This triggers both meta-cognition and deepens the understanding of the topic. This is particularly effective because the students learn from grading other students and then grading their own work again. Since the grades are not used as a summative assessment, the focus can really be on learning, rather than making the mark. This whole would be cumbersome with assistance from technology. Coordinating, distributing, and tracking are easily done using administrative platforms that facilitate submitting and commenting of work.

Based on the input from step 2, the learning proceeds to the next step. Step 3, determining what materials to offer and at which pace, requires variation in format (oral, video, textual), pace (fast, or slower, with or without revisiting), and timing (in the morning, the evening, during a break). A lecturer cannot deliver different formats all at once. So she needs to rely on different sources that provide the content in different formats. Formats that vary according to need. And formats that allow students to fast forward or slow down. Technology offers the ability to do all that. The lecturer can explain a topic to a subgroup of students, while others are individually watching a video. The video can be rewound and paced. The lecturer meanwhile can keep track of the students watching the video through a specific app. Yet other students can read some materials online. Using special software, they can set the reading pace. This tool provides a small ruler that sets the pace for the eyes of the reader. By doing so, it helps the reader focus and find the right pace without distraction.

Finally, step 4, providing students with feedback on their achievements to help them in their learning. Feedback and feedforward, whether it is formal or informal, is key to enhancing understanding and continued learning. Just telling students they made the mark or not is not very helpful. Teachers all do know that. Yet, time constraints often lead to sparsely annotated markings, and relatively little time for reflection.[15] Technology will by itself not remedy this lack of time. That is a matter of conscious choice by schools. It can, however, facilitate the reflection, enable input from a wider range of sources, and provide richer content. Many of the works, though definitely not all, by students can be submitted in an electronic format. Physical objects can be photographed, videos, audio files, electronic documents, computer code, 3D models, presentations, etc. Submitting electronic artifacts for grading feedback can be solicited easily from other sources such as parents, professionals, and peers more easily. That feedback can be presented as annotations to the work. Other people giving feedback can relate not just to the work, but also to the feedback already given.

---

[15] At New Engineers we try to reserve at least 15% of the available time for reflection and feedback. Some institutions, such as KaosPilot, have a guideline reserving up to 25% of the time for reflection.

This will work best if somewhere earlier in the learning process joint definitions of "good" have been developed. A shared frame of reference is necessary for the feedback to be valuable. And, in the same way as face-to-face feedback, online feedback must be governed by shared rules on how to ask for, give, and receive feedback, probably even more so, since online feedback is more often asynchronous. The provider cannot assess how the feedback is being received and correct if tone-of-voice or intentions are misunderstood. To facilitate learning, the Lean coaching Kata routine involves a series of questions that focus on understanding the thinking process of the pupil, on facts, the enhancement of understanding on the part of the pupil. Learning is understood as a series of small experiments in which hypotheses are tested. This means we ask a student what she wants to achieve (to learn, to be able to do). This is often in part related to general standards and norms of what students need to know at a certain age and a particular study or school type. Next she is asked to reflect on where she currently stands in relation to the goal, what the obstacles are, what the next steps are, and, finally, when and how we will see the results of the next step. This routine can be supported well through electronic formats. As part of this process, specific elements of the student's work can be annotated with more sources that the student can use to deepen his understanding, refer to more exercises, etc.

It is extremely important that a school starts on this journey with a vision and strategy on where the school is headed and how it wants to achieve its goals. All kinds of factors figure into such a strategy. What kind of students does the school cater to? What is its socio-economic background? How many students does it expect to serve? How easy or hard is it to attract teachers? What are the age groups of the students? Does it see itself as a provider of narrowly defined skills and knowledge sets, or has it a broader social, religious vision? That is why we cannot make generic recommendations. A school needs to tune the available technologies to its needs and abilities. This is what the strategy is about. Formulating a vision in a way that it can be translated in a concrete, coherent strategy is difficult. Often the vision is there, but it is very general, multi-interpretable. The strategy kicks in to help provide guidance on concrete policies of staff hiring, class sizes, materials, and also on the application of technology. That is why a complete chapter is dedicated to the formulation of a strategy (see Chapter 8).

HANDS ON!

The systematic introduction and use of information technology across a school is a challenge. It will in all likelihood involve multiple technologies, tools, apps, and platforms. Since a complete design with a big bang introduction is out of the scope for most schools, costing too much money and requiring know-how and resources that are not simply available on demand, a step-by-step approach is probably best. Even if resources would be available in abundance, a big bang approach would be undesirable. Changes are fast paced and profound. To make sure that students and teachers are all on board, a step-by-step approach of continuous improvement and innovation provides better learning opportunities and chances of success.

This is also key because it is not just technology that is introduced. The technology must serve the staff not curtail it, it must support the pedagogical vision not constrain it. In short, there is a lot of coherence required. Teaching experts and teachers need to formulate their pedagogy and convey it to technology experts. The experts in turn must explain the possibilities and drawbacks of each technology so that pedagogical experts understand how to best harness the power of technology, and teachers understand how to deploy the various technologies.

Following the next steps will help a school setting up its own IT support for learning and teaching.

1. Formulate the vision on the role of technology in learning and teaching. Why would the school introduce digital innovations at all? What is the intended role: a small supportive role for technology, or a ground breaking one? Is the drive primarily novelty and technology driven? Make sure that the technologies chosen have either their own clear pedagogical underpinning or are clearly and explicitly tied to the school's pedagogical vision

2. Introduce a system in which the evidencing of impact is an integral part of the school's way of teaching. This goes for everything a school does from pedagogy to housing, and particularly for technology. What is the impact of the digital technologies on the learning outcomes and costs? If there is not clear evidence of time savings for teachers, for example, and of impact on the learning of students, one should question the use of the technology. This is not to say that

everything can be measured, but the effort to do so will clarify the perspective and understanding

3. Consider the collection and use of data. What data are needed to support learning and teaching? Is it likely that the school will be able to collect data in the near future? If not, do not introduce data collection. If yes, look for models of students, learning outcomes, and learning strategies. This way a school can build a coherent view. That view can be used to determine requirements for apps, tools, platforms, etc. Data collection is also a delicate and sensitive endeavor. Make sure to consider privacy issues from onset

4. Develop the capabilities of teaching and professional services staff regarding digital tools. Ensure sufficient implementation support during the selection, deployment, and use of digital tools. The selection and purchase of tools are one thing. If implemented poorly, all effort is lost and wasted. The capabilities include leadership, and leadership support throughout the whole cycle. Introduction of new tools is bound to come with hick-ups. Persistence is crucial and requires ongoing attention and commitment

5. Look for cooperation with other schools on data sharing, joint purchasing, national guidelines, and offers. Syndicating with other schools is one of the more powerful ways to deal with the complexities associated with information technology. It requires from the school a fundamental openness and willingness to cooperate. Even if it means change in some of the ways in which learning and teaching are organized[16]

6. Compile a list of apps, tools, and platforms. Implement in small iterations. Draw from existing research and evaluations of tools. Evaluate this list on pedagogical innovativeness and scalability. Fullan and Donnelly offer a valuable index that can be used to evaluate technologies.[17]

---

[16] It will help schools overcome unwillingness to adopt other practices if they know that intra-school variation in quality and student attainment is bigger than inter-school variation.

[17] Fullan and Donnelly, "*Alive in the Swamp: Assessing Digital Innovations in Education*," 28–35.

3

Education and the Future

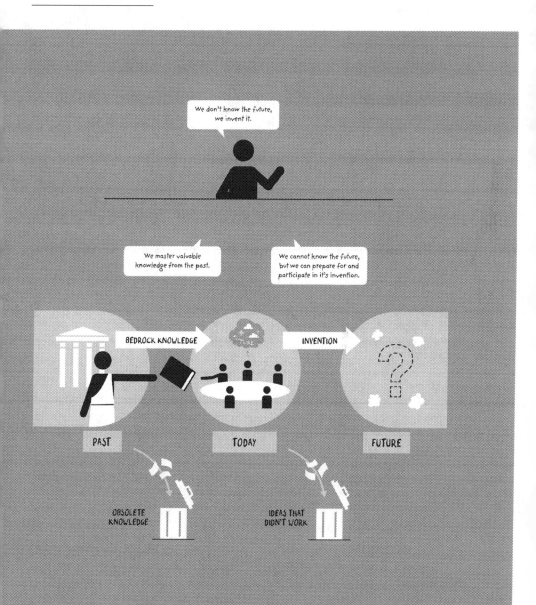

The future is a foreign country, they do things differently over there.

A variation on L.P. Hartley

INTRODUCTION

We do not know the future, we invent it. Hence, we cannot educate for the future. But we can prepare for it, and, as schools, participate in its invention. And that is a major step forward from teaching yesterday's stuff. Contrast this with, for example, the Dudenstadt report on engineering education: "We are educating engineers for the 21st century, with a 20th century curriculum at 19th century institutions." Ben Levin notes in a similar vein that all efforts to the contrary, "…most of the basic features of schooling remain largely unaltered even over a century." Schools should be much more than a conduit for knowledge from the past and knowledge created elsewhere. They would also benefit greatly from being much more integrated with social groups and organizations, be it research institutes, companies, government, and special interest groups. And, together with them, have our students actively participating and creating in frontier projects. Then schools as a whole will be exposed to the future as it is being invented.

Let me make two things clear at the outset. One, the past has generated much valuable knowledge that should not be discarded at all. There is much to be learned from the past so at no point should we be disdainful of our ancestors and what they achieved, quite to the contrary. Two, many schools are open toward society and have their students actively involved in projects. That is no mean feat. I propose to take things one step further still, and bring the future and the outside world to the core of our schools. We can do so by participating in concrete research programs, by having outsiders not just reflect on what we are doing, but by engaging them from scratch, by enlisting their help in teaching, etc. Various cases and chapters throughout the book will address this topic.

To manage this transition, schools need a stronger core on which to build a more agile and adaptive program. The core consists, among other things, of a system for strategy-based continuous improvement and innovation, a pedagogical philosophy, a learner agency program, a set of critical skills for the twenty-first century, and a core body of knowledge.

ADAPTIVE AND AGILE SCHOOLS

Schools have been presented with unwanted change quite often. Change has been done to the people working in schools rather than them being the drivers of change. The educational system needs changes to deal with new demands of our future citizens and employees and to incorporate opportunities that new technologies and pedagogies offer. These opportunities must be owned and driven by teachers and school administrators. Change can be managed best if initiated from a safe and stable basis. In our educational system, our schools need core stability as a basis to become more adaptive and agile. Adaptivity is the ability to respond to lasting, large scale changes in the environment. In the case of education, this means changes in technology and economy, among others. Agility refers to the ability to move quickly and easily in response to changing circumstances within the system.

The call for stability on the one hand and adaptiveness and agility on the other hand might seem contradictory. Stability could imply a certain heaviness and slowness. Adaptiveness and agility could imply a flightiness and flimsiness. I intend it in a different sense. The core stability provides education with a basis that focuses on the long term.[1] Learning and developing as individuals is a lifelong pursuit. It deals with large numbers and huge amounts of resources. These cannot just be changed on a whim. They need a fundament that everyone can rely on. At the same time, schools must be adaptive, have a core that is stable yet able to notice changes in the environment and adopt a new course. Within that system and on a solid basis, we need schools that are able to adapt to local needs, that are able to faster incorporate changes in knowledge and skills that are required of our students.

The question then is: What does this core entail? And, which part of the system should be agile? These questions refer to some extent to the definition of value a school, a country, or a community adopts. Based on cultural, historical, political, and religious grounds, schools will adopt different definitions of value. There are also some elements of value that can be identified as part of the basis that we can still include regardless of

---

[1] This reflects the first Lean management principle that states that organizations should base their decisions on a long-term philosophy, even at the expense of short-term gains. Jeffrey K Liker, *The Toyota Way: 14 Management Principles from the World's Greatest Manufacturer* (New York: McGraw-Hill Education, 2004), 71–84.

cultural, historical, political, and religious considerations. The twenty-first century skills are such an example. Value is at the heart of Lean Education thinking. Defining what constitutes value is left to the users, students, stakeholders, and administrators jointly. Lean Education does not presume to prescribe what constitutes value. However, some suggestions will be made.

There is another part of the core stability of schools: the system by which its processes are managed and monitored, the way in which the workings of the school are improved. This process focus leads to a predictable way of working and a controlled way for change. Content and methods of teaching and learning can be changed, the way in which that is done remains the same. That way is the way of Lean Education. Schools are not just organizations for learning, they are learning organizations. That learning must be based on critical self-reflection and continuous improvement and innovation.[2]

DESIDERATA OF AN ADAPTIVE AND AGILE SCHOOL

To educate with an eye on the future, there are a few essentials. These follow from the trends sketched in the previous chapters: fast paced technological change, pedagogical insights, social and economic pressure to deliver more, and differently educated citizens and employees. Schools need to be adaptive and agile. Given the magnitude and pace, schools cannot expect, nor be expected, to address this all by themselves. Content wise and capacity wise, they need a fundamental openness toward the world. Without stability as a basis, schools would be tossed around responding to every whim and latest fad. Adaptiveness and agility require a solid core around which change can take place. The core is made up of a vision on what constitutes value and the key elements of knowledge and skills for any future. The pedagogical philosophy adopted by the school will also be a key part of the school's core stability. Whatever pedagogy is adopted, it will need to focus on developing learner agency in students. Self-directed learning activities based on ownership of the learning is crucial in light of lifelong

[2] This reflects the 14th Lean management principle. I added, however, the continuous innovation element. Under the relentless change of technology, improvements will not be enough. We will need to innovate the way we do things, and not just do them better. More on Lean thinking and learning organizations in Liker, 250–265.

learning. Bringing stability are two additional system components. One, crucial is a system of active, controlled collection of feedback in relation to the goals that have been set, the analysis of the feedback, and interventions to make improvements. Knowledge is created through application and testing of existing knowledge and new ideas in practice. It involves the running of experiments.[3] The outcomes of these experiments are fed back into the curriculum and learning and teaching practices. This is a system of short cycled feedback loops in which students and external stakeholders are closely involved, a system of continuous improvement and innovation. Two, the other element is a filter that weeds out the key changes from the latest fads, the fundamental from the peripheral. Otherwise, the educational system and schools will be overwhelmed.

These are the desiderate for schools engaging in education with an eye on the future and a drive to be involved in its invention.

1. Core stability
2. Agility and adaptiveness
3. Fundamental openness toward society, science, and business
4. Systematic, short cycled feedback loops and active filter
5. A program of application and experimentation.

The core stability provides the basis for more adaptive and agile schools. Adaptiveness and agility will benefit from openness toward society, science, and business. In order to make this an orderly and workable proposition, schools will need a systematic way to process the input it receives from external stakeholders and to direct its own efforts at change. This will include an active filter to prevent schools from being overwhelmed and chasing wild gooses. Creating new insights that will benefit society at large will involve schools in inventing the future. If we are able to integrate the application and creation of knowledge into the scope of learning, we will effectively create a huge research and development (R&D) network. By including schools in a R&D agenda, we increase even further the relevance and impact of our schools and the joy of learning for our students. I will now discuss each of the five desiderata.

---

[3] Applying and experimenting is not exclusive for older students. I envision children in kindergarten engaged in small experiments just as well. What will change over time is the conscious agency involved. Early on, applications will probably be focused more on the recreation of knowledge. That will remain an important element of everyone's lifelong career as a student. Over time it will be mixed with a growing element of directed effort to test hypotheses and develop new ideas.

Core Stability

The core of a school consists of five components.

1. Learner agency
2. Pedagogical philosophy
3. Critical skill set: Twenty-first century skills, lingual and analytical skills
4. Fundamental and formative knowledge (mathematics, history)[4]
5. System of process management with strategy deployment, continuous improvement, and innovation.

Figure 3.1 shows how the core is built up. A school ideally solicits and receives input from a large array of stakeholders. This input is processed through a system of continuous improvement and innovation and strategy deployment. These drive adjustments to both the content and pedagogy, which in turn strengthen learner agency and increase the value provided. The circle can also be viewed from the core outward. Based on the school's vision on value and learner agency, its pedagogical vision is developed. That pedagogy then drives the curriculum with the skills, knowledge, and attitudes. The execution is driven through policy deployment and continuous improvement and innovation activities, as well as generating the evidence to demonstrate that learning is taking place and is improving. The result is an adaptive and agile school system.

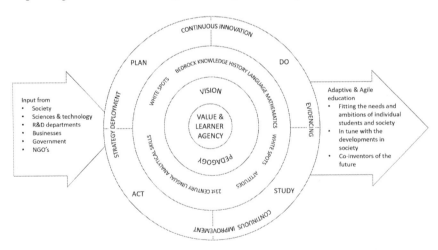

FIGURE 3.1
The core as basis for adaptivity and agility.

---

[4] What is contained in this component is open for debate and specific to culture, history of a country.

Most schools have a vision statement and a strategy. The biggest challenge is to formulate these in a way that drives all activities in a coherent and actionable way. Recent case study research (see Chapter 9) shows that even though elaborate vision and strategy statements are available, staff is only superficially acquainted with them. Their department, team, and individual activities are at best loosely tied to these statements. Based on the vision and strategy, the staff should make sure that the resources of a school are deployed in a way that does not waste them. There is abundant evidence that in addition to the waste of talent, other forms of waste occur often.[5] In order to eliminate waste, a system of continuous improvement is required. The Lean Education way of continuous improvement is through a simple and structured six step process (see Chapter 8). Continuous improvement is not only concerned with improving processes, but also on the evaluation of the pedagogical methods and the impact on students. Incremental steps of improvement are not always enough. Step change in the form of innovations are also required. A process of continuous innovation complements continuous improvement. The focus of continuous innovation is on the introduction of new pedagogical methods and new technologies.

To fulfill the vision, a school will need to select one or more pedagogies that best fit the vision of value, the needs of society, and students. There are many different strands of pedagogy. Pedagogies express views on what knowledge is, how people learn, and ways for teachers and students to interact. For the purpose of the book, I will define it loosely as the art and science of teaching. Pedagogies are complex combinations of psychology, philosophy, and epistemology. They are expressed through teaching and learning methods and approaches. Just to name a few: constructivism, constructionism, behaviorist-directed learning,

---

[5] M L Emiliani, "Special Issue: Lean Six Sigma for Higher Education Evolution in Lean Teaching," *International Journal of Productivity and Performance Management* (2016): 1–17; M L Emiliani, "Improving Business School Courses by Applying Lean Principles and Practices," *Quality Assurance in Education* 12, no. 4 (2004): 175–187, doi:10.1108/09684880410561596; M Robinson and S Yorkstone, "Becoming a Lean University: The Case of the University of St Andrews," *Leadership and Governance in Higher Education* 1 (2014): 42–71; Vincent Wiegel and L Brouwer Hadzialic, "Lessons from Higher Education: Adapting Lean Six Sigma to Account for Structural Differences in Application Domains," *International Journal of Six Sigma and Competitive Advantage* 9, no. 1 (2015): 72, doi:10.1504/IJSSCA.2015.070104; Vincent Wiegel and Lejla Brouwer-Hadzialic, "Lean Education," in *The Routledge Companion to Lean Management*, ed. T H Netland and D J Powell, Routledge Companions in Business, Management and Accounting (New York: Routledge, 2017): 422–434. W K Balzer, "Lean Higher Education: Increasing the Value and Performance of University Processes" 1 (2010): 1–312.

student-centered learning, project-based learning, transformative learning, dialogic learning, and critical pedagogy.[6] Not every teacher will be aware of the various pedagogies available, nor necessarily of the one(s) he has adopted. It would seem that pedagogical awareness is, by and large, bigger at the level of primary and secondary school teachers than at university level. At all levels, critical reflection on pedagogical choices and the effectiveness thereof could be improved.

At the heart of everything are, of course, our students. Regardless of the level of teaching, the focus of the study, the subject matter, there is a set of qualities that we try to install in our students. Learner agency is a key quality. The student takes ownership over her learning, is self-aware, and displays growing degrees of self-management and self-efficacy. She has an intrinsic drive for learning and a growing degree of autonomy in the process. The student and her questions, interests, and motivations are the focus of the teaching.[7] These are qualities that require careful nurturing over a longer period of time. The better that schools succeed at achieving these qualities, the higher the school impact. The core component of continuous improvement must therefore in part be focused on evidencing the impact our teaching has on our students.[8]

Part of the core is the skill set that is expected to be of critical importance in the decades to come. These are skills that are related to the advances in technology and the new ways in which society and businesses are organized. There is a general consensus on the impact that new technologies have on work and life in the twenty-first century,[9] by which is generally meant the 1st half of the century. Many jobs will disappear and new ones will be created. This is a phenomenon that is not new. The Luddites weren't the first nor the

---

[6] There are many good sources on pedagogy with different focuses. The number is overwhelming as are the publications. For readers interested to read more, I include here a few references. These are by no standard a complete or balanced overview. Eunbae Lee and Michael J Hannafin, "A Design Framework for Enhancing Engagement in Student-Centered Learning: Own It, Learn It, and Share It," *Educational Technology Research and Development* 64, no. 4 (2016): 707–734, doi:10.1007/s11423-015-9422-5; J Hattie, *Visible Learning for Teachers: Maximizing Impact on Learning* (Taylor & Francis Group, 2012); F Dochy and M Segers, *Creating Impact Through Future Learning: The High Impact Learning That Lasts (HILL) Model* (London, UK: Taylor & Francis Group, 2018); M Resnick, *Lifelong Kindergarten: Cultivating Creativity Through Projects, Passion, Peers, and Play* (Cambridge, MA: MIT Press, 2017).

[7] Dochy and Segers, *Creating Impact Through Future Learning: The High Impact Learning That Lasts (HILL) Model*; Hattie, *Visible Learning for Teachers: Maximizing Impact on Learning*.

[8] D Wiliam, *Embedded Formative Assessment* (Bloomington, IN: Solution Tree Press, 2011); J Hattie, *Visible Learning for Teachers: Maximizing Impact on Learning*.

[9] Twenty-first century skills are a bit of a misnomer. Providing a list of required skills to deal with a fast-changing world that is fixed for a whole century. There is no knowing what skills will be needed by 2080. The name twenty-first century skills is appealing, widely adopted. Hence, I will stick with it.

last to fear for their jobs and way of life. The pace of change has gone up. The largest companies make more money with fewer people than their predecessors from the previous century. The number of jobs that will be made redundant through automation is estimated to be between 30% and 50%.[10] This is not just a matter of a more profitable business model. The work is markedly different, the skills required are different and trump ready knowledge (though knowledge remains very important). Different researches list largely overlapping sets of skills that are key, now and in the future. The skills can be roughly categorized in three groups: meta-cognitive, meta-functional, and functional. Meta-cognitive skills are a group of higher-order thinking skills that relate to the ability of a student to consciously reflect on, direct, apply, and change his ways of acquisition and development of knowledge, skills, and attitudes. The skills are thus *reflecting on, directing of,* and *changing of.* Meta-functional skills refer to skills that allow a student to perform in different functions. It entails being aware of the value in, and necessary additions to, her current knowledge, skills, and attitudes to perform well in miscellaneous functions. Functional skills are those skills that relate directly to the execution of specific activities. They are part of what makes one an expert. They can be generic, such as mathematical skills, or very specific, such as the effective use of media. The list in Table 3.1 Skills is an example meant to illustrate the breadth and support for skills. It is by no means a complete list. Schools have to make their own selection.

The final part of the core is the knowledge that every student must master. Again, as with the skills, there is not one universal set. What knowledge is a part of the core will depend on the type of school, the culture, and tradition of a community, the focus of the school (e.g., vocational vs. generic), etc. Some developments have a global scope and are likely to feature in this set of core knowledge, e.g., globalization, environmental change, and digital technologies. I would also assume that some theories that relate to important skills will feature more prominently in the core knowledge. Innovating and creating feature on most skills lists. Theories on what constitutes creativity and on innovation are therefore likely to be part of the knowledge part of the curriculum.[11]

---

[10] In 2017, Apple was the most valuable business with a value roughly 40 times bigger than AT&T in 1962 employing just a fifth of the workforce. Darrell M West, "Future of Work," in *From The Future of Work: Robots, AI, and Automation,* 2018, doi:10.7864/j.ctt1vjqp2g.7.

[11] Here, again, I would like to stress that this applies to the whole spectrum of education, from kindergarten to academic and vocational studies. A theory on innovation might sound unduly "heavy" for primary school students. I do believe that topics like these can, and ought to, be included in all curricula. In appropriate format, depth, and context of course.

TABLE 3.1

Skills

Meta-cognitive	Meta-functional	Function
Learning skills—ability to obtain new insights through searching, selection, and critical evaluation of information, working, and learning in teams (1) (2)[a]	Job flexibility—the ability to perform in varying functions (1)	Digital skills (3)
	Job crafting—the ability to design one's own job (1)	Entrepreneurship (3)
Just-in-time (JIT) learning—ability to recognize in an instant either what must be learned or what the value is of previous learned material (1)	Interpersonal skills—working in teams (1)	Analyzing and interpreting data (3)
	Lateral thinking—ability to apply knowledge, skills, and attitudes obtained in one situation to other, diverse situations (1)	Creativity (4)
		Leadership (4)
		Media, information, and Information and Communication Technology (ICT) literacy (4)
Learner agency/self-directed learning—making choices regarding what and how to learn and taking responsibility for these choices (1) (2)	Creativity (4)	Mechanical and electrical engineer (5)
	Leadership (4)	Mechanical and electrical engineer (5)
	Flexibility (4)	Automated manufacturing (5)
Problem-solving (5)	Accountability (4)	

[a] (1) Dochy and Segers, *Creating Impact Through Future Learning: The High Impact Learning That Lasts (HILL) Model.*, (2) Victor A Benassi, Catherine E Overson, and Christopher M Hakala, "Applying Science of Learning in Education: Infusing Psychological Science into the Curriculum," *Annals of Anthropological Practice* 37, no. 1 (2014): 303, doi:10.1111/napa.12013., (3) E Brynjolfsson and A McAfee, *Race Against the Machine: How the Digital Revolution Is Accelerating Innovation, Driving Productivity, and Irreversibly Transforming Employment and the Economy* (Lexington, Digital Frontier Press, 2012)., (4) Partnership for 21st Century Learning, "P21 Partnership for 21st Century Learning," *Partnership for 21st Century Learning*, 2015, 9, http://www.p21.org/documents/P21_Framework_Definitions.pdf. (5) Darrell M West, "Future of Work."

Agility and Adaptiveness

We have taken a look at the core of education, the first of the five desiderata. It is conditional for the second desideratum, an agile and adaptive school system. Take a moment to consider a recent innovation that needs to be incorporated in the curriculum. Usually it takes a while for new technologies and theories to get noticed. Once the need to incorporate them into the curriculum is established, the educational wheels are set in motion. Ideas are discussed, meetings scheduled, and various experts consulted. Once agreement has been reached about the content, scope, etc., committees are put together to (re)design the curriculum, create materials, and select appropriate sources. A typical process like this might easily take several years, let's say 3 years, from the moment the need for change has been established, was several years after the need arose the first time. Then the first students start on the new course of study. They take somewhere between 4 to 6 years to graduate (for most bachelor studies, primary and secondary schools). So, it is at least 7 years before the first student graduates from her school with the new insights. And this is an optimistic scenario! Schools need to adapt to developments in sciences and technology faster than ever. Seven years is not fast by any standard and certainly not by today's pace of technological change. Consider the advance of DNA sequencing, data storage capacity, and 3D printing advances. These are each in its own right developments that will have a huge impact on how we live and work, and therefore on education. So, schools need to find ways to develop and introduce new curricula faster (adaptive) and make courses and studies more open to on the fly change (agile). In Chapters 7, 8, and 10, cases and methods are described that help to gain greater adaptiveness and agility. Adaptiveness and agility require certain organizational capability. This capability to respond and adjust swiftly is made up of a curriculum that is stable in the core with white spaces to be filled up at a short moment's notice. A short-cycled feedback loop is also key. Finding out what is currently relevant, what questions are asked in organizations, which problems need solving, and also insight in recent scientific advances allow a school to adjust swiftly. The external focus is important. Why else would a school adapt, to what would it respond? It is a fundamental openness toward society, science, and business in which schools actively listen for and solicit input from outsiders.

Fundamental Openness toward Society, Science, and Business

Most teachers are rooted in the middle of society, and schools play active roles in their community. Schools are, however, on the whole, self-contained worlds in which the outside world is put at arm's length.[12] Educators and schools can have an aura of closedness and inscrutability. They have the sole right of passing judgment on a student's achievements and his fitness to qualify for further education. This almost absolute prerogative comes

---

[12] To be sure, most schools get their more than fair share of social problems inside their classrooms! What I mean is the integration of research, business, and socio-economic forces into the school. For example, the technology, politics, and economics of developing actual wind farms and the organizations that are involved.

with a duty that teachers educate at a highest level of quality possible. To ensure this quality, a complex system of norms, rules, and oversight has been installed. It is this very system that renders education inflexible, inscrutable, and closed to outsiders. Given the failure to provide affordable and world class education, the closedness and primacy of educators and educational institutions becomes untenable. Top universities charge tens of thousands of dollars per year. Private schools for primary and secondary education charge easily many thousands of dollars. They deliver world class education, better than most schools, and beyond the reach of most people. The purpose of this book is to build on the many achievements and innovations of public schools, so that it can provide world class education to all.

Openness refers to agenda setting, curriculum development, teaching, and questions to be addressed. In a strive for uniformity, agenda setting and curriculum development are often organized along highly institutionalized, centralized bureaucratic processes. Stakeholders are involved, but often through representatives of interest groups who are bureaucratic institutions. Individual members from stakeholder groups rarely are actively involved or know someone who is and who they can talk to. The stakeholder involvement is restricted to a few and rather short instances across a multiyear period.[13] It is paramount that stakeholders get and take some ownership of education. And, that these stakeholders are locally, regionally, and nationally embedded. They need to have firsthand experience with education and its students. By this I mean, for example, local government staff that hires its civil servants from among the graduates of the local schools and colleges. Staff that is aware of key issues facing the community and to which it needs fresh ideas to solve them. This might be graduates with knowledge of wind powered turbines and green energy. The development of wind farms sometimes divides communities that want sustainable energy, but have a hard time dealing with the drawbacks of huge wind farms. These issues can also feature as projects and challenges that our students work on as part of their education. Not in order to replace existing staff or consultancy, but as a means that highlights the impact and application of specific knowledge, and to practice necessary skills and hone certain attitudes. Introductions and guidance on these projects can well be provided by staff of local government

---

[13] Accreditations of a study, for example, might take place every 3 or 4 years in which mostly members of other educational institutions and special interest groups meet over a few days at most to assess a multiyear study. This never allows for the in-depth familiarization that is needed to have a frank in-depth conversation about the quality and future of a study.

officials and companies that are involved.[14] This is not something to be done in an off-hand manner. It requires rigorous thought and preparation. A structural cooperation with a continuous dialogue is key to its success. Some interesting examples of experiments run include cooperation between primary schools and hospitals in which students are taught with help of physicians and nurses about the human body. I was involved in an experiment in which students from different secondary schools and a university studied industrial robotics within the context of an industrial company. With experts from the FieldLab for industrial robotics, engineers from the company, and teachers, students learned about the workings of robots, the way a company is organized, and how to improve working conditions and productivity using robots.

The final element of openness concerns the teaching itself. There are several additional sources of teaching capacity. Staff from companies, NGO's, and governments all have some relevant and actual knowledge that benefits students. They do not have the training as a teacher. And make no mistake, teaching is a profession that requires skills that are not easily obtained. Not just anyone with some expertise can teach. Some professors and experts in their field are notoriously bad teachers as many students can attest. But requiring these experts to complete a master's degree in pedagogy will not work for obvious reasons. Some minor instruction for these experts in a more structured setting might work very well. We could imagine the certified teacher taking on a different role. In addition to regular teaching, she would be involved in guiding the research and development employee, looking into more advanced work forms that let students integrate the materials much better, etc. The time freed up by involving "outsiders" can be put to use for these activities. When we educate our pupils in various learning strategies, they are better equipped to deal with pedagogically less skilled experts. A final source of teaching capacity is the student themselves. An old saying states that, "the one who teaches learns most." When we make our students first aware of their own learning preferences and next of various learning strategies, these will make them better able to transfer knowledge to other students. I ran an experiment in which students with a bachelor's degree taught their fellows. They did not want to let down their fellow students and therefore studied the subject

---

[14] I have personally seldomly met organizations and people that were not willing to dedicate some of their time to education, often, voluntarily. People enjoy working with other people to transfer some of their acquired knowledge and know-how. They are rightly proud of what they and their organizations have achieved and delight in sparring with fresh minds.

they were meant to teach with extra attention. They did indeed learn the most. The other students learned as much as, if not more than, in traditional settings. As teacher, my role was to make sure they would not teach nonsense and provide a safety net in case they could not master the topic. As teacher, I monitored the students progress in preparing the classes and acted as stand-in in cases of blackouts. The different teaching methods (each for every student teaching) brought welcome variety, the other students paid attention. Overall, my effort was not less, but the teaching was more effective and more fun. One of the intended side effects was that the students became more versatile in articulating and transferring what they know. That is an important skill for their careers. In many jobs, people have to address, involve, and help colleagues. In all likelihood most of the measures proposed in this book will not make education cheaper. But it will make it dramatically better and more impactful. It will allow schools to meet the growing demands without simply asking for more resources. It supports a more agile organization.

A final word of caution in this context. At times and places, it was and still is necessary to create safe havens of learning, free from intervention by the outside world. Bringing the outside world in means running a risk of our schools becoming a pawn of social, political, and religious forces. This is something that should be avoided even though they have a say on what constitutes value in education. Exposing teachers and students to these outside forces is something good and valuable in educating for the future.

Systematic, Short Cycled Feedback Loops and Active Filter

All teaching activities, the content, and the formats are based on assumptions of relevance and effectiveness. The content must be relevant to the goals of the school and student, the format must be conducive to the learning. The content must also be relevant to society at large, businesses, and other organizations. There are three levels at which we work when teaching: individual student, class/group, and school. At all levels, the key idea is to evidence the impact our activities are having. In most current educational practices relevance is determined once every couple of years, when a course is designed, when a school is accredited. But if you think about it, each year with each student that graduates we have an opportunity to establish the relevance and effectiveness of what has been taught and learned. When a student moves from kindergarten to primary school, from primary school to secondary school, and so on, till she starts working, the relevance and effectiveness of the previous education is being tested. It is tested in the extent in which the previous study has prepared the student well for her next step. With every student that starts working, we have an opportunity to verify the relevance and effectiveness of our educational efforts. We should actively seek and value the feedback. By using the opportunity for feedback, we can adjust faster than we currently do. The same applies for classroom teaching. During and at the end of each school year, we establish how well we have taught. We hardly use that feedback to adjust the teaching program and methods. The program has been determined for at least a year and often many years ahead. There is no room for adjustments. Any adjustment must be the student's. That is a lost opportunity. We have an opportunity for feedback at a more frequent interval and at a larger scale then we currently do. That is an opportunity for adjustment and improvement. For an agile and adaptive educational system, feedback is a necessary component. Lean Education has several simple instruments to collect and evaluate feedback which will be demonstrated throughout the book. In pedagogy, there is also a development that focuses on the use of information on students' progress to steer the next activities. In *High Impact Learning that Lasts*, Dochy and several other authors advocate some just-in-time learning, adapting learning materials on the spot.[15] They also propose to change assessments from assessment-of-learning to assessment-as-learning. The former is about establishing what the student has learned, whereas the latter views assessment and learning as two activities that are intertwined. The learning happens also during assessment, and during learning feedback is sought on a highly regular basis on formal, but more often informal basis.[16]

---

[15] Dochy and Segers, *Creating Impact Through Future Learning: The High Impact Learning That Lasts (HILL) Model*, 33. Dutch version.
[16] Ibid., 79.

A Program of Application and Experimentation

The last of the desiderata relates to the engagement in the creation of (new) knowledge. Contrast this to schools as a conduit for knowledge. The pace of the growth of knowledge is high, and we cannot just keep transferring knowledge at a faster pace. We need to engage more in the act of creating knowledge. It might be new knowledge for our students or even add some new insights to the existing body of knowledge and know-how. We can take this act of creation quite literal. In the act of creating we learn. Through the construction of objects (tangible and intangible), a deeper understanding of a theory arises. By having to deliver a functioning construct, a proof of concept one has no short-cuts, cheating is not possible. Things cannot be assumed to be unproblematic, they have to be tested and proven to work. Something either works or it doesn't. We learn as we make things, and in making things, we demonstrate that we have learned. Traditional classroom teaching at best creates awareness. In the doing, the teacher observes what the actual thinking of the students is.[17] This is a constructivist orientation that not every reader will necessarily adhere to, but it illustrates what application and experimentation might amount to.

Without subscribing to a particular pedagogical and epistemological view, the value of applying knowledge and experimenting will be apparent to all. Some students have a more practical inclination than others. They will be better served by learning through making. There is no reason why different learning strategies should not work together. Successful teams in companies are often made up of very diverse people working in different ways who complement each other. In schools, however, we often rely on one strategy only: the theoretical, analytical approach of storing and retrieving theoretical knowledge.

Finally, if we want schools and our students to make contributions to the growth of knowledge and to society, they will have to create things that can be used, tested, and verified. It is only in testing that a hypothesis can be validated. If our schools are a testbed for a strand of research, what better way than to conceive applications in a context that our students are familiar with. It will produce demonstrable effects, observable instances of the theory at work. It will enhance learning.

---

[17] M Rother, *Toyota Kata: Managing People for Improvement, Adaptiveness and Superior Results* (Maidenhead, UK: McGraw-Hill Education, 2009), 186–187.

EDUCATING IN THE FUTURE

We foresee education trends which require higher quality education, accessible to more at less cost, "the more-for-less" challenge.[18] Students and teachers will need to prepare for a future in which flexibility is a driving theme because there will be less predictability and less security. Teachers, currently bogged down in non-value adding work, need to be freed from the routine chores. Technology will come to our aid here, automating a lot of routine work. Similarly, technology will help with profiling needs of individual students using big data and machine learning. This will also affect the employment of new specialists at schools. The amanuensis of old might be replaced by a data scientist or a process analyst. Offering of learning materials will be technologically mediated providing teaching from the best experts around the world. Rather than teaching all materials themselves, teachers will be adding much more value by tailoring the external offerings to individual needs and guiding the application of what has been learned in practice. This scaffolding of learning is key in the learning process.[19] Taking diversity among students as a given and something we need to address, future teaching will be more varied and richer. Much of the teaching will be dedicated to tuning the learning environment to the individual needs of our students.[20]

Through the application of theories in practice by students, teachers will gain a lot of new insights into how specific theories work. Thus, the applications and experiments generate knowledge and help teachers keeping up-to-date. By collecting the output of applications and experiments, systematically, teachers can make valuable contributions to many different fields of research (pedagogy itself, business, technology, innovation, etc.). So, research and inventing the future will enter the schools. Some amazing, and admittedly exceptional, examples are provided by

---

[18] R Susskind and D Susskind, *The Future of the Professions: How Technology Will Transform the Work of Human Experts* (OUP Oxford, 2015). This documents some of these trends convincingly in Chapter 3.

[19] Lee and Hannafin, "A Design Framework for Enhancing Engagement in Student-Centered Learning: Own It, Learn It, and Share It"; Christine Redecker et al., *The Future of Learning: Preparing for Change-Publication, Publications Office of the European Union*, 2011, doi:10.2791/64117.

[20] This trend and its methodical implications are documented in Wiegel and Hadzialic, "Lessons from Higher Education: Adapting Lean Six Sigma to Account for Structural Differences in Application Domains."

Jack Andraka,[21] Angela Zhang,[22] and Boyan Slat.[23] Prodigies are of all times. My point is that there is more potential for students of all ages and their teachers to make their mark, in perhaps somewhat less dramatic, but no less valuable ways.

A word of caution here as well. I am not an unconditional technology optimist. Technology has several downsides as well as limitations. One of the risks of employing too much technology is that the realm of phantasy and creativity is confined. Try as we may, technology is not (yet?) very good at being creative, let alone recognizing playful boundary crossings that are the hallmark of a creative mind. Technology can be very good at stimulating creativity though.[24] I also believe that there is pedagogical value in playing the truant. Relentless technological observation might make it much harder for truant behavior to go unobserved. That would be a loss for human society.

---

[21] http://www.smithsonianmag.com/science-nature/jack-andraka-the-teen-prodigy-of-pancreatic-cancer-135925809/. Accessed August 12, 2018.

[22] https://www.smh.com.au/technology/17yearold-girls-cancer-breakthrough-20111212-1oq7v.html. Accessed August 12, 2018.

[23] https://www.theoceancleanup.com/milestones/how-it-all-began/. Accessed August 12, 2018.

[24] Resnick, *Lifelong Kindergarten: Cultivating Creativity Through Projects, Passion, Peers, and Play.*

Section II

Lean in the Classroom

4

Lean and Pedagogy

INTRODUCTION

The core processes of education are learning and teaching. They are formed by pedagogy. For Lean Education to be successful it has to relate to pedagogy, that is understand what it is about and how it might align to and help increase the effectiveness of pedagogy. There are many views of what constitutes pedagogy, teaching, and learning. It is empathically not to Lean Education to say what is, and what is not a good pedagogy. Through an overview of various pedagogies, this chapter discusses how Lean Education relates to pedagogy. As it happens, Lean thinking and many pedagogies share a common outlook and underlying philosophy which makes it easier to relate the two. They share a process orientation where goals are established, progress toward those goals are tracked, and interventions designed. They can be natural allies in a bid to improve education. Lean Education supports schools through creating "flow" in the work by seamlessly integrating processes, eliminating non-value-adding activities. Lean brings a wide range of tools and techniques to support flow and prevent the waste of talent.

LEAN EDUCATION AND PEDAGOGY

For the purpose of this chapter, I shall loosely define pedagogy as the discipline that is focused on theory and practice of teaching and influencing learning. A pedagogy refers to a specific theory on teaching. Every pedagogy will have a view on what constitutes learning and what constitutes knowledge (epistemology). Pedagogies will have often been "translated" into a set of methods that together implement the theory. I will call this the pedagogical approach (sometimes this is called a design framework). For example, student-centered learning is an approach to teaching that is rooted in constructivist and constructionist theories on learning and epistemology.

The purpose of this book is to show how Lean Education can help schools deal with the challenges of this age. It is not a pedagogical treatise. Moreover, the readers, I assume, will be more or less familiar with various pedagogical theories, some certainly more than I. The goal in this chapter is to establish the affinity between pedagogy and Lean thinking.

This affinity shows how Lean thinking and education share common ground. This common ground allows these two different worlds to be combined, and let Lean Education strengthen pedagogy and schools.

There are many theories of pedagogy, many views on what teaching and learning is about, and what they should be about.[1] It is now the place to relate Lean thinking to pedagogy. From a Lean Education perspective, there is no position on which pedagogy is best (even if there is such a thing as the best pedagogy). Just as in Lean manufacturing, there is no statement as to what is the best designed car or what is the best machine to press steel in a specific form. But Lean Education is not separated from views on pedagogy. The way we organize our processes is not independent of our view on what constitutes good teaching, what learning is about, etc. Given what we value in education, given our view on pedagogy, Lean Education will help arrange our activities in such a way that they help us in achieving our goals. The overview of pedagogies is not meant to be representative or exhaustive. Several theories will be discussed. I have chosen a few without any claim to the quality of these pedagogies. Though as a lecturer, I do have preferences and specific views, again, this book is not on pedagogy.

There are a few limitations on pedagogy when the Lean Education thinking is adopted. The student is the primary recipient of the value generated in education. What she defines as value has to play a part, though certainly not exclusively, in the way we organize education. The first principle of Lean thinking states that the recipient of the values is a prime source of the definition of the value. Starting thus from the perspective of the student the most important process, the one that generates the value, is the process of learning. Supporting this process of learning is the process of teaching. A lot of learning is taking place outside the scope of the immediate teaching process. The learning taking place outside the classroom is definitely influenced by the teaching, but it is not fully controlled and there are other factors influencing the learning, e.g., the situation at home, friends, and family. So, whatever pedagogy is adopted, it will have to be student-centered and consider all student activities in- and outside the classroom. This means we focus on the student as the "locus of control." The student has more control than teachers over many of the aspects of the learning process. This is not a new revolutionary insight. It has been around for many years. Macleod and Golby make this point, as many

---

[1] Knud Illeris, *Contemporary Theories of Learning: Learning Theorists ... In Their Own Words* (London, UK: Taylor & Francis Group, 2018).

before and after them have done.[2] What is surprising though is that many discussions, much work of teachers, are still about the teaching rather than the learning. The discussion often focuses on what the schools have to offer in terms of buildings, classroom materials, group sizes, organization of classes, introducing electronic boards, etc. And of course, these elements have an effect on the learning. The starting point is, however, not the learning, but the teaching. It is very much an inside-out approach. I would ask the reader to listen closely to discussions with colleagues, at boards, committees, etc. and observe we talk about teaching instead of learning, the school instead of the student.

There are various elements in pedagogies that are not addressing the teaching and learning itself, but focus on the process. For example, there are goals to be achieved, such as a certain proficiency level in reading. Whether they are collective or individual, whether they are relevant or not, however we pursue them, there is the bare fact that there is something we want to achieve. This also means that there has to be a way in which we can assess whether the goals have been achieved. It also implies that our students are in a certain starting position, and we need to define a way to get from A to B. Without engaging in a discussion whether being in A is good or not or in whether pursuing B is worthwhile, Lean Education is instrumental in organizing the processes of establishing what A is, of where B is, of how we are doing in getting from A to B. It is in fact this close affinity of the Lean Education process-oriented way of thinking to the meta-aspects of most pedagogies that makes them close allies. There is an overlap, but also a complementary element. This is why Lean Education makes so much sense. Lean Education brings to education a long tradition and rich know-how of process thinking, establishing current conditions and tracking progress. It adds execution power to education. And, perhaps most importantly, it contributes a culture and mindset of continuous improvement.

To illustrate the above arguments, I provide a short overview of some pedagogies and show how they link to Lean Education. Directed instruction. Directed learning and instruction are focused on creating reproducible behavior and understanding through a stimuli-response model. Correct (incorrect) answers or desired (undesired) behavior is rewarded (punished) and thus reinforced (extinguished). This is a

[2] Flora Macleod and Michael Golby, "Theories of learning and pedagogy: Issues for teacher development," *Teacher Development* 7, no. 3 (2003): 345–361, doi:10.1080/13664530300200204.

behaviorist approach toward agency. The underlying epistemology states that certain facts are objective and knowable. Directed instruction is teacher-centered. The teacher is the more knowledgeable person in the student-teacher relationship and directs the learning. Under the guidance of the teacher, the student obtains certain objective knowledge and is able to reproduce and apply this knowledge. The learning goals are defined by the curriculum.

Student-centered learning. "Student-centered-learning (SCL) is a learning approach during which students generate learning opportunities and reconstruct knowledge dynamically in an open-ended learning environment [...] students assume increased autonomy and responsibility for their own learning."[3]

SCL is based on the idea that highly and intrinsically motivated students achieve better learning outcomes. The degree of motivation is in turn influenced by the degree of autonomy and competence. So, fostering autonomy and building competency is a way to get students to engage in their learning tasks more actively. Students show greater ownership. They set their own goals and will pursue them even in the absence of external drivers such as affirmation, recognition, or rewards. This idea of self-determination is complemented with a constructivist epistemology which presupposes "a relationship between learner, context and understanding."[4] The learners create their own learning by using the cognitive and other abilities to obtain and process knowledge, rearrange facts and insights. So, rather than passively receiving and storing knowledge, they construct knowledge, often in interaction with others (peers, experts, ...). SCL is further elaborated through a constructionist dimension which states that as students construct artifacts, they share their understanding of the world. The artifacts are representations of their understanding. In the design, the production, sharing, and reflection of their creations, knowledge and understanding are created and refined. It is an interactive process in which students invent the tools they need to increase their understanding. Affect, the personal meaning attached to the project they work on, is a key element in a growing investment in the learning. It enhances student performance.

[3] Eunbae Lee and Michael J Hannafin, "A design framework for enhancing engagement in student-centered learning: Own It, Learn It, and Share It," *Educational Technology Research and Development* 64, no. 4 (2016): 708, doi:10.1007/s11423-015-9422-5.
[4] Ibid., 713.

Art & craft of learning spaces. The KaosPilot is a Danish a hybrid business and design school.[5] It is the leading experimenter in higher education. Its pedagogy and culture are narrowly intertwined and aligned with the objectives of the education. That means they live the things they would like their students to develop. Students and the outside world have a clear say in the working and content of the study. Its set-up is experimental and aimed at both the transfer and the development of new knowledge. Students are engaged in real life projects that are the core around which a lot of the teaching takes place. As such, it can be characterized as student-centered learning annex project-based learning. Students are encouraged, and even required, to take increasing ownership of their learning. This dynamic setting offers an excellent stage for the development and acquisition of not just knowledge, but also of skills and attitudes. The learning spaces are envisioned as the space contained by a learning arch. The arch is initiated by a joint "set" phase in which the participants direct the intentions for the learning. They envision where they want to go with the learning and how to get there. The arch closes the learning space with the "land" phase in which the extent to which the goals have been met is discussed. It is a phase of explicit reflection on the learning. In the pedagogy, reflection and landing play a crucial role in ensuring that the learning actually sticks. During the learning, in the hold phase, the learning activities are interlaced with small informal moments of reflection. These moments allow students and lecturers to take stock and change course if necessary.

High Impact Learning that Lasts. The High Impact Learning that Lasts (HILL) is a pedagogy that resulted from a Flemish and Dutch research project regarding teaching practices.[6] In the HILL-model, learning starts from a clearly stated and felt problem that must be solved. The problem, the hiatus creates urgency and relevance. From the engagement created through urgency, the development of the student is focused on self-management and learner agency. In close cooperation with others the student develops his knowledge, skills, and attitudes. The students receive feedback as they interact with others. This might take place in communities of learning and inquiry. The learning itself is a continuous process where various modi are closely integrated. Online and offline, synchronous and asynchronous, and individual and group activities are mixed into a hybrid

---

[5] www.kaospilot.dk The art & craft of learning spaces and the vision backcasting methods generate from Simon Kavanagh and KaosPilot school.

[6] Filip Dochy and Mien Segers, *Creating Impact Through Future Learning: The High Impact Learning That Lasts (HILL) Model* (Taylor & Francis Group, 2018).

learning experience. Learning requires practice and preferably in real life situations. As the projects are seldomly isolated, individual settings learning also means sharing. Mistakes are made, openly shared, and used as a valuable source of learning (contrary to many current practices where to make mistakes is to receive lower grades). The setting within which the learning takes place, the learning space, must be flexible. There is room for spontaneous learning as unforeseen developments insert themselves into the open learning space. Finally, the assessment is constituted to maximize the learning. Learning and assessment are no longer delineated. An assessment is a moment to practice, which provides insight into both the mastery of a subject matter and the learning process. It informs both student and mentor, and motivates the student toward the next steps.[7]

SHARED CHARACTERISTICS OF PEDAGOGIES

All the above discussed pedagogies as well as many others share some basic characteristics. There is a goal to be attained (A). Students are provided with means to master the subject matter based on where they currently are (B). Along the way at various stages the progress is tracked (C). Pupils learning mathematics might have a goal of mastering matrix algebra at basic level. They are provided with reading materials that explain the basics of matrix algebra, they get instruction from the math teacher, and make exercises to practice. At the end of a teaching period, they make some exams that show how they have progressed and whether that have mastered the basics of matrix algebra.

> All teaching really boils down to three key processes [...]: finding out where the learners are in their learning, finding out where they are going, and finding out how to get there.[8]

The differences between various pedagogies lie in how these three steps are designed. Students might, or might not, have a say in the goals. Pupils might, or might not, be involved in collecting materials for study and,

---

[7] New Engineers is an engineering school (see Chapter 10), where we implemented a pedagogy inspired amongst others by HILL and the KaosPilot. The students do not receive traditional grades and have no formal exams, though they need to submit various proofs of their progress. Yet our students tell us that 'though we do not get grades, we've never studied so hard'.

[8] Dylan Wiliam, *Embedded Formative Assessment* (Bloomington, IN: Solution Tree Press, 2011), 45.

might, or might not, be studying together on projects. The test might or might not be frequent, formal, in fixed formats. These decisions ought to be based on evidence on how the chosen practices impact the students in their journey toward the set goals.

> We know that the major source of controllable variance in our system relates to the teacher, and that even the best teacher has variability in the effect that he or she has on his or her students. The message [...] is that teachers, schools, and systems need to be consistently aware, and have dependable evidence of the effects that all are having on their students—and from this evidence make the decisions on about how they teach and what they teach. The evidence is that it is about student learning—particularly progress—provided that the learning intentions and success criteria are worthwhile, challenging, and become meaningful to and understood by the students.[9]

So, whatever the culture and pedagogy of the school, it will need to have insights in goals, starting position, and progress. Based on the gap between goal and current state, teachers initiate various interventions. To be effective, schools need to consider how to define goals and make them easily sharable with students, how to measure progress, and how to assess the current state. The analysis of gaps is a complicated activity in which it is key to get to the root of the gap. It is exactly this thinking that forms the core of Lean thinking.

LEAN THINKING

Lean thinking is a philosophy about how to the best run the processes of an organization. Lean thinking is foremost process thinking. It starts its conception of how to best organize processes by investigating what it is that the clients, customers, patients, or students of the organization value. It is radical in this respect.[10] It is not the organization that determines the definition of value. Then, thinking backward from the moment the service or product is delivered, the processes steps are analyzed on their

---

[9] John Hattie, *Visible Learning for Teachers: Maximizing Impact on Learning* (Taylor & Francis Group, 2012), 170.

[10] It may not sound radical, as many organizations profess the importance of the customer. But when it comes to everyday working, almost every organization reasons starting from its own capabilities, capacity, etc. and then tells its customers what can and cannot expect. Which is in fact the opposite of customer-centered thinking.

value-adding capacity. If a process step does not add value, we call it waste. It is by striving to eliminate all waste that Lean becomes amazingly effective. Rather than optimizing activities, Lean eliminates waste. This is also more radical than it might seem. Since most activities are not value adding, optimizing value adding activities deliver fewer results than eliminating the non-value adding activities. Lean uses the principles of flow and pull to effectively organize the process steps. These principles are understood intuitively. Imagine yourself in a shop or at the hospital. All the waiting is annoying and does not add value to what you came to do, i.e., get a diagnosis or buy the birthday present. The principle of flow says that a service or good should "flow" through the organization. At any moment, someone from the organization should be working on the product or service and add value. Simply stated: "no waiting." The pull principle ensures that all the work is done just in time based on the real demand of the client, customer, patient, etc. Finally, in Lean, we acknowledge that things are never perfect, the world keeps changing, so we need to have a practice of continuous improvement.

Lean is often associated with industry and mass production. This sometimes leads to the impression that Lean does not apply to services that are very specific, let alone to education. But consider the core of Lean, starting from the client's definition of value. Lean is radically focused on what each client needs. That makes it actually well suited to education. The challenge is to maintain this focus while scaling up to organizations and processes that work with hundreds up to tens of thousands of clients. In education, we acknowledge that every child is different, but provide all children with roughly the same education. Educating hundreds of pupils, thousands of students, based on their individual needs while keeping education affordable is the great challenge of education! We need to provide higher quality education on a more individualized basis at lower costs. I described in part I the need for more, life long, broader scoped education. The current way of education is not scalable. Just throwing more money at it is not going to deliver the education we need, though additional budgets may very well be requested due to past underfunding and for support of the transition.

Lean Education works well to eliminate waste in education. This frees up some resources that can help implement new pedagogies and technologies to work toward a school that provides the students what they need, how they need it, and when they need it. By this, I do not mean that we should provide our students with just whatever they feel like. Just as a physician does not prescribe a painkiller whenever the patient asks for it, but considers the medical appropriateness, in the same fashion teachers and schools have an ethical and professional responsibility to use their knowledge and experience to keep students from harm. That is, however, not to say that our pupils are incapable of formulating how they see the future, what moves and motivates them, and what they think should be on the curriculum. Over the many years, I have always been pleasantly surprised by the enormous sensibility and responsibility of children when given room to decide for themselves. And not only that, they also show great energy and engagement when working on stuff they care about. In doing so, they are also open to advice and direction from more experienced people. Resnick in his wonderful book *Lifelong Kindergarten* provides some good illustrations.[11] I'm always puzzled by the fact that we let our students drive cars, buy a house, get children, yet fail to engage them on the education beyond a mere occasional committee membership and some post-year evaluations. In Chapters 7 and 10, two cases are described (New Engineers and Crossing Educational Borders) that illustrate how to engage students deeply in the development of the curriculum and the execution of the courses.

RELATING LEAN EDUCATION AND PEDAGOGY

From the preceding sections, two questions arise. One, how do we go about eliminating waste? Two, how do we use Lean to develop schools that cater for the individual needs of our pupils at a higher quality level and at lower costs? These two questions drive the remainder of this book. I first discuss how Lean and pedagogy relate and how Lean thinking helps making pedagogies even stronger. The next chapters will illustrate in detail how • Lean Education works in practice.

Remember the core three steps of every pedagogy. "There is a goal to be attained (A). Students are provided with means to master the subject matter based on where they currently are (B). Along the way at various stages the progress is tracked (C)." This thinking is at the core of Lean thinking. For each of these steps over the many decades of Lean practice, concepts and simple tools and techniques have been developed to execute these steps.

[11] Mitchel Resnick, *Lifelong Kindergarten: Cultivating Creativity Through Projects, Passion, Peers, and Play* (Cambridge, MA: MIT Press, 2017).

Establishing where the pupils need to be (A) can be supported through the following Lean techniques. Observing and engaging various stakeholders while active in their own work environment (going to the shop floor, genchi gembutsu), establishing performance criteria as critical to quality (*CtQ*) aspects, listening in to semi-structured discussions of students regarding their education (*client arenas*), defining together with stakeholders a "bounty island" (*future state*), and defining and organizing requirements as qualities (functions) of the education (*quality function deployment*).[12] Next, providing the students with input (B) can be done using just-in-time techniques (*Kanban, POLCA*). By standardizing inputs (*standardized work*), by introducing visual management (*5S*), both the inputs and the activities involved in providing the inputs are divided in small components that can be offered at a pace fitting individual students. They "pull" what they need. By having the teaching materials in configurable formats (*configure to order, CtO*) and extensible formats, teachers can tune the size and make-up of materials offered. Or even better, the students can do so themselves.[13] Finally, tracking progress (C) can be done using *performance boards*, that depict the goals and the development toward the goal. Using again visual management and standardization, the goals and progress are made concrete, tangible, tractable, and easily accessible.

Just how important it is to strengthen this cycle is illustrated by Hattie. His research finds that variance is often greater within schools than between school systems. This means that the teacher is probably the single most important factor in school outcomes. It is not what teachers do per se, but what an individual teacher does, that matters. The difference between "high-effect" and "low-effect" teachers is expressed in five dimensions: (1) high levels of knowledge and understanding of the subjects they teach,

---

[12] Each of the techniques can be deployed in various degrees of rigor. In full, they can be overwhelming. They scale down easily without losing much of their value. I recommend that schools pick only one or two and start with small steps. Just the very fact of starting already brings great benefits.

[13] An important consideration in this context is the element of co-creation. Learning is by its very nature something that is done by the student. The teaching process is intertwined with the learning. Students are therefore inseparable from the process and create their value together with teachers. The learning is not done unto them, all too often teaching is done unto our pupils. In this respect, Lean Education differs from many traditional applications in which providers of services and products create the whole service and then hand them over to their customers. Increasingly, other applications of Lean encounter the same phenomenon of co-creation. Think of therapy in which physician and patient are both actively involved, or the design of client specific products and services which require heavy client involvement during the design phase. See Vincent Wiegel and L Brouwer Hadzialic, "Lessons from Higher Education: Adapting Lean Six Sigma to Account for Structural Differences in Application Domains," *International Journal of Six Sigma and Competitive Advantage* 9, no. 1 (2015): 72, doi:10.1504/IJSSCA.2015.070104.

(2) guide learning to desirable surface and deep outcomes, (3) successfully monitor learning and provide feedback that assists students to progress, (4) attend more to the attitudinal attributes of learning, and (5) provide defensible evidence of positive impacts of the teaching on student learning.[14] Now this is exactly where Lean Education provides teachers with the tools and techniques to support them as described above. Lean Education does so in the firm belief that every teacher has the potential to become a high-effect teacher. Respect for people is one of the key values of Lean, and it translates into a mindset of support toward growth.

Next, Lean Education provides a concise and tangible frame of reference through the value definition. Using this definition, every activity can be assessed on its value-adding or value-distracting nature. Using the systematic approach of continuous improvement (Kaizen and Kata), pupils, teachers, support staff, and administrators can work systematically and gradually toward the removal of waste using the A3thinking technique. Value is defined by the students (in conjunction with other stakeholders), and the teachers are supporting the student learning. Teachers are in turn supported by professional services staff for whom the definition of value derives from student and teachers' needs. Lastly, in support of all others, administrators work to create an organization that delivers what society and students need. They do so by formulating a strategy in a way that involves many stakeholders, gathering their input in a systematic way (strategy A3) that is also easy to share and communicate. They direct the school's means toward the value adding activities and build a culture of continuous improvement and innovation.

There sometimes is a certain aversion toward such a rationalist, businesslike approach. Education is for many of its professionals something of the heart, a passion and social engagement, and idealism in raising young people and helping in their growth. That idealism I share, the sheer joy of seeing people learn and getting excited! Yet, for all of us it goes that a day still contains only 24 hours, a week no more than 7 days. In order to make the most of our ideals, we must be economic with our time and scarce resources. There is nothing inherently contradictory between pursuing ideals and being efficient. If anything, it makes the case for efficiency even stronger. The more efficient one is, the more of one's ideals can be realized. The anthroposophical schools in Flanders realized this long ago when they engaged me in some introductory Lean work. These schools are by their

---

[14] Hattie, *Visible Learning for Teachers: Maximizing Impact on Learning*, 2012, 25–28.

anthroposophical nature far removed from cold, economic rationalism, and yet saw and appreciated the need for a stable, efficient organization that takes away some of the strain of running a school. Doing so frees up the time and mental energy to build an environment for joy in learning.

STRONGER PEDAGOGY WITH LEAN EDUCATION

So, there is an affinity between education and Lean. That makes Lean Education feasible. It does not necessarily follow that we should wish for Lean Education. The key question is "Why should schools engage in Lean Education?" In Part I, I painted the background of fast changing technologies and new requirements on our schools to meet that fast-paced change. So far, schools have, by and large, demonstrated that they cannot keep up with the pace. Teachers are often overworked and bogged down in bureaucratic work. This distracts them even further from what is already often only middle of the road quality. Quality that is, in addition, varying substantially across teachers, across schools, and across countries. And finally, the price of education is too high to be affordable for all.

Attempts to improve are of course made. And good work is being done. Schools often lack, however, execution power. Improvement initiatives are fragmented across politized organizations. Traditional high degrees of autonomy for both schools and individual teachers makes concerted efforts at improvement hard. Improvement cycles are long. Evaluations are done only at the end of a teaching cycle, often at the end of a school year. By that time, it is too late for improvements for the current cohort. When it is about time to start the run of the course, many of the improvement ideas have been forgotten, or it is too late to implement them. Staff working in education is mostly highly educated themselves and verbally powerful. In combination with high degrees of autonomy and a strong professional identity, change gets easily bogged down in long talking sessions.

What makes Lean a preferable way to help schools are the following arguments. Lean Education stands out and differentiates itself because it is:

- Easy to master. The Lean Education theory, methods, and techniques can be understood by everyone working in education
- A good fit with pedagogy. Lean thinking has a close affinity with pedagogy. It aligns naturally which makes it easier to get buy-in

- Action oriented. Lean is complementary by adding an action-oriented outlook to 'verbose' organizations
- Concrete and measurable. Lean forces organizations to establish concrete, measurable targets to match their strategies
- Short cycled. Lean offers a system to improve by small steps frequently. This helps achieving early successes, freeing up some time, and impacts current cohorts rather than future cohorts only
- Integral. It offers support for both staff working on the primary processes of learning and teaching and for professional services staff and administrators. Thus, it is one of the few improvement philosophies that offer an organization wide support
- Credible. Lean has a history of success across many sectors, over many decades, dating back to the early twentieth century.

Lean Education is not a magic wand. It is hard work and requires change. There are sufficient successes, but also several failures. Most of all a cultural change is needed. Lean is always about change.[15] Bringing people on board is a challenge. But it is worth it as testified by the various examples of schools that make headway toward education that is more satisfactory for both student and teacher.

HANDS ON!

To get started with Lean Education:

1. Get a first understanding of Lean and Lean Education
   Most inspiring is to visit other schools. In addition, you can read about Lean in Education and attend conferences or workshops. You can also invite some experienced people to share their stories
2. Prepare interviews with students/organize student arena
   Bring students from different backgrounds together and let them discuss what school and learning means to them. In an arena there is a facilitator, but no other participants (teachers, parents) partake in the discussion. They observe in a second ring the discussion. After the discussion in the first round has been closed, the observers

---

[15] Vincent Wiegel and John Maes, *Succesvol Lean* (Amsterdam, the Netherlands: Pearson, 2013).

get to ask some questions to clarify elements from the discussion. They cannot argue in favor or against things they have heard

3. Get input from other stakeholders

   Organize interviews with people from industry and government. Also for primary school programs, it is important to involve them

4. Develop the definition of value

   Distill from the discussions and interviews what students and society want. You can add the school's philosophy. Take also the cultural and socio-economic context into account. A good value statement should not be longer than couple of sentences, a paragraph at most

5. Plot student journey

   The student journey involves every step a student (and his parents) take to select and enroll in a school, to study, and graduate. Take the position of a student and take her perspective in everything. Try not to insert knowledge of what you think should happen or what a student should do. Plot the journey as it actually happens. Map the journey on a very large, horizontal piece of paper (a meter high, or so, 2 meters wide, sometimes called brown paper, from the large roles of paper to wrap goods in). Write down each step of the student on a sticky note and stick it on the brown paper. Write down time involved in doing and waiting. Next, put up the steps taken by the teachers and support staff. Again, write down also how long it takes, how much waiting is involved. Discuss the findings with colleagues, and mark all wasteful activities, quality issues, rework, missing information, and so on

6. Elaborate on the pedagogical vision

   Each school has a pedagogical vision. Using the output from the previous steps, revisit the vision and elaborate it. Test the vision by testing it on various scenarios, e.g., school trips, exams, and industry visits. Determine how you evidence that learning is actually taking place and not just through summative tests. Ensure that all teachers understand the vision and know what it entails for their classes and teaching routines. Understanding a vision is different from listening to it. Do not assume because the vision has been emailed around or addressed in a town hall meeting that everyone can actually live it

7. Identify for each step in the journey whether it adds value and what is needed in pedagogical terms.

   Using the definition of value and the pedagogical vision, you can now assess the value of each step of the student journey. This is important from the student's perspective. It also offers the school an opportunity to save scarce time, money, and energy by eliminating steps that do not add value. Expect some 30%–50% of the steps to contain non-value-adding activities.

Follow-up by organizing small steps to improve school activities:

1. Assign school improvement leadership
2. Establish goals for each class
3. Develop a varied and extensive set of informal formative assessments
4. Discuss with colleagues how to provide evidence that learning has taken place
5. Set-up small improvement events (with a Lean coach for the first few times)
6. Organize discussion about quality among colleagues on regular basis
7. Organize regular class visits by colleagues to identify opportunities for improvement.

LEAN EDUCATION: VALUE FOR THE STUDENT

One of the core principles of Lean thinking states that value is the driving factor for all activities. Value is defined by the student. This is a challenging and difficult proposition for education. Many of our students are not yet of an age where they can effectively decide what value is for them. Parents have an opinion that matters as well. And so does society at large as represented by government and special interest groups. In the definition of value, the student should be at the core. The prerogative is not absolute. Just as a patient has not an absolute say in what he wants. Nurses and physicians do have a moral and professional obligation that arise from their knowledge and their long-term commitment to the patient's well-being. But neither do we ignore the patient wishes, he has an acknowledged stake and right to be involved in his treatment. The Lean value proposition for education is to be read in a similar vain. The students do have a say in their education. One that goes beyond the token involvement we often see. But neither is it absolute. The say should grow as

LEAN EDUCATION: VALUE FOR THE STUDENT (Continued)

students demonstrate a clear grasp of what their education is about and have demonstrated the ability to autonomously choose and execute their learning strategies to good effect. As educators and parents, we should think from the student's perspective as much as possible, rather than thinking for them.

Before we continue discussing what constitutes value, we should note that students are not just passive consumers, but active participants, co-producers, and co-creators of their learning. In this sense, talking of a customer is missing an important point. Moreover, the lifelong pursuit of learning and of personal growth is something that has a larger meaning and goes beyond the narrower ideas of commercial transactions of producing and consuming. The discussion about terminology has a clear danger of distracting from what should be the focus, the value.[16] For the purposes of this book, I shall mean students among several other beneficiaries and active participants when referring to customer in the old Lean sense.

In the process of defining value we should be careful to avoid one of the fallacies often encountered in organization: confusing the indicator for the goal, and the measurement for value. Obtaining a diploma is an indication that one has acquired a set of knowledge and skills. And that is the goal. Often though the diploma is confused with the goal and passing an exam is confused with knowing something. We should be careful to make sure that we understand and agree about the goal of education: for example, growing as an individual or being able to function as an autonomous individual within society. To that end, we try to equip students with certain skills, knowledge, and attitudes (SKAs) that will help them to continue to be and grow as a

[16] Steve Yorkstone, "Lean Universities," in *The Routledge Companion to Lean Management2*, ed. Daryl Powell and Torbjorn Netland (New York: Routledge, 2017), 449–462; Jan Riezebos, "Lean Schools," in *The Routledge Companion to Lean Management*, ed. Daryl Powell and Torbjorn Netland (New York: Routledge, 2017), 435–448; M L Emiliani, "Special Issue: Lean Six Sigma for Higher Education Evolution in Lean Teaching," no. June (2016): 1–17.

LEAN EDUCATION: VALUE FOR THE STUDENT (Continued)

citizen, employee, etc. Students have their own ambitions, dreams, and ideals. If we ignore these except at a few moments where they get to make some choices between the subject of a presentation, a show and tell, or course in their study program, we do them an injustice and end up with less engaged students.

Hence, the definition of value is something that should be left to students and their schools with input from the parents. However value is defined, there are a few generic characteristics that should inform the discussion on value. They relate to meta-cognition, the knowledge about knowledge.

Learning is a conscious process. Acquiring new knowledge is one of the key goals of education. Having knowledge and knowing that you have it are two different things. Our students often learn new concepts without being conscious of it. This is even more pronounced in the case where skills and attitudes are trained and developed. As part of the development of a skill—say negotiation—content topics are covered such as the subject of the negotiation—that are not the obvious focus of the learning. Still the student acquires new knowledge. Also the reverse is the case. Acquiring new knowledge is never just that. The knowledge is captured. If the student uses, for example, a mind map to capture a theory her meta-cognitive skills are also exercised. This may be done without explicit awareness. The value delivered goes unacknowledged. As such, it does not yet exist for the one to whom it is delivered.

The process of learning requires information on the progress of that learning. If the SKAs acquired are not mentioned explicitly and their progress not tracked, there is no steering information for either the teacher or the student or both. This lack of information hampers both learner agency and the ability of the teacher to steer the learning process and determine what is the next thing that ought to be done.

SKAs that go unacknowledged cannot be consciously exercised and applied. As a consequence they might, deteriorate through a lack of exercise. Even if they are consciously acquired there is a risk of atrophication. SKAs that are not applied or exercised will deteriorate quickly. This is demonstrated, for example, by the fact that students

LEAN EDUCATION: VALUE FOR THE STUDENT (Continued)

will unlearn 10%–25% of what they have learned, over the course of the summer holiday.

Furthermore, the student might miss the benefits that come from the actual application of the SKAs. This is missing out on the value that would be generated had the SKAs been explicit and used. The missed value can range from better learning, earning money on a side job, or engaging more effectively in community activities.

Whatever definition of value students, schools, and other beneficiaries agree upon, they would be well advised to include meta-cognition, progress tracking,[17] exercising, and applying of acquired SKAs in that definition. To summarize, the definition of value for the student should include mechanisms that ensure that:

- Value is defined through a joint, ongoing process in which students have a substantial say, and other stakeholders and beneficiaries take care to think through the students' perspective
- What is being learned is made explicit
- The conditions for application are indicated as far as possible
- The acquired SKAs are consciously exercised and applied.

---

[17] Strictly speaking progress tracking is a part of meta-cognition. It is mentioned explicitly to single it out because it has importance not just for the learning, but also for the process of continuous improvement and innovation.

5

Lean in the Classroom:
Goals and Progress

INTRODUCTION

The first thing in learning is knowing where students want to go. Then, step by step, to help the student grow and develop toward that goal. Setting goals and tracking progress is key to Lean Education. There was a time when the goals were predetermined and every student had to achieve the same goals. And that still is the case for the very large majority of students around the world. A trend is emerging, however, where students can increasingly set their own goals. Whatever is the case, goals have to be set, shared, and tracked. Good goals have to meet a specific set of criteria that will facilitate both the learning and tracking. Knowing where a student is in her learning journey is key to determining what content must be offered in what format and when. The acts of setting, sharing, and tracking goals are in and by themselves powerful tools in learning. Lean has a long and rich tradition of setting and tracking goals. Based on the progress and the learning, improvement activities are initiated by Lean organizations. In education, the same principle applies to both the learning of the individual student and the way the school organizes the teaching and learning. The lean tools and methods of A3 thinking and performance management are the beating heart of a learning organization.

GOALS

Goals function within a broader setting for which aims have been defined. An aim is a general and high-level description of what must be achieved. Various goals objectify the aims and make them concrete. For the minor World Class Performance we run at the HAN University of Applied Sciences, the aim is to deliver Lean practitioners that have mastered the theory of Lean and are capable of independently running tactical improvement projects in varying industries. This is translated into a set of goals (indicators in our school jargon) that jointly ensure that the aim is met. The goals in this case relate to mastery of important Lean concepts, change management skills, and general communications and presentations skills.

For a goal to be effective, all involved must know what the goal is. What does success look like? How do we know the goals have been achieved? If the goals have been achieved, what do we see, what do we hear and say? Defining the success criteria for a goal is hard to accomplish. There is a series of requirements for a good goal and its criteria. A goal in this context is an intended outcome of an educational unit (be it a course, a study, a class). It is concise, but still abstract. Related to the goal is a set of criteria that: (a) translate the goal into concrete, verifiable statements and (b) when all are met, ensure that the goal has been attained. These success criteria have a set of characteristics which define good criteria. The role of goals and goal setting are widely documented. Their importance is widely agreed.[1] Day to day practice in education is often much different. Goals are often not shared except for a general reference to documentation on the school's intranet. Goals are also sometimes confused with measurements. Passing an exam is not a goal, but a measurement. The goal is to learn something, the exam measures to what extent the learning has been successful. The discrepancy between what we know about goal setting and everyday practice can be explained, in part, by the difficulty and time-consuming nature of goal setting. The value of Lean Education is not in arguing the importance of goals, but the practical help in doing so.

In order to work, goals and their criteria must be[2]:

- Owned
- Understood
- Shared
- Relevant
- Attainable
- Challenging
- Balanced
- Measurable & measured
- Visual

Owned: This is perhaps the most important and complicated characteristic of a learning goal. A goal should be owned by the pupils. It is their learning after all, and they are the beneficiaries of the

---

[1] Mit, "Institute-Wide Task Force on the Future of MIT Education Final Report," *Institute-Wide Task Force on the Future of MIT Education*, 2014, 85, http://web.mit.edu/future-report/TaskForceFinal_July28.pdf; Michael Brooks and Bob Holmes, "Equinox Blueprint," no. April (2014); Eunbae Lee and Michael J. Hannafin, "A Design Framework for Enhancing Engagement in Student-Centered Learning: Own It, Learn It, and Share It," *Educational Technology Research and Development* 64, no. 4 (2016): 707–734, doi:10.1007/s11423-015-9422-5; Claudia Ott et al., "Illustrating Performance Indicators and Course Characteristics to Support Students' Self-Regulated Learning in CS1," *Computer Science Education* 25, no. 2 (2015): 174–198, doi:10.1080/08993408.2015.1033129.

[2] Vincent Wiegel and John Maes, *Succesvol Lean* (Pearson, 2013). 112–119.

learning. Paradoxically, they often have little say over what they have to learn. Unless a goal is owned, the efforts to attain the goal are extrinsically motivated. Extrinsical motivation is less effective than intrinsic motivation.[3] "Students who pursue intrinsic goals tend to engage their learning tasks more actively than those who pursue primarily external affirmation, recognition by instructors, or avoidance of negative consequences."[4]

Understood: A goal can only be really owned if it is understood. A student must understand what is expected of him, what it means for him to have attained the goal. What will he have done that marks the attainment of the goal? How can he himself determine whether the goal's success criteria have been met?

Shared: In order for a goal to be understood and owned it must be shared. Goals and their success criteria must be shared extensively and explicitly with the students and teachers. Sharing is not referring to a guide or manual in which they are described. Most school systems require the goals to have been documented. But that does not mean they are really shared. Goal setting should take a substantial part of the teaching time.[5] The goals and subgoals of smaller teaching units should be discussed with (not just told) the students in order for them to really understand what they are about. In the process of discussing the goals, teachers "accidently" find out what the students are thinking about their study and learning. That is extremely important input for their teaching.

"The more transparent the teacher makes the learning goals, the more likely the student is to engage in the work needed to meet the goal. Also, the more the student is aware of the criteria of success, the more the student can see and appreciate the specific actions that are needed to attain these criteria."[6]

---

[3] The reader might recognize in this section, and several others in this book, thoughts similar to those exposed by Maria Montessori. This book and the ideas presented are not intended as Montessorian even though I'm sympathetic to some of the Montessorian ideas. The ideas are applicable to most if not all school types and philosophies.

[4] Meece et al. quoted in Lee and Hannafin, "A Design Framework for Enhancing Engagement in Student-Centered Learning: Own It, Learn It, and Share It." Similar points are made by F Dochy and M Segers, Creating Impact Through Future Learning: The High Impact Learning That Lasts (HILL) Model (Taylor & Francis, 2018); J Hattie, Visible Learning for Teachers: Maximizing Impact on Learning (Taylor & Francis, 2012); M L Emiliani, "Special Issue: Lean Six Sigma for Higher Education Evolution in Lean Teaching," no. June (2016): 1–17.

[5] There is not a fixed amount of time. Some best practices such as the KaosPilot readily take up to 10% of the teaching time to setting the goals.

Relevant: A goal must be conducive to reaching a higher-level aim for the student. Whether it is something that brings him joy or furthers a career, it has to be something the student cares about. In this way, it is relevant for the student, and he will engage more intensively with the learning. In the most minimal version of relevance, something helps meeting external requirements ("My parents want me to get a diploma"). Though there is some value in learning to do things you do not want, this type of relevance should be minimal.

Challenging: Most students like a challenge. A good challenge motivates pupils to explore and to engage with a learning task. In particular, the reward after the hard work is a feeling of achievement that helps to keep students engaged and intrinsically motivated.

"...setting challenging goals is more motivating than either possessing easy goals or urging people to 'do your best'".[7] The learning becomes secondary to completing the challenge. Which it is why setting a goal which is challenging and relevant is so important. Moreover, not all students like it, and not in equal measure. Dealing with challenges thus is both a motivator, but also something, an attitude, that has to be learned.

Attainable/Within sphere of influence: A goal that is beyond the reach of a student will only demotivate. Finding the balance between being challenging and unattainable is a delicate exercise. Finding out the balance rather than getting the balance right the first time is the key objective. The goal must be such that it takes the student out of her comfort zone into stretch mode, sometimes bordering on panic. Getting it wrong sometimes is a useful learning experience in itself. At New Engineers, we deliberately push our students into panic mode in order for them to learn their limits and to say "no".[8] Being attainable implies that the means to attain the goal must be within the reach or sphere of influence of the student.

---

[6] J Hattie, *Visible Learning for Teachers: Maximizing Impact on Learning* (Taylor & Francis, 2012), 51.

[7] Victor A Benassi, Catherine E Overson, and Christopher M Hakala, "Applying Science of Learning in Education: Infusing Psychological Science into the Curriculum," *Annals of Anthropological Practice* 37, no. 1 (2014): 303, doi:10.1111/napa.12013.

[8] It is obvious that this must be done very carefully, taking the individual student's mental condition into account. Doing things like this requires a safe environment, and students that have gone through sufficient personal development to be self-aware and demonstrate some learner agency.

Balanced: Goals are seldomly formulated on their own. There are multiple goals within one teaching unit. There are multiple units that are to some extent dependent, sometimes by the mere fact that a student has to work on them, and they compete for her limited time. This dependency needs to be managed for the learning to be possible and effective.

Measurable & measured: A challenging goal stimulates. But unless progress toward the goal can be tracked it is meaningless. Progress tracking means that the goal and the student performance have to be measurable. And they must be actually measured. Measuring goals is notoriously hard. The risk is of artificial measures. If conceived wrong, a measure might actually stimulate behavior opposite of what is intended. This part is key as it feeds into aggregated levels of information on how teachers, classes, and schools do. "...the key component is providing quality evidence to create the right debates [...] and it is important to focus on the overall teacher judgements that are made about progress."[9]

Visual: Making goals visual has various benefits. It makes them easier to grasp and share. Through visualization, they are easier to be "present" physically and thereby in the minds of pupils. Visualization is also key in progress tracking and feedback. After every task is completed, pupils and teacher can check whether the completion of the task has actually gotten the pupils closer to their goal. Thus, the visuals bring the goal into the heart of the teaching and learning.

Looking back at this list the reader is probably aware of these criteria and, also, to at least some extent in agreement. It can be a daunting list. One of the dangers in this setting is trying to be complete and right the first time. Setting good goals is a craft that requires hard work, feedback, and rework. In actually starting with some goals and reserving some time during the year to work on them is a good way to get going. While tracking progress, new insights will come that help in refining the goals. At the end of the chapter an example will be discussed.

---

[9] Hattie, *Visible Learning for Teachers: Maximizing Impact on Learning.* p. 173

TRACKING PROGRESS AND GUIDING LEARNING

Achieving goals means taking action. To assess whether an action was effective, information is needed. The action, in education that is the learning spaces and teaching, is discussed in Chapter 6. We now focus on tracking progress toward the goals. Tracking progress is what Hattie calls evidencing the effect a teacher or a school has on its students.

> Feedback is among the most common features of successful teaching and learning. But there is an enigma: while feedback is among the most powerful moderators of learning, its effects are among the most variable.[10]

In order to turn progress information into valuable feedback, goals must meet the above-mentioned characteristics. The progress information regarding the attainment of these goals must be:

- Individualized
- Frequently polled
- With room for error in the learning.

Each pupil's way of thinking, background, and frame of reference differs. Given these and many other differences, progress information must be interpreted against the individual background. It is the student's thinking that should be the focus. As a teacher, part of the job is to understand what the student has understood and how she reasons. Through that understanding, interventions can be initiated more effectively.[11] The longer a deviation from a course goes unnoticed, the harder it is to correct the course. Frequent polling of progress is therefore important. That fits also with attention spans and planning horizons of most students. Assessing progress is a core element of learning and should be integrated as an element of the learning process. There are multiple, plausible courses toward a goal. Finding out which one(s) work for a student amounts to running experiments. The importance

---

[10] Ibid. 129.

[11] Here, and hopefully throughout the book, the idea and challenge of Lean Education will surface in apparently smaller elements. Understanding the students' reasoning is a challenging task. Doing so for a classroom full of students is daunting. Coming up with personalized interventions is a next level that is almost unimaginable. Yet, that is exactly what we must strive for. That is a lifelong pursuit.

of high frequency is even bigger given that there must be room for experimentation and for error. If there is no real room for error, there is no room for learning. If tracking of progress is done in terms of good or wrong, as a formal assessment that carries weight in decisions other than learning, e.g., access to university, school career choices, the learning will be reduced.

Wiliam argues convincingly, "All teaching really boils down to three key processes [...]: finding out where the learners are in their learning, finding out where they are going, and finding out how to get there."[12] Learning thus entails investigation, uncertainty, and error. With frequent feedback, these errors are a big source for learning. Information on progress is input for a decision on what to do next in the learning and teaching processes. The teacher and student should pull the information when and where they need to decide where to go next. Rather than having a fixed format, fixed time assessments designed by others, teachers should focus on designing small, frequent, informal formative assessments to guide the learning.

To obtain the information on where the students are, informal formative assessments are a powerful means to track progress in a way that is conducive to learning. It is important that the information obtained from the assessment is turned into immediate and extensive feedback. The feedback is placed in a wider context of the learning goal, prior knowledge, and preceding and future teaching activities. These future activities consist of asking questions and giving tasks.[13] Student and teacher can map the student's trajectory through for the student's unchartered waters. This way it becomes assessment-as-learning.[14] The student obtains insight in her own learning process. The informal formative assessments are small units that help assess whether the pupils have actually grasped the meaning of a lesson and mastered a skill that has been exercised. A teacher might mark essays without explanation, for example, and return them together with three essays judged to be well written. And then he distributes these among all students and ask them to consider and compare them and rewrite their own essays.[15]

---

[12] Wiliam, *Embedded Formative Assessment* (Solution Tree Press, 2011), 45.

[13] Martinez and Lipson (1989) quoted in F Dochy and M Segers, *Creating Impact Through Future Learning: The High Impact Learning That Lasts (HILL) Model* (Taylor & Francis, 2018).

[14] Ibid. 79.

[15] Wiliam, *Embedded Formative Assessment*, provides a host of powerful formats for embedding formative assessment in the classroom.

LEAN SUPPORT

Lean provides several powerful tools that help implement goal setting and progress tracking: A3 thinking, Kaizen and Kata techniques, and visual progress boards. A3 thinking is a technique in which a whole project is consolidated on an A3 paper. It contains everything from background and scope, to past performance and goals, analysis of the gap, plans to close the gap, and progress tracking. The format is the A3. The structure is based on Kaizen, a change for the better. Lean thinking is based on continuous improvement. As such, it fits seamlessly with the process of learning. The A3 and Kaizen techniques provide support for larger chunks of learning. For the everyday small step learning and teaching activities, A3 and Kaizen can be complemented with the Kata coaching. The Kata is a series of small coaching steps toward a next goal. The whole progress along the way is tracked via visual progress boards.

The idea behind both the Kaizen and the Kata techniques is that people and organizations navigate territory that is to some extent unknown. The key in being successful is finding fast the right information to make the next step. Also key is visualizing the future state. And then, based on the current state, devise the next intermediate target condition. Once that condition has been achieved the next step is planned. The Kaizen approach can be used as a plan for a pupil's entire year at school and for special projects. It consists of a six-step approach.[16]

1. Understand and define the desired learning and the learning gap concisely
2. Analyze the gap and find the root-causes
3. Generate learning strategies
4. Make a plan
5. Execute the plan
6. Check and safeguard the learning

---

[16] Experience Lean practitioners will that I have adapted the six-step approach to the educational context and language. The general practice of focusing on a problem is maintained, but the phrasing is changed. In a business, problems are good news, though it takes quite some effort to change the culture to that realization. Focusing on a problem is creating a frame. By rewording the steps toward the desired learning and leaving "problem" out of the description the mindset is positive. The material integrity of the approach is maintained. The learning gap is the problem. I find it problematic to frame something a pupil has yet to learn in terms of problems. It is a chance, an opportunity, and something that is natural. One cannot be expected to know what you have come to school to learn.

What is the problem the pupils are working on? This could be their own learning as such or a school project for which they need to acquire certain skills, knowledge, and attitude. By defining the desired learning and the learning gap concisely, they deepen their understanding. It is a crucial step in learning. The learning gap can be described as a gap between a goal and the current situation or between a norm and the actual knowledge. A student needs to understand, for example, his nineteenth century history. What history and why does it matter? What does he currently know of the events in the nineteenth century? He visualizes how he knows and demonstrates that he has mastered the subject. Then he researches various sources of knowledge about the nineteenth century. Next, knowing how he best studies, he devises, possibly with input of the teacher, various ways to obtain the necessary information. This could be a regular class, but also other sources such as a local museum, the Internet, etc. He makes a plan of how he will gather and process the necessary input and turn it into evidence that he has in fact understood the subject. These are his learning strategies. Where will he study, who will he approach for help, in what form will he demonstrate his understanding? Next, he goes to work, and at smaller steps, notes the progress he is making. The teacher and the pupil will discuss progress and check whether the learning strategies are delivering the envisioned result. Finally, he demonstrates his learning and thinks of ways to add what is not yet understood.

A great additional value of this approach is that it is used also in the support and administrative functions of the organization. It thus supports affinity across functions in the schools and supports an organization-wide culture of learning and growth.

Within the everyday setting of project work and classroom teaching, the Kaizen approach is complemented by Kata coaching. The idea behind the Kata is to develop a standard problem-solving approach and attitude. The Kata coach is asking questions on a regular basis.

1. What is the target condition?
2. What is the current condition?
3. Which obstacle do you face right now?
4. What is the next step?
5. When will the results of this next step be visible?

The Kata works from the same philosophy as Kaizen. It focuses on smaller, intermediate steps. The educational equivalence again is easy to derive.

What does the student want and need to learn? What does she know/can do right now? What does she still have to learn during the next day or two? What does she not yet grasp, what understanding evades her? How can she tweak her learning strategy? When and how does she want to show that she has bridged the gap? This way Lean Education helps the teacher to act as coach for the student's learning. At the same time, it tasks the student to engage with the learning goal, self-reflection, and learning strategies. All these elements are conducive to learner agency.

Using progress tracking boards and A3's, the student and teacher visualize the target condition. This offers also a great opportunity for students to engage each other through peer coaching. Students that have mastered a topic will come to the aid of those that haven't yet. Both learn in the process. In the Lean Education culture, it is accepted that not everyone progresses at the same rate and toward the same goal. Some students have useful prior knowledge which allows them to go further. Traditional education would hamper them since they already made or easily make the bar. Of course, traditional education does acknowledge and accepts the differences. But it does so in a more marginal sense. There are some extra-curricular activities for faster students, for example. But the frame of reference is the standard that has been set for every specific school type and age group. The room to acknowledge and accommodate deviant performances is very small. In Lean Education, students tune their own goals in the process of writing their A3. They investigate how far they want and need to progress. When I supervise a student's thesis work, one of the first things I ask him is what final mark he wants to achieve. Then we discuss the marking criteria and investigate to what extent his knowledge, skills, and thesis topic allow him to achieve that mark and what still needs to be done. Over various meetings, we'll revisit the criteria and his progress. These are, of course, not the only topics of conversation. We venture into the content and relevant theories as well. The investment in time is somewhat larger than usual. That investment is, in my personal experience, more than compensated for in terms of higher impact and fewer revisits.

A brilliant example is of primary school pupils discussing with their teacher at the classroom board a grammar rule. The teacher asks how they will know whether they have understood the rule. The pupils ponder this question and ask the teacher to write down several sentences of which some are incorrect. They discuss the sentences and try to determine together which are correct. They find out they got it wrong. The next question the teacher asks is how they could learn the rule better and offers halfway through the discussion some suggestions.[17] It is a delicate balance between questioning and suggesting. The teacher will need to make room for all pupils, ensuring each gets want she needs. He could split the group into smaller groups according to their understanding, or mix students with differing advancements, and have them actively involved in each other's learning and teaching.[18]

TRACKING PROGRESS ON PERFORMANCE BOARDS

When navigating unknown territory, it helps to have something like a map and a tracker of the steps one has made, and to map out the next steps. Performance boards are simple visual means to map out goals and progress, to indicate hurdles, learnings, and actions. There are many forms a progress board can take. It can be tuned to culture, means, and needs of classes and schools. Whatever the form, there are a few perquisites for a successful progress board. One, it is owned by the group and not the teacher. Two, students use it to track and report on their progress. Three, the atmosphere in the group is safe, respectful, and constructive. Performance boards provide students a means to exhibit ownership not just over their progress, but also over the class, the materials, and topics covered.

By jointly building, for example, the week's program on the progress board, the students provide input for the program, they can track the progress, and during the week reassess their progress and possibly make changes to the program. We ran such a model at New Engineers during a week in which Dave Gray came teaching. The students had read various materials in preparation. They worked on their own, real-life projects and were asked to research how Dave's theories could help them. On the Monday morning, the students constructed a week plan on the windows dividing the week days in pre- and after lunch sessions. Next, they built a list of artifacts they wanted to produce as part of the week's learning. These artifacts, and the theories needed to construct them, were spread out

---

[17] From personal conversation with Jaap Versfelt of *Leerkracht* foundation. A foundation that actively supports primary schools and vocational schools with the introduction of Lean Education.

[18] Various schools already have students helping each other out. Mostly, the more advanced students help the less advanced students. There is room to task the more advanced students with, for example, meta-cognitive assignments while they help out others.

over the week, also stuck on the window. The students and Dave discussed them till it fit most of the objectives of the students. Over the next days, they marked topics successfully covered and discussed necessary changes. This approach gave them ownership, established rapport between Dave and the students, and a deeper understanding of what they were getting to work on.

In another format, we draw a horizontal line across the entire length of a classroom wall. Then we ask the students what the left- and right-hand side represent in terms of mastery of a topic. The left usually stands for novice status, the right-hand side for expert level. Since "novice" and "expert" are not well defined and dependent on context, the students are asked to debate together what expertise means in their context. This is a very useful exercise that requires them to engage with the topic deeply and jointly. Next, they position themselves on the line, first where they think they stand, and next where they would like to get to. Over the course of the teaching they are asked frequently to reposition themselves and provide evidence. In some powerful cases, students show awareness that cause them to reposition themselves more to the left indicating that they now better understand the topic, and what they actually know or can do, and what they would like and need to know. The scale is thus itself part of the learning and not an external given. The scale might even change! This, of course, is an anathema for traditional education with its externally fixed standards. Changing scales reflect growing and deepening under-standing on the part of the students. This does not mean that anything goes. Teachers and other experts challenge students and steer the process based on their understanding and expertise. They intervene when the dis-cussions get off track and serious damage could result. The intervention is, however, not the heavy-handed "I'm the expert and I'll tell you how it is" type. Rather, it focuses on the understanding that got the students to this point and brings them around to understanding why their track is headed in the wrong direction. Some topics and settings will allow this flexibility, some not, or not fully. When formal accreditation requires the scales to be formally and externally set, it is important that the norm is shared.[19] Still, the students discuss what it means and position themselves.

---

[19] Healthcare or operating industrial machines, just to name two, are examples where some form of external norms are called for that are non-negotiable. But even in healthcare not all standards are absolute. What constitutes a good physician-patient relationship is a topic on which one can imagine there being some room for discussion.

LEARNER AGENCY

In Lean thinking, a process is owned by the people working on it. In education, this means it is owned by students and teacher together. Given that the process of learning takes place in, but also outside the classroom, Lean in the classroom covers only a part of the learning process. The student must own his learning for the teaching to be effective. Ownership is something that must be given (by teacher, the school) and also accepted (by the student). Giving ownership can be difficult given the drive and engagement of the teacher and the responsibility she feels. Letting go of some control is difficult. Taking ownership is also difficult. It must be learned. A teacher cannot just tell the students they now own their learning. One of the important tasks of a school and its teachers is to help students taking ownership. The various Lean Education techniques are working toward the transfer of ownership. By having students draft an A3, a process starts in which they think about their learning. Writing A3s is about discovery and gaining deeper understanding. In that same process, the teacher gets a feeling to what extent she can let go. Through progress discussion, using their performance board (see Figure 5.1) students own up to their work. It is their assessment of progress rather than the teacher's assessment. In the Lean philosophy, managers are also coaches of their staff. The key in that role is asking questions instead of passing judgment or giving instructions. In a similar vein, a teacher can ask questions about the student's assessment of his progress instead of saying he is wrong. The great benefit of this approach is that it provides the teacher a better understanding

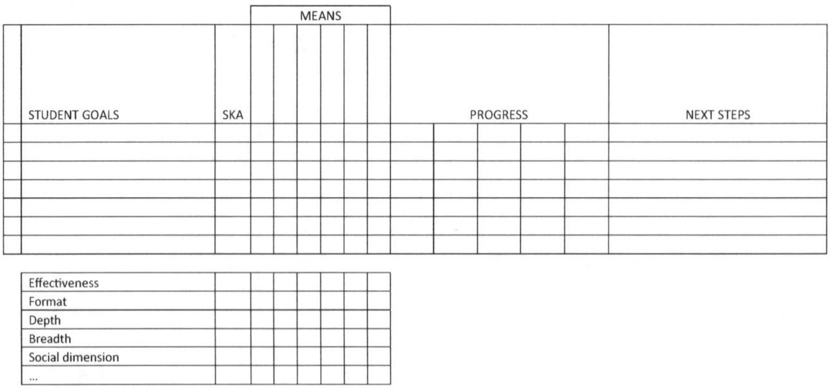

FIGURE 5.1
Student performance board.

of the student's thinking and thereby gains better insights into how to support the student's learning with additional learning strategies. This will work best when the goals are clear and defined according to the characteristics defined at the beginning of the chapter. In the process of tracking the progress goals can be revisited. They might require clarification. It is a joint process of discovery.

HANDS ON!

There are six steps that together help students and teachers create the backdrop against which the learning process can be organized and progress tracked. This framework is easy to understand and apply. I encourage teachers and students alike to experiment. Using this framework as a basis, try what works best for the students, class, and school.

1. The student reflects on why she wants to go to school, what she wants to learn, and why.[20] What does she aim for? Based on a (self)reflection on where she is now, one or more learning strategies are devised. A plan is made which starts from the teaching plan, but allows for individual variances. A key question to ask the student is: how do you know when you have achieved your goals? The student A3 captures all this (see Figure 5.2). It is a living document that gets updated several times over the course of a semester (or whatever teaching period is applicable). As a student progresses through school and becomes more mature, there might be multiple A3's addressing different subject matters. In that case, it is advisable to maintain 1 overarching A3. These A3's together effectively constitute the student's portfolio

2. Elaborate on aims and goals by formulating more concrete goals. These goals can be derived from a generic set defined by school and industry. But the students should also be able to define their own goals. Goals relate to knowledge, attitudes, and skills. It is strongly advised to limit the number of goals to about five per period. Formulating the goals entails also defining what it means to have achieved them, how achievement can be evidence, and how the progress can be tracked

---

[20] This applies to students of all ages and is not restricted to older students. For the youngest ones, the format needs adjusting.

3. Design a (set of) learning strategy which consists of a mixture of different sources and formats that will allow the student to gain and develop the knowledge, skills, and attitudes necessary. The school and each teacher will have a set of different formats and sources, based on their pedagogical vision, the purpose of the school, and the culture

4. Over time, at least weekly, a student reflects on the progress being made. Progress tracking involves relating to the goals, for example, by means of a rubric and showing evidence. Students can do so first by themselves and then in discussion with either peers, the teacher, or both. It is important to remember that progress is not linear

5. Based on the progress, establish the effectiveness of the learning strategy. Did the format work, was the content rich enough, complex, but not too complex, etc. Let the student at least try to express what they have learned through a knowledge A3. Why is the topic at hand relevant to the student in light of the goals, what does she know/is able to do/what is her attitude? And what gaps does she still have? How did she learn? What does she now know/can she do/how does she look at the world? How can she apply what she has acquired? This should show that she gets closer to her goals and overarching aim. And finally, is there anything left for her to still focus on, or can the topic be closed for now?

6. Detail the next steps. This includes both adjustments in the learning strategy and the content of the learning. The student might switch to a different format for learning (e.g., moving from a group activity to an individual assignment) and to different or more complex content.

Setting up this cycle initially involves some work on part of the teacher. It will foster greater ownership and motivation on the part of the students. This first and most importantly enhances the effectiveness of the learning. It also saves the teacher time down the line that she can spend on designing or improving formats or on more individual coaching.

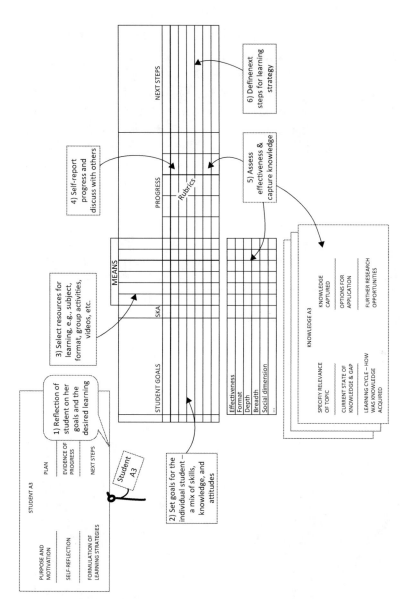

FIGURE 5.2

A3 and performance.

PEER REVIEWS AND PERFORMANCE BOARDS: TWO POWERFUL WAYS TO ASSESS AND TRACK LEARNING PROGRESS

As part of their study, students run an improvement project. First, they are taught core concepts and methods. These they then apply on real cases with the help of companies, healthcare organizations, etc. Concluding the project and reporting on their progress and learning is part of the formal, summative assessment. We are convinced that results of the assessment should not be a surprise. We guide and coach the students along the way. And, more importantly, the students guide themselves and their peers.

We have defined a set of criteria that measure the attainment of the goals. Each criterium has 5 grades ranging from 0 to 4, 0 indicating that the required insight or behavior is absent, 4 that it is fully fulfilled. For each grade, there is a short general description. In our case, there is an overarching goal for the project. That goal is sub-divided in sub-goals, one each for the ten major aspects of the projects.

We share and discuss the criteria together with students. These are the criteria that we will use when grading their work. We are fully transparent on what we expect of our students. We describe, in terms of Lean Education, the future state of their work. We share and discuss this in peer groups. A peer group is a group of students that will maintain contact as they go out and work on their individual projects. They will come back to school together to share experiences and get coaching from the teachers.

Early on in their project, we assess and discuss together the first version of project reports of each of the students in the peer group. This way we illustrate what the criteria mean and how we interpret them. This provides an opportunity for the students to explore and deepen their understanding of the criteria. They are also instructed on how to provide constructive feedback.

Having thus set a standard and explained it, students then proceed to self-assess their work and review other students' work. They use the input, the project reports, and the peer review form to assess the project report. They write a short explanation for each aspect detailing how they derive the grade. In the next meeting they share their assessments. As the students assess the work of others, they learn a lot. The "fresh" look from a distance to a project they are not involved in creates a deeper understanding.

**PEER REVIEWS AND PERFORMANCE BOARDS:
TWO POWERFUL WAYS TO ASSESS AND
TRACK LEARNING PROGRESS (Continued)**

Understanding that evades them when they are solely looking at the project they are running themselves. There is a certain myopia when looking at your own work. With the fresh perspective they are better able to look critically at their own work. Moreover, through assessing of multiple project reports, there is a repetition that is conducive to learning. From the second session onward, the students have an important role in the running of the performance board and peer review sessions. The teacher monitors the progress, but is no longer the sole owner of the sessions. She will review the reports and check a sample of student peer reviews. If, and when, necessary she will voice an opinion or share an assessment. She will be able to spot students that are struggling and intervene sooner than is the case with solely final exams. Individual students can be provided with pointers to additional materials that are relevant. Thus, we can also tune their learning materials based on their individual needs.

The progress of the students is tracked also via a performance board. Our performance boards are made of simple sheets of brown paper, about 2 meters wide, 1 meter high. There is a row for each student in the peer group and a series of columns that correspond to the aspects of the project. The students share with each other their ambition and their progress. The progress is based on the self-assessment and peer reviews. In each session, the students are asked to analyze the gaps between the ambition and the actual progress. They must find the root causes for their delay, if any. Next, they list the actions they are going to take to remedy the gap.

The materials used are basic. The time involved for the sessions are limited. A performance board session takes about 15–20 minutes for a group of on average five students. The review sessions are scheduled every 3 weeks with a teacher. These sessions take on average 1.5–2 hours. As the students slowly take ownership for the sessions and their learning, the teacher's active involvement decreases. The students develop some skills in addition to the theory they have learned and discussed in the sessions. Leading a session requires, for example, withholding judgment, an open mind, empathy, and presenting in a concise way.

PEER REVIEWS AND PERFORMANCE BOARDS: TWO POWERFUL WAYS TO ASSESS AND TRACK LEARNING PROGRESS (Continued)

Overall, we find that by the end of the semester there is little discrepancy between our judgment and those of the students and also between teachers. If, and when, there are discrepancies, we discuss them. These discussions may lead to an alignment of views, an adjustment of teaching materials, or an agreement to disagree.

ASSESSMENT DOCUMENT FOR PEER REVIEW AND FORMAL GRADING:

There are ten aspects on which we assess the work of a student. These range from specific knowledge to attitude and analytical skills. This example shows aspect four, root cause analysis (Table 5.1).

TABLE 5.1

Peer Review Document with Rubrics

4. Root Cause Analysis

	Is able to identify the causal relations between causes and consequences of a problem. Can visualize and analyze problem statements using adequate methods rigorously and consistently.
0	• There is no or only superficial analysis. There is no description of logical cause-consequence relationships.
1	• Cause-consequence relationships are unclear and illogical. Root causes have not (sufficiently) been identified. • The validity of the analysis has not been based on traceable, verifiable data and facts.
2	• …etc.
3	• …etc.
4	• Complex causal relationships have been identified and laid-out clearly and concisely. • An original approach (not discussed in class) has been used to identify root-causes without ambiguity.
	Resulting score with explanation.

**PEER REVIEWS AND PERFORMANCE BOARDS:
TWO POWERFUL WAYS TO ASSESS AND
TRACK LEARNING PROGRESS (Continued)**

The assessment of this aspect and the other nine aspects together provide a view on the overall progress of the student's work. Not all aspects are equally important. We apply a weighing factor. The grade for each aspect is entered (Table 5.2).

TABLE 5.2

Assessment Document for Peer Review and Formal Grading

Overall Assessment Document			Date:	
Student	Student no:	Student name:		
Weight	Sub-item	Indicators / Rubrics	Score [0..4]	Explanation
10%	1 Background			
19,0%	2 Current State			
5%	3 Goals and Target Condition(s)			
19,0%	4 Root Cause Analysis	Is able to identify the causal relations between causes and consequences of a problem. Can visualize and analyze problem statements using adequate methods rigorously and consistently.	2,5	First causal relationships have been defined. Impact on quality and cost is not yet clear. Several explanations for root causes are offered. These contain, however, several unvalidated assumptions.
	Etc. 5–10			

**PEER REVIEWS AND PERFORMANCE BOARDS:
TWO POWERFUL WAYS TO ASSESS AND
TRACK LEARNING PROGRESS (Continued)**

All taken together give an overall mark for the project. This mark will be low in the beginning and increases over time as the student's work progresses and he improves his work. We extend the marking process by:

- sharing and discussing the criteria up-front
- have students assess each other's work
- tracking progress visually and for all to see
- having formative assessments at regular, short intervals.

The goal is not the grade. The grade reflects the extent to which the student has learned. The goal is learning and proficiency. That is what this practice of Lean Education fosters.

6

Lean in the Classroom:
Each His Own Together

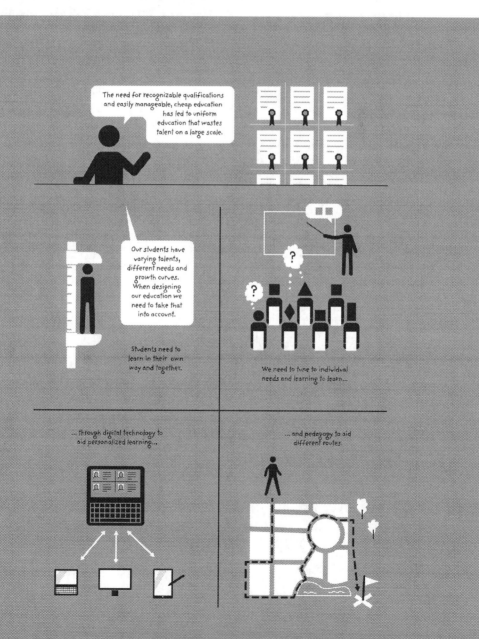

INTRODUCTION

There is a growing awareness that each student has her own specific individual capabilities and ambitions that require an individualized provision of learning opportunities. Education is still often large scale and uniform. As a consequence, we waste talent on a large scale. Once we acknowledge differences in starting points of the learning journey, differences in preferred ways of learning, and allow for differentiation in goals, we cannot but provide each student customized, personalized learning paths. New technologies as well as pedagogical innovations make that possible.

Education needs to provide higher quality and differentiated education at lower costs. And, importantly, it should be more fun and engaging for both students and teachers. Just doing the same slightly more efficient will not work. As it is, teachers face already a heavy workload. Smarter teaching means deploying other resources and deploying existing resources more effectively. In order to stay relevant, schools need to do more than hanging on. Beginning to teach each student according to her need is a beginning of an innovation journey that will also address the other needs of higher quality and lower cost.

EACH HIS OWN—THE PRINCIPLE OF PULL

If we accept that each pupil is different in a way that is meaningful for education, than this ought to have implications for how we teach. This may sound unrealistic, especially if we have already heavily burdened teachers and class sizes that many feel are too big. How can we differentiate our way of teaching such that it fits individual students' needs? That is the challenge we face. The traditional trade-off between size of the class and individualization needs to be overcome. Lean Education provides the framework to achieve this. A note of caution. This is obviously not going to be easy. Had it been easy, it would have been done already. Nor will it be the same for every school. Each school needs to experiment using the Lean Education framework to find the way that best fits its students, the school, and community.

Differentiation or Personalized Learning Requires

- Understanding and classification of various drivers for learning (modalities, timing, physical setting, group vs. individual)
- Modularized approach to development of teaching materials
- Flexible physical and digital settings to allow students to pull learning materials
- Student ability to pull information

One starting point is my adage that, "If I'm working hard something is wrong since it should be the students who are working hard." As a teacher, everyone will have had the experience of a lesson that was hard going. You do your best, and then try even harder. Still the group will not come along. It is our feeling of responsibility that gets in the way. It is not our learning! Even though we are paid to teach, we cannot learn. We engineer the environment in which our pupils can learn. So, if we stop just teaching in one format for the whole group first, we gain a lot of time, and prevent a lot of waste of talent.[1] Evidence shows students forget a lot of what they have heard during class. Finding more effective ways to teach saves teachers time. We could either teach less extensively or fewer topics. Formats in which students, engage together and are actively involved, even teaching other students will be up to an order of magnitude more effective. We should also teach in a way that relates clearly to the prior knowledge of our students. We often define what the entry criteria are for a course. Based on these, we design and execute our teaching. This becomes problematic if we consider the following. The entry criteria are implemented as: "the students have passed earlier exams." In the meantime, between those classes and the new class students may have acquired new, relevant knowledge, attitude, and skills. They might have forgotten some as well. The actual prior knowledge is not established. And that is problematic.

> Anyone who has ever taught a course knows that students are not a homogeneous group. They come into our courses with differing levels of knowledge about subject matter content, broad ranges of intellectual and metacognitive skills, and a variety of beliefs and attitudes toward

---

[1] Redecker et al., *The Future of Learning: Preparing for Change—Publication.*

the topic and toward learning. In fact, prior knowledge is one of the most influential factors in student learning because new information is processed through the lens of what one already knows, believes, and can do.[2]

An additional problem is that there is a huge variety in a group of students. If every individual meets at least the criteria, there must be many who exceed the entry criteria. All the teaching then is geared toward the lowest shared achievement. This means a lot of waste. If we were to aim at the highest repeatable performance, i.e., the achievement that has been attained by more, not exceptionally gifted students, we would gain immensely in achievement.

Taking all this into account, the first focus should be on effective learning. We have evidence that there is substantial variance among teachers with regards to the effect they have on learning. Expert teachers, "...seem not to be just more knowledgeable but more effective in the way they present materials, relate to prior knowledge, ...".[3] Theories on learning styles and preferences are heavily debated and controversial. I argue that students should devise their learning strategies in which they mix various sources, formats, and modalities of learning. Ultimately, students and teachers ought to provide evidence of the effect. What we do know is that students, left to their own devices without critical coaching will choose formats that are easier rather than effective. Therefore, it is critically important to start fostering learner agency early on. Timing of lessons, both starting time and duration, have an effect on the impact of the teaching and learning. Group and individual learning formats have different effects on different pupils. This gives a rich set of variables teachers and students can use together to tune the provision of learning materials and formats.

> No document should prescribe teaching methods in exact detail, of course, because no single method will work best in every circumstance. The learning process is complex and variable; research has just begun to scratch the surface of the question of what methods will help students learn most effectively.

---

[2] Ambrose and Lovett in Benassi, Overson, and Hakala, "Applying Science of Learning in Education: Infusing Psychological Science into the Curriculum."
[3] Hattie, *Visible Learning for Teachers: Maximizing Impact on Learning.*

It seems clear, though, that different methods have different strengths and weaknesses, especially when considering the specific background and preferences of individual learners. Different methods will also be optimal in different cultural contexts. Some methods will be better at conveying facts; others at fostering creative thought. Some will work for the most academically advanced students, other for the most dexterous students; others may be superior for those who need more guidance and support. Alert teachers will be able to employ different learning methods as the situation dictates, and modify their approach continually depending on their results...[4]

In a hybrid learning environment, students construct various learning strategies that are a mix of online and offline activities and materials, theoretical and applied work, solitary and group work, and free and heavily formatted. There are multiple ways of knowing, multiple ways of interacting, and multiple opportunities for practicing.[5] There is a wide range of meta-cognitive strategies that students and teachers can make use of to find ways of knowing and learning that fit the students well.[6] At New Engineers, for example, we ask students to work on their subjects and produce exercises that will let other students practice the subject. This provides us with insights into the students' thinking and understanding, it enhances the students' mastery over the subject, and it provides us with more exercises and thus saves time.[7]

PERSONALIZATION AND STANDARDIZATION

We have established the potential drivers for learning. To match the teaching to individualized learning, we need to modularize offerings in the learning space. The learning space encompasses the physical and digital environment, the content and materials, and the various formats,

---

[4] Brooks and Holmes, "Equinox Blueprint."

[5] Hattie, *Visible Learning for Teachers: Maximizing Impact on Learning*, 113–114.

[6] Dochy and Segers, *Creating Impact Through Future Learning: The High Impact Learning That Lasts (HILL) Model*; Wiliam, *Embedded Formative Assessment*; Hattie, *Visible Learning for Teachers: Maximizing Impact on Learning*; Ott et al., "Illustrating Performance Indicators and Course Characteristics to Support Students' Self-Regulated Learning in CS1."

[7] The time saved is spent on assessing the students' thinking and assessing the quality of the exercises. So, overall, we do not save time, but the level of understanding is remarkably better.

plus the participants, i.e., student, coach, and expert,[8] and the intended learning outcomes. The question here is how to create a learning space that is manageable and personal. Again, the Lean toolkit helps. Lean product development contains various methods and tools to provide services and products that meet individual clients' needs. Even for a car, there are so many features and variants a customer can choose from that hardly any two cars are the same. We call this mass customization. Schools, in contrast, have been remarkably uniform in their teaching programs. This stems from both the need for uniform output (students meeting the same standards) and old economies-of-scale thinking. Combined with a teacher's own preferences, we get uniformity (for all students in a class) and unwanted variance (between teachers). Students would be better off if the teaching is tuned toward their learning based on evidence. Evidence that is shared among the teachers and among schools. In order to be meaningful, evidence must be based on a shared standard. So, there is a strong case for both standardization and personalization. These two demands might seem contradictory, but actually go hand-in-hand. If teaching materials are standardized in a way that allows configuration and parameterization,[9] teachers will gain a lot of time, students will be able to pull materials better suited to their needs, and data will be comparable.

There are a manageable number of dimensions that need to be variable in order to meet individual students' needs.

- Format: text, visual, audio
- Speed: how fast can a student work her way through the materials
- Intensity: how deep can a student delve into a specific subject
- Extensity: how broad can a student extend a subject
- Social setting: individual, small group, large group
- Timing: when, and for what duration can a student study
- Feedback: intensity, frequency

---

[8] Coaches and experts are part of the learning space proper if they have their own learning intentions which they want to satisfy as part of the learning that takes place in the learning space. This is an insight that arose from the discussions with José Cuperus that have been very helpful.

[9] Configuration means putting various elements together to form a greater whole. Which elements and the way in which they are put together is to some extent open. A class, for example, is the configuration of some frontal teaching, individual exercise, and online videos that are discussed in groups. Parameterization is the adjustment of an element according to a fixed set of variables. A test might contain 10 or 20 questions, the duration of a teaching session could be 30 or 40 minutes, i.e., the pace being slower or faster.

If we can modify a lot of the teaching along these dimensions, we can achieve real personalized learning. Even though there are only seven dimensions, the number of variants is enormous. And, even if it is not perfect, it is a whole lot better than one uniform way of teaching. This, of course, is not something that is easily done. There are two key issues to address. One, how to design learning materials that are configurable and parameterizable? Two, how to organize learning and teaching accordingly?

DESIGNING LEARNING MATERIALS

When designing learning materials, there are many different formats and dimensions. We can have recorded, animated slides; traditional classroom teaching; recordings of cases with comments explaining the theory in action; on demand materials, with conditionals on grasp of prior materials; linking materials thematically, skipping strict age cohorts, allowing students to fast and slow pace into other groups; group related work, e.g., project-based learning, action learning; self-timed group work; feedback from peers, annotated work, coaching sessions; pull of learning materials based on progress board discussions; self-tests; etc. The list is almost limitless.

When it comes to designing different ways of learning and teaching, relatively new pedagogies such as project-based learning, problem-based learning, simulation-based learning, constructionist, and constructivist learning provide ample formats that will allow teachers to modify their teaching. Technology comes to our aid as well. Platforms such as Coursera show how topics can be explored in-depth and in-breadth. Various suppliers offer high quality materials that can be viewed by students at their own pace and at their own time. They can revisit topics, follow-up, and additional references for more depth and traverse to adjacent topics. It is a wonderful world, not just for students, but also for teachers. It provides a means to stay up-to-date and find materials that challenge their students and help them close gaps. Since this wide group of providers all differ to some extent in tone, format, analogies, speed, etc., it offers students opportunities to investigate what works best for them.

In order to be configurable, teaching materials must be clearly delineated in terms of the topics covered. The description should indicate which knowledge, skills, and attitudes are covered and at which level. During the design of a new course, class, or study, these are important considerations. This provides students with various paths through the learning space: broadening, deepening, and both. The learning space is like a store with virtual and physical shelves from which students and teachers pick various resources to form their learning strategies. The education or the study defines the bandwidth of the paths a student can choose. A medical study might pose stricter conditions on which subjects are covered and in which modality. Making an incision, for example, cannot be studied in theory alone. A school's vision or a country's culture might likewise put restrictions on the paths that are open to students.

STRUCTURING THE LEARNING

Throughout this book, I have stressed the importance of learner agency. The chapter on goals elaborated the role of goals in learner agency. A third key factor in learning are meta-cognitive skills. These three elements come together in the learning process and the design and execution of classes. To illustrate how this works, consider a type of learning process called LAMDA: look, ask, model, discuss, and act.[10] This is the Lean way of learning and of developing new knowledge. One starts by looking, observing, and testing the object of study. Then, by asking probing questions, you try to understand what is at the heart of an issue or topic to be understood. This can be done through study, reading, visiting labs, workplaces, etc. Based on the growing understanding, a student models his understanding. This model should be good enough for the students to make predictions about the topic that demonstrate his understanding and possibly add new insights the existing body of knowledge. This model is discussed with other students, teachers, and outside experts to evaluate the model and collect input for refinement. Finally, the model is implemented and tested. The learnings and insights are collected using a knowledge A3. This document, named after the A3 paper size, structures the knowledge that is gained. Why is it worthwhile to investigate the topic? What is already known about the topic? How is the model set up, what did the learning cycle look like? Based on the discussion and act steps, what

---

[10] See, for example, https://www.lean.org/lexicon/lamda-cycle accessed December 3, 2018, 15:00.

new knowledge was generated? How and when can it be used? What is the next step in the learning and development of the topic? This way a student demonstrates her understanding of the topic, is conscious of the learning process itself (meta-cognition), and has a piece of understanding she can share with other students, outside stakeholders, and teachers for future use. The student becomes one of the experts on this topic who might support other pupils in their learning and thus alleviate the teacher's burden. The steps in this learning cycle, and the knowledge A3, tie in nicely with the student performance board discussed in Chapter 5. The student's learning goals are the trigger. The learning strategy consists of the means on the performance board and is documented on the A3. The progress along the LAMDA steps is tracked on the performance board. The final iteration on the performance board lists the next steps, which are documented more extensively under the A3 header of application and future research.

Over time a student collects multiple A3s regarding his plans and ambitions and the various topics he has studied. Together with multiple captures of his performance board these constitute his portfolio which demonstrates the things he has learned, and how he has learned.

DECOUPLING SUMMATIVE ASSESSMENT FROM TEACHING

One of the tenets of Lean thinking is that there are multiple solutions to a challenge. Locking into one solution too early deprives you of the opportunity to gain more information and to learn. In teaching it is the same. There are many ways to master a subject. Through the close connection of assessment and teaching, too much teaching and learning becomes focused on making the exam. The exam is not the goal, the learning is. By making the exam the goal, measure and goal are mixed up. This often happens in organizations. Profit is not the goal, sustaining the business over a longer period, providing the customers with what they need, and the employees with a chance to grow and make a living, that is the goal. And profit is *a* measure. Passing the exam is a measure that means that a subject has been mastered. It is not a very good measure at that. Many students are able to reproduce the learned materials without really having mastered them. Being able to reproduce knowledge is a valuable ability. The idea that students can just look stuff up on the Internet is misguided.

You cannot ask a meaningful question without having some prior knowledge, and you cannot assess the value and correctness of information without prior knowledge. Just reproducing knowledge, however, will leave students with surface rather than deep knowledge. Therefore, it would be a good idea to decouple the summative assessments from the teaching. Instead, we can ask our students how they would like to prove that they have mastered the subject,[11] and ask professionals what they would like to see as an indication that a student has sufficiently mastered the subject. We still will have exams for purpose of comparison, use the input of exam boards as a valuable source, but work toward a richer assessment in which learning is the purpose. The very discussion on how to measure mastery is an incredibly effective learning activity. By decoupling exams and the learning, we also stimulate a more varied supply of teaching and learning offerings.

PULL

If we can make students pull the materials they need, it is better tuned, but also a time savings for the teacher. Pull is a well-established principle in Lean thinking. In many settings, it is challenging to implement. The challenge is due to change that is required in the provider (a preceding step in the process, a supplier). In education, it is the other way around, at least in the beginning. The assumption in general Lean thinking is that the customer knows what he wants. In the case of a student, that is not so clear cut. I do believe that students are mostly capable of making important choices also regarding their education. This ability is not absolute. And it comes with a caveat. We will have to teach students how to take ownership. Just giving it is not enough. In a system where we often made students unlearn their curiosity and drive to explore, they will have to relearn how to take ownership, and how to investigate what interests them. Pull requires our pupils to direct their own learning. As long as our assumption is that they cannot do so, and we as teachers are to play the most important part in the learning, we are not going to make the transition.

---

[11] The impact of self-assessment is great tool in which students show themselves to be accurate assessors. Hattie, *Visible Learning for Teachers: Maximizing Impact on Learning.*

TYING IT ALL TOGETHER: ORGANIZING FOR PERSONALIZED LEARNING

As part of their learner agency students devise learning strategies. This process is facilitated through the modularized, configurable, and parameterizable learning modules. We discussed these elements above. Now, the question is how to tie these elements together. It is a six-step approach (see also Chapter 5). It starts with the student expressing (the form depending on the age and abilities of the student) why she goes to school, what she would like to learn, and why. She also investigates how she learns best and most effectively (not necessarily most pleasurably!). Based on the school's overall mission, vision, and purpose, the student with input from teachers and other stakeholders selects various goals relating to subject matters, knowledge, skills, and attitudes. She thinks about what the evidence of attaining that goal looks like. Next, she selects sources to construct learning strategies. These can be selected from a standard offering by the school, but will also consist of sources from outside the school. Regularly, she tracks progress, on a weekly basis at the very least. This self-report is shared and discussed with peers, teachers, and others. Student and teacher evaluate the effectiveness of the learning strategy. Based on the output from the coaching, she defines the next steps. Over time as students mature, and depending on their personality and preferences, this process might be more freely organized in terms of choices of materials, learning strategies, and persons with whom to discuss progress.

DEPLOYING MORE RESOURCES, AND DEPLOYING THEM MORE EFFECTIVELY

As said before, this is not something done easily. It is not as hard as it might seem either! There is a lot of waste in the system as it is. Getting rid of that waste is a first step. By reducing the number of meetings and their duration, a school saves a lot of time. Most meetings repeat themselves, are talk shops, and lack a clear focus. Primary schools that partake in the Leerkracht initiative[12] typically organize 15-minute meetings to replace the existing ones that often lasted an hour or more. During these regular, short

---

[12] https://stichting-leerkracht.nl/accessed August 18, 2008.

meetings there is a simple agenda and a few rules on what can and cannot be discussed. Items that need more extensive discussion are referred to separate meetings or groups that seldomly involve all the teachers. It thus saves many colleagues a lot of time. The teachers involved value the new way of meeting as it frees up time for teaching.

It is a good idea to review cumbersome processes. If they feel cumbersome, bureaucratic, in all likelihood they are. An example is the yearly procurement process in which teachers indicate what they will need for the coming year, and all gets ordered at once. Though it seems efficient, it causes a lot of waste because no teacher knows what he will need throughout the year. So, the school ends up with too much of some material and too little of another.[13] There are many other simple and harder interventions that would make education more effective. Summer holidays, for example, as they are currently organized leave pupils much time to forget up to 25% of what they have learned. Talking of waste!

By using teachers time more effectively time is freed up that can be used to guide "outside" people and sources in the school. As mentioned earlier, there are many valuable sources available, e.g., experts in industry and online materials. These are referred to as open educational resources. Using these sources makes it easier to stay up-to-date on a topic, provide more levels, and a greater variety in formats that are unthinkable for a school in a regular situation. These sources, however, cannot just be deployed. To date, the use of these resources has remained limited. They require expansion and adaptation of current professional practices.[14] Teachers have to assess and select, deploy, and evaluate the open educational resources. To do so they must acquire new knowledge and skills not unlike the skills their students must learn, e.g., digital literacy. Throughout this book, I will make the point that if we position ourselves as teachers that are students of our own teaching practices and new technologies, rather than all-knowing, we create a more effective and stimulating learning space where we can all learn and become better teachers.[15]

---

[13] These examples are from the "Leerkracht" foundation. The foundation provides help for schools moving toward more impact on learning through the application of Lean. https://stichting-leerkracht.nl/werkdruk-in-het-onderwijs-verminderen/ accessed August 18, 2018.

[14] Hood and Littlejohn, "Knowledge Typologies for Professional Learning: Educators' (Re) Generation of Knowledge When Learning Open Educational Practice."

[15] Hattie, *Visible Learning for Teachers: Maximizing Impact on Learning* makes a similar point convincingly.

BREAKING THE VICIOUS CYCLE

All this requires, evidently, a lot of work. It can be daunting to consider all these changes. Of course, it is something not to do all at once. Consider the metaphor of the woodsman who has a lot of work felling trees. So much work that he has no time to sharpen his ax. As his ax becomes blunt the felling is taking increasingly more time. Which leaves him no time at all to sharpen his ax. Teachers need to break this vicious cycle. That requires courage, creativity, and a go-do-mentality. First, consider whether the current situation is sustainable. Remember next where all the waste is. How much of what you have taught has exactly made an impact? Consider what you would like to do differently, and which activities do not add value. Then, don't be afraid to let go of wasteful activities and tasks. Just kill them. This is the hardest part because many outsiders have an opinion. So before doing so, as a school, inform your stakeholders of the experiment that is coming and why you are doing it. Engage students and external stakeholders. Many will happily pull their weight and support you. If explained properly, I found that students are more than willing to engage.[16] If they are addressed as responsible actors, they will act accordingly. And, in the process, learn a lot more! As a teacher, you become a creator and curator of a learning space with as many assistants as you are willing and able to take on!

HANDS ON!

1. Establish what the students know, can, and have (Skills, Knowledge, Attitude—SKA)
   Running a series of formative assessments at the very beginning is a good start. Prior qualifications state what students (ought to) know, can, and have. That can be something different from what they actually do. Devise assessments that will appeal to different skill sets so that there is a broad spectrum against which students can show what they are capable of

---

[16] This does not just apply to adult students, but also to pupils in primary and secondary schools. It never ceases to amaze me how much they already can and are willing to do if treated properly, that is as responsible individuals with a stake.

2. Discuss learning goals with students and relate sources to these goals
   Have students tell, show, and write what they hope to achieve and how school will contribute to those achievements. There are no wrong answers here. Whatever it is they want to achieve, that is where they get their drive from. Most important at this stage is to create a safe place where the aspirations can be shared. Ask questions that clarify and make clear what they think the future situation will require from them, what they think they will need to know, be able to do, and have to get there. Next, share the goals that you, the school, and society have for them. Together, they constitute what the students need and want to achieve

3. Establish a match with individual learning preferences and strategies
   Given what students and you know about what is envisioned, set out to design the overarching learning strategies for the month, semester, or year, depending on how mature the students are. Giving the students a "language" to craft their strategies is key at this stage. The learning arches from the KaosPilot are a good candidate, but there are more. Find one that works for you and the students. For the more mature students, you can point out that at this stage you are engaging in a meta-cognitive process

4. Mix and match materials to meet a student's need
   In the design of the course, ample time and attention will have been paid to the needed SKA's, various formats, and materials. So, when starting out, you can rely on an extensive toolkit. There will, however, also be white spots on purpose. These are for you to fill once you get going. First, you will help students design their learning strategies by what is at hand—which usually is a lot. It is a wise course to first start with small iterations that will allow students and you to find your way toward a good working strategy

5. Use SKA's different requirements to mix student groups that can learn together regarding different SKA's
   One of the most challenging elements of this kind of learning is to give each his own while maintaining a sense of the group and work as a group. Here, the heterogeneity is both the problem and the solution. Differentiating is hard when it concerns just knowledge, for example. But you can combine exercises in which some students can work on knowledge related things others can work on skills, e.g., some students collect data while other manage the process or set-up communications

6. Have students search for additional sources

   Further down the process, white spots will appear more often. Certainly as students mature they will feel more confident to express their needs. At this stage it will be harder for you to supply all the sources, let alone the substance. Now is the moment to enlist "outside" help. In my experience, there are few, if any, experts that will refuse to help students. You will have to explain what and why and respect their limitations. You will have to be more flexible regarding timing and location. Try not to force external parties exactly into the time frame of educational season and rules. These are means and not goals, the goal is learning. The strategy should address how the schools create an environment that is more flexible. Make work of networking outside the school!

PERSONALIZED LEARNING

One of the promises of big data, online learning, which generates the data, and learning analytics is personalized learning. Each student studies the materials online. The system "observes" when the student is struggling, scrolls back to a previous section indicating that the previous materials might not have been completely understood. Next time the course might include a refresher before moving into the new subject matter. Using smart technology, specific information relating to the student's needs can be offered rather than the student having to sift through all the general information. This would make life a lot easier for the student. This is what I call passive personalized learning. The norms, the content, and the pace are all still set by an external party (the lecturer, the accreditation board) and not by the student.

Active personalized learning happens when the student takes ownership for his learning. He determines what he wants to learn, makes decisions as to which sources to use, when, and in which pace. The systems and lecturer still make recommendations, but the student decides. Also, the student can pull content from the system, ask his lecturer to provide additional materials, etc.

This is not a matter of good or bad per se. The key thing here to recognize is that there are two forms rather than one. As the student matures and is better informed, we might move from passive

PERSONALIZED LEARNING (Continued)

to active personalized learning. The extent to which this is possible depends also on the external requirements of society. We require, for example, that a physician has completed certain courses. A student has got no say in this if he wants to be a physician. However, most studies from primary school onward leave at least some room for an active involvement of the student.

Active personalized learning requires ownership on the part of the student. This is a particularly challenging concept in education. Traditionally, the lecturer and curricula committees and administrators have been considered the guardians of quality. Students have been, and mostly still are, treated as a passive participant to whom the learning is done. The norm still is no active involvement on the part of the student. To some extent, the student gets to decide which courses he takes, which school he attends, but once chosen, he has no, or little say in what transpires.

There is a lot to say for more ownership for the students. They are not incompetent beings. Depending on age, they might even buy houses, drive cars, etc. Also, at a younger age they do make informed decisions. More ownership gives them a bigger stake and commitment in the education. Resnick makes this point convincingly when writing about the Computer Club Houses and the Scratch programming language.[17] In the Scratch programming environment, students can create their own project online, design their own games, share these with other students in the online community, and ask for advice. Ownership in itself is already a large booster for learning impact.[18] This is not to say that they should always get to say what they want to learn, nor that they are the only ones to decide. I'm arguing that they should get involved early in the design of the curricula, that sometimes they should be

---

[17] Resnick, *Lifelong Kindergarten: Cultivating Creativity Through Projects, Passion, Peers, and Play.*

[18] Both Hatti and Dochy argue that the ownership, as part of learner agency, is a key element in success. Hattie, *Visible Learning for Teachers: Maximizing Impact on Learning*; Dochy and Segers, *Creating Impact Through Future Learning: The High Impact Learning That Lasts (HILL) Model.*

PERSONALIZED LEARNING (Continued)

allowed to make their own informed decisions on what they want to learn. Learning is an inherently joint process in which teachers and students work together to achieve the learning goals. Learning is a process co-creation.

This brings along certain risks. A student might make a wrong decision. Who then is to blame? It is exactly this question of responsibility that is both important, but also a blockage toward larger student involvement. Growing up and raising children is an inherently risky business. Avoiding the risks is probably not going to help avoiding accidents. And, if one reflects a little, there is something odd with the passivity with which we treat our students. While they are at school, we will not afford them a say, but as soon as they leave they might start their own business, they will take up jobs that require them to make important decisions, etc. The change is rather abrupt and not involving them might not be helping our students preparing for a future in which they have to make important decisions continuously. It is of course not the case that currently our students get no say at all. But the choices are very limited and within very clearly delineated borders.

Lean Education is about the student. Our job is to get our students what they need. Finding out what they need and getting what they need to them can only work when they are actively involved in the whole process.

7

Developing New Classes Faster and Better

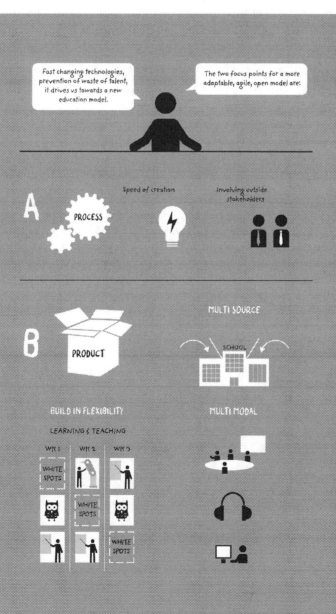

INTRODUCTION

Demands on education grow fast over time. New skills and knowledge that our students must master grow at a pace faster than we can keep up with. Our curricula must be more adaptable to change to reflect the fast-changing technology and socio-economic developments. To support personalized learning and higher quality teaching, the curricula need to allow for on the spot adaptations, and the agility to benefit from opportunities for serendipitous learning and adjustments to individual needs of students. This is a tremendous challenge. The key is to create leverage in order to speed up. New technologies and pedagogies can be leveraged to deliver up-to-date and personalized content. The idea of relatively fixed and stable curricula is outdated and needs to be replaced by the idea of continuous innovation and education in motion. Adaptivity and agility need to be at the core of the curricula we design.

FROM STATIONARY EDUCATION TO EDUCATION PERMANENT IN MOTION

Education used to be, and in many schools still is, a fairly static affair. Curricula are developed, rolled out, and taught for many years. This is not to say education has not changed. There have been many policy changes and other interventions that have rocked schools, sometimes to their very foundations. But all these changes, some misguided and downright failures and some valuable, had the same characteristic. They were step changes mostly done unto the schools. The proposal in this chapter is to have fewer radical changes and create a culture and organization in which changes take place at a somewhat slower pace, but continuously, changes that are driven by students, teachers, and stakeholders outside of policy circles. If we put more focus on the design of education in which flexibility and adaptivity regarding the content (skills, knowledge, and attitude) and format are ingrained, we lay the groundwork for continuous innovation and improvement of education. When we combine this with new technologies and cooperation with students and outside experts and stakeholders, we create the leverage we need to keep education up to the challenges of the future. Peter Goodyear formulates it nicely, "...teaching traditionally—in the literal sense of teaching as one was taught oneself—is unable to cope with the changes now besetting higher education. Shifting resources towards design for learning, and adopting more effective design practices, is a credible strategy for improving the quality of higher education while managing with tighter funding."[1]

This leads to two demands: one, a demand for shorter lead times when developing new curricula and two, greater flexibility within existing curricula. These two demands are related. In the development of new curricula, space for the yet unknown demands and needs should be designed in. If done right, these more agile curricula should lessen the demand for curricula to be (re)developed. These demands are discussed already in Chapter 3. In this chapter, we discuss how by using Lean Education and various pedagogies these demands can be met.

MAKING CLASSES AGILE

Being able to take on new subjects, on the fly as it were, generates a certain open-endedness. This is something that society and education have not been comfortable with. We want to know the value of a diploma. And, traditionally the value has been tied to both teaching practices and a promise of a certain curriculum. We have set up various committees, instated inspectors, etc. to safeguard the quality of the diplomas. Thereby, we also created slowness in the system and risk avoidance. An educational experiment gone wrong is sure to lead to headlines in the news, and local and national politicians crying shame.

Our challenge is to create a more agile education, keep the high-quality standards, but get rid of institutional sclerosis. This requires a shift in mindset of all involved, teachers, politicians, parents, and administrators. We are working and teaching in complicated and sometimes complex situations. Some fields pose difficult questions to which we do not yet know the answers. Some best practices have been developed, but these are challenging and require expert input to implement them.

---

[1] Peter Goodyear, "Teaching as Design," *HERDSA Review of Higher Education*, 2, no. 2 (2015): 27–50.

In Lean, we like to create good processes that deliver good results. The process is designed with the quality criteria in mind. It is the process that matters. By managing the process rather than the specific outcomes, we create more flexibility. A process of teaching that is set for one specific set of outcomes rather than a whole bandwidth is less flexible. A process in which the level of teaching and learning are designed in the process and the ability to come up with validated adjustments fast will be better able to cope with change.

There are three key changes to the system that would allow more flexibility.

- More providers of high-quality content
- White spots in the curriculum
- A mechanism for generation and validation of proposals for curriculum changes

By accepting that content can be provided by other parties than the school itself, the range of providers grows immensely, both in quantity and in breadth. It also grows in pace! These other providers can be other educational institutions, industry, and private educational initiatives. We should accept that there are many knowledgeable, capable people that know how to present a subject and present it well. This is not the prerogative of a school's own teachers. And, to be honest, based on the laws of statistics, chances are that the best teachers and subject matter experts are not teaching at your school and are not you. This is not a judgment on teachers! Everyone knows there are many good math teachers, for example, that are not best in their field. There are just a few really top-notch teachers. And, some of those can teach very well. This goes for me as well. As a professor at the HAN University of Applied Sciences with two master's degrees and a PhD, I do know a thing or two. And, I'd like to think I'm good at what I do. Still, I do know various colleagues around the world who are better teachers and/or better subject experts. This does not imply that I do not add value, or the math teacher does not add value. It does, however, force us to reconsider our roles now that technology offers so many chances to share materials and teaching. Coursera, Udemy, and Khan Academy show how an expert and good teacher can reach many thousands of students at once. As there are many around the world who keep developing new, relevant materials, this is a source that neither a teacher nor a school can keep pace with. Never! A school might, in a niche, be a provider of such world class expertise combined with like teaching skills. Companies run large laboratories and Research & Development (R&D) departments on par and often better equipped than many schools and universities. Why not engage them in the provision of some materials.[2]

To insert new materials and subjects into a class or course, there has to be room. So, the next question is how to design and organize so that there is room in our curricula. The easiest way is to allow white spots in the curriculum. Because of the uncertainty about what will be needed, and the freedom we want, this I believe is the best solution. It is also the most radical, though certainly not unknown. Various education institutions allow for this. It offers room for the unexpected, for serendipity. If we give students a serious and substantial say in the way the white spots in the curriculum are filled, it fosters ownership. This freedom works best if it is explicitly managed and not filled in one big step. It can be divided up in smaller parts as the situation requires, as long as it is not squandered or used as a stopgap to solve other problems. The alternative of offering several options to choose from is still inferior as it tries to second guess what will happen. It also takes away some of the responsibility for the curriculum. This will reduce the freedom and also require possibly wasteful effort upfront. It is, however, a lower risk option because the options can be controlled upfront.

There is a better way to reduce some of the risks. That is by upfront defining and agreeing on a process for the generation of proposals and of criteria for what is and is not admissible. If progress is monitored regularly, at least on a weekly basis, it will soon become clear which students struggle with what subjects and which students need additional challenges to keep them interested. By involving external stakeholders in this process, external developments will enter the radar earlier. The steps to generate and assess the value of a proposal are the same as in the formulation of learning strategies. Based on self-reports of students on their progress, their goals, and external developments, they select sources for their learning strategies. In this case, they might construct new sources as well. The key questions to them will be,

- How will it contribute to achieving the learning goals?
- Which of the current obstacles does it help overcoming?
- When and how will we see evidence of the impact?

---

[2] I believe this can be done without being eaten alive by a company. Individual researchers are often also responsible parents, professionals that are proud and behave in an ethically responsible way. Engaging them will not mean being exposed to marketing or recruitment efforts, for example.

The role of the teachers and experts is to coach the students on the development of their proposal and to assess the quality of their sources. As the students act as primary agents in the search, selection, and accessing of the sources, it does not require a lot of time from the teachers. As coach, they ask questions to the students and ask them to argue their choices. Teachers will need to share upfront the criteria by which sources will be judged. Sharing success and quality criteria with students has been demonstrated to foster better learning.

DEVELOPING NEW CURRICULA FASTER

More agile classes will reduce the need for wholesale redesign of classes. Given the faster pace of change, (re)designing classes and courses will still be necessary. And this will have to be in a much shorter time frame. The key to fast and effective design of courses are the following rules.

- Starting from the end state and reason backward[3]
- Involving many stakeholders and co-create the curriculum
- Allocate the available working time in a short time window with all decision makers available for on the spot decision.

The first steps in the development of new classes is determining what value is going to be delivered to whom. Traditionally, we define desired learning outcomes or competencies for a class. These describe what the student is able to do or knows after having attended the class successfully. It is often assumed that: (a) these are valuable, and (b) these are the only value that should be considered. These assumptions contain some serious misconceptions and lead to less than desirable outcomes. Though there is nothing wrong about competencies per se, the question is whether the specific competencies, knowledge, etc. are the ones that are actually desired. The learning outcomes are: (a) reviewed on an irregular basis with often many years in between and (b) derived through an opaque process in which stakeholders are at best superficially involved. Given the fast changes in society and technology, the

---

[3] The best and most inspiring example of this is the Vision Backcasting approach as designed and practiced by Simon Kavanagh and the KaosPilot in Denmark.

relevancy of curriculum taught is questionable. As one of my former bachelor students phrased his predicament as he pursued his master study in innovation management: "I'm studying the history of innovation management." The underlying assumption is that the academics, pedagogues, teachers, and course developers do know what is required because they are the experts in their fields. This is an untenable assumption in a complex and fast changing world. Another assumption is that the quality (part of the value) is guaranteed through a lengthy process of peer reviews and once every so many years a review by outsiders from academia, industry, and students. The length of the process seems to guarantee materials that are outdated. Many of the peers are in the same position as the authors of the course and are therefore not in a position to contribute much added value.

Value, moreover, includes also dimensions that are not (directly) connected to competencies and knowledge. These include such things as recognition of the value of the education different from the standard diploma's, access to networks of experts and organizations, and capabilities such as self-regulation and meta-cognitive abilities. These values are identified more easily by other stakeholders such as students themselves, industry, etc. The underlying assumption seems to be that the delivery of these values is either outside the scope of education, or that they are not valuable. A point in case is cultural awareness. When several colleagues and I developed a course for engineers, we included industry and students from the very start (see Chapter 10, New Engineers, a case study). The need for cultural awareness in an engineer is not something that had crossed our minds. Industry representatives pointed out, however, that most of their business was done outside of the country on other continents, and that it included heavy customer involvement. Engineers interacting with customers from all over the globe for sure had to be aware of cultural sensitivities.

The process of developing curricula contains a lot of waiting time. As various stakeholders and decision makers inside the organization need to be involved, the process can be drawn out. Also, not having had a joint start, as I advocate, will lead to a series of misunderstandings about what is to be achieved, what is needed for decision making purposes, and what is ultimately to be delivered. This lack of joint understanding leads to unnecessary activities, missing information, wrongly formatted information, and many back-and-forths. The mere spreading out of available working time will lead to waste. If the course developers have to put down their development work for other work and restart in even just 1- or 2-weeks' time, they will need to get re-acquainted. Shortening the lead time will ensure more efficiency. Errors can be corrected faster.

Reducing the waiting time can be achieved using Lean techniques as value stream mapping, waste elimination, and standardization. The development of a curriculum of a master study can be achieved in under 6 months from start to finish. Waiting time is waste in Lean Education and leads to other wasteful activities, such as re-engaging in materials already partially dealt with before, updating new staff that join mid-process, requirement changes that necessitate adjustments, etc. A shorter lead in itself means the process can be started later, thus ensuring that the most recent insights, materials, and information are used. If the lead time is 3 years instead of 6 months, that means that 2.5 years of recent development will be ignored.

It took us less than half a year to design and develop the first year of a 2-year master-level engineering course. By cutting out a lot of the waiting time, by involving all stakeholders at once, and over a condensed time, we reduced the opportunities for misunderstandings, changing views, being caught up by new developments, etc. The momentum this condensed working creates fosters also ownership outside the group of educational designers: it engenders relationships that can be used throughout the course later. The pressure cooker approach amazed everyone involved and created confidence.

INCLUDING TECHNOLOGICAL AND PEDAGOGICAL INNOVATIONS

The new curricula have to be richer in content, address skills and attitude as well as knowledge, allow personalization, and a greater degree of student autonomy. Education as it is currently practiced will not deliver this agenda. This agenda requires a high degree of "tuning" with multiple providers and on the spot changes. To achieve this, we need both different pedagogies and technological support. Remember that individual education is not difficult. It is expensive, however. We want to achieve personalized learning in group settings that is affordable. This means each student must be able to work and study on his own specific needs and goals while being part of a class, cohort, and peer group. These goals will overlap with the goals of other students, but not be identical. She will work and study according to her learning strategies that will share similarities of those of other students, but not be identical. The result is a rich, varied, heterogenic teaching construct. It is not unlike a multi-player, multi-level game in which the teacher is the game designer and game master, and students co-design the game's rulebook which evolves continuously and sometimes might take the role of game master. In this analogy, the students have their learning strategy (game strategy) to explore the subject domain (the imaginary country in a game) and work toward a goal (a game level). The teacher helps the students by scaffolding (providing clues to progress), striking deals with other students to form teams to help each other (team formation to deal with threats), and obtaining external help from experts (obtaining new tools, more energy, lives). This multi-dimensional image of teaching with shifting rules is challenging, but also fun. The design requires the teachers and experts to have a deep understanding of the subject matter and of the students' possible learning strategies. It is complex and uncertain.

The power of the metaphor is conveyed nicely in Mitchel Resnick's *Lifelong Kindergarten.*[4] He describes the use of Scratch, an online environment in which students create their own games, learn to interact with others in the community, shift their strategies, and have evolving goals. This is an example of a constructivist approach to learning. It is one of several pedagogical approaches that supports this type of learning and education. The "Art & Craft of Facilitating Learning Spaces"[5] is another example of a pedagogy that is very powerful in creating these rich learning environments. They can be supplemented with various technologies. Schools can use machine learning algorithms to monitor students progress and generate suggestions for next steps automatically. Applications will allow monitoring of student progress while they are working on an assignment or digesting new theories. At the same time, students can pace their study according to their own need, instead of having to fall in line with the teacher's pace, which will be too slow for some and too fast for others.[6] The key aim for pedagogy and technology alike is to foster ownership on part of the student. This means setting goals, selecting sources, and accounting for their progress.

---

[4] M Resnick, *Lifelong Kindergarten: Cultivating Creativity Through Projects, Passion, Peers, and Play,* (Cambridge, MA: MIT Press, 2017).

[5] https://www.kaospilot.dk/philosophy/.

[6] One of many applications that support this varied paced learning is provided by EdPuzzle, https://edpuzzle.com/.

The design and execution of learning and teaching in this setting is what we at New Engineers call the creation and curation of learning spaces. It requires abstract and creative thinking, strong empathy skills in combination with lateral thinking, and strong interpersonal skills in order to relate to the students. Each student brings his own practice, his own work-related projects, ambitions, and talents. To personalize the learning and yet also learn as a group, the learning curators need to abstract across projects to find common themes that can be addressed together and translated back to the individual settings. We create assignments that focus on different sets of skills, attitudes, and knowledge in which some students work on their attitudes while others deepen their knowledge or hone their skills. What the students need and want is not always obvious upfront and will change over time. The requires the curators to "listen" and "watch" the students closely to determine where they are in their learning, something that cannot be determined by exams alone.

From an administrative and professional services point of view, a new set of requirements and support needs arise. Schools need an updated vision on teaching and learning in the twenty-first century. Teachers need to develop new skills and acquire knowledge regarding both educational technologies and pedagogies. The physical and digital infrastructure of the school needs to support the more varied teaching and learning. Learning at varying paces will require the school to offer flexible facilities in which groups of students can be formed and (re)configured at a moment's notice, and, preferably by the students themselves so that it fosters ownership. It will require a digital infrastructure to include external parties through video-conferencing, file-sharing, virtual tours, and facilitate travelling between different locations of both school and industry partners. The important role of professional services and what Lean Education requires is discussed in Chapter 9, On the importance of processional services.

All the above is a larger than life bill. No one organization can just do this unless very well endowed. The argument in this book is that this is not necessary and probably not even desirable. Schools, teachers, students, and other stakeholders should jointly develop toward a next level that befits their specific situation and needs. Lean Education provides the framework for schools to form their own vision, implement their own, specific strategy and processes. It is a journey of discovery.

HANDS ON!

This approach can be daunting. Though I have no doubt that you and your colleagues are up to it if you decide to go for it. To help you along your way, there are a few tips to start with.

1. Visit other schools. There are already many good examples of schools and lecturers that have embarked on this innovation journey. Look them up and visit them. They will be more than happy to share their experiences
2. Get some basic training. It helps to have some understanding of how these new pedagogies play out in practice. Though not required, it helps to get some training
3. Reach out to industry and the community and do not be afraid to ask. Share your plans and ambitions with the community and industry. Explain what drives you and solicit their input. Ask for help based on a vision of which they are a part and not just to mend some holes. There are very few people who do not take an interest in the education of our children. As schools, teachers, and students, we have much goodwill. A note of warning: do not let the bureaucratic ways of education get in the way and do not hide behind regulations
4. Embrace the uncertainty and trust your professional qualities. Though there are popular complaints about the quality of our teachers, it is my strong conviction that teachers are good professionals that, if not hampered by the system, will deliver good work. Trust in your qualities and actively seek opportunities to reflect and improve. With that frame of mind and trust, you are ready as need be to embark on the experiment and the uncertainties in entails
5. Do limit the lead time to 6 months. Whatever you are changing, a class or a curriculum, make sure you do it fast. It is about learning for you as well. Learning and change work best in small iterations that allow you to feed forward and create the first successes that will sustain you in your journey
6. Involve your students, they will love it. Tell them what you are about, and that the outcomes are uncertain. Be honest and open. Make them partners in your discovery, and they will help and back you. In my

experience so far, they never shy away from partaking. Provide leadership, especially on the occasions when the going gets a bit tougher. When we talk about skills and attitudes our students must develop, never forget that you as an administrator, lecturer, and professional staff member must also develop them.

LEAN EDUCATION CASE: CROSSING EDUCATIONAL BORDERS—TEACHING FROM THE STUDENTS' PERSPECTIVE[7]

Enrico is a highly motivated and dedicated student of business economics. He has his own ideas and research interest. He would like to organize his thesis work in an unusual fashion, testing theories by setting up his own company. He meets with resistance at his institution. "What you want does not fit the curriculum." And, "Thesis work needs to fit a specific frame, what you would like to do does not fit the standard." How would a student feel when meeting this response to his well-intended efforts to direct his own learning? There are many ways in which a response could have been more constructive and stimulating. But in his case, the standard had become the goal.

When we conceived our idea for a different educational set-up in which students from high school and university would learn together with their teachers and workers in industry, we went looking for students to join us in this experiment. Enrico was the first to come forward. With his extra-curricular activities learning about robotics and big data, he was highly motivated and well-suited.

WHY

Keep Enrico in mind when we take a step back to look at the bigger picture. Our economy has always been knowledge driven and

---

[7] This experiment was made possible through an educational innovation price awarded to New Engineers by GAK and NSVP.

LEAN EDUCATION CASE: CROSSING EDUCATIONAL BORDERS—TEACHING FROM THE STUDENTS' PERSPECTIVE (Continued)

only more so over the last decades. Borders between disciplines are permeable, and most innovations are so big they require large, multi-disciplinary teams to conduct the work. To find solutions to our current socio-economic and environmental challenges, we need people that can transcend divides between classes, economic sectors, and disciplines. We need creative solutions for our hard problems. Creativity in turn requires settings in which deviating views are nurtured and enriched by the latest developments and insights in science. In terms of Lean Education, this is what constitutes (a part of) value. The ability and knowledge to operate in such an environment.

Contrast this with our current educational practices. The emphasis is mostly on the development of cognitive abilities. Though many schools today acknowledge the importance of competencies, of skills, and attitude, in effect, most time is still spent on one-directional, frontal classroom teaching. Moreover, there is a strong mono-disciplinary, uniform approach toward education. Students are grouped by cognitive ability, cognitive skills are valued over manual skills, and age groups are uniform. There are fixed, impermeable borders between students and workers, students of vocational and academic backgrounds, between sciences and arts. There is a lot to be said for focused, uniform groups, at times, in terms of effectiveness of learning. And yet, by this exclusive focus, we also create a big gap between school and work, we deprive industry and its employees of learning opportunities and society of creative solutions. The current system does not deliver all the value that is demanded and needed.

From this view on value, we set out to design an experiment in which we could deliver the previously unaddressed value components. The goal of the experiment was to create a learning space

**LEAN EDUCATION CASE: CROSSING
EDUCATIONAL BORDERS—TEACHING FROM
THE STUDENTS' PERSPECTIVE (Continued)**

in which students, their teachers (!), and employees from industry
would form a team that would learn together, devise new solutions,
and apply these in practice. They were to learn from each other and
experts, develop twenty-first century skills, and become a professional for our times. Our hope was and is to prepare our students
in this way for professions that do not yet exist. Ideally, they will be
able to keep learning so that they can adapt to changing conditions
in the work place and even craft their own job. That would facilitate a change from job security (which is for many already a faraway
notion) to work security.

WHAT

We ran an experiment to cross the borders between different educational institutions and types, and between industry and schools.
We called age borders, subject matter categories, and sources of
knowledge into question. We developed new teaching formats to
facilitate the heterogenous group of learners and away from the
narrow paths of predominantly cognitive teaching programs.
In this experiment, we actively sought approaches toward personalized learning.

The project's ambition is to connect different educational types:
high school, vocational, and academic, and at the same time connect working people, students, and teachers. Thus, we cross at least
two borders. Bringing people of different ages together, we created a
dynamic that one would never see in homogenous cohorts. For example, learning each other's language. This is, of course, not the native
language, but the language of work, of the street, the language of
business, etc. All learners had to face the need to understand the
perspectives of the others and develop the skills to do so. Some of the
most important skills that are thus addressed are boundary crossing, cooperation, job crafting, and reflection.[8] Working together on

LEAN EDUCATION CASE: CROSSING EDUCATIONAL BORDERS—TEACHING FROM THE STUDENTS' PERSPECTIVE (Continued)

real live projects with a heterogenous group also appeals to the attitudes, like curiousness and openness (towards the other), empathy, and entrepreneurship. The knowledge and know-how required for the project was available through experts, literature, the Internet, and if these do not suffice, the other sources that the students identified themselves. We worked on the reduction of fear of learning and working together to create something new. Our students (all the learners involved) would in all likelihood have not mastered (or even addressed) any of these aspects if they had stayed within their "regular" learning setting.

We created a learning space for all people involved. The learning spaces encompass the physical and digital environment, the content and materials, and the various formats, plus the participants, student, coach, and expert, the intended learning outcomes, and subject matters. The learning spaces exist for a limited time as long as the people involved in the (research) question are working together on that question. It is more limited in scope than a learning community. The physical space is a place that excites, challenges, and inspires cooperation and creativity. Within the learning space, all participants say what they want to learn, in which way, and under which conditions. We identify together what help is needed. Within the learning space, there is a place for everyone individually and for the group. We free up time and energy for the learning strategy of each participant and his own prior knowledge and ambitions. Within the learning space,

---

[8] Dochy and Segers, *Creating Impact Through Future Learning: The High Impact Learning That Lasts (HILL) Model*; Partnership for 21st Century Learning, "P21 Partnership for 21st Century Learning"; Redecker et al., *The Future of Learning: Preparing for Change – Publication*; Scheer and Plattner, "Transforming Constructivist Learning Into Action."

LEAN EDUCATION CASE: CROSSING EDUCATIONAL BORDERS—TEACHING FROM THE STUDENTS' PERSPECTIVE (Continued)

we work on real live projects, not theoretical cases. The people involved in the case participate in the learning space. This provides an extra impulse, motivation, and urgency to work together and get to a solution.

In our experiment we work on a robotics challenge. In the production process of the factory where the physical learning space is situated, the work is done mostly manually and is physically demanding. The process is also time consuming and error prone. The assignment is to look at opportunities for process optimization and the deployment of robots. The mixture of students, production staff, teachers, and experts ensure that practical, relevant knowledge and know-how are available. The learning experience thus is richer, more relevant, and inspiring. We cross several boundaries, and everyone learns.

WHO

The experiment was joined by nine high school students and four high school teachers from two different high schools, three bachelor students, one academic lecturer, three employees of the industrial company, two robotics experts, and two process facilitators.[9] Everyone involved had at least one role: learner. An important condition for the creation of a learning space is the active involvement of all involved, an open mindset, and an appetite for uncertainty (or at least a willingness to endure uncertainty over a longer period). Some participants had additional roles, at varying moments during the experiment. The plant's participating staff

---

[9] The following organizations participated: School federation Quadraam (Scholengemeenschap Quadraam), school federation Gelderse Onderwijsgroep and Overbetuwe college (OBC Bemmel), the FieldLab Industrial Robotics, the company Bruil EBM Beton, and HAN University of applied Sciences and New Engineers.

LEAN EDUCATION CASE: CROSSING EDUCATIONAL BORDERS—TEACHING FROM THE STUDENTS' PERSPECTIVE (Continued)

are learners, and during the tours and analysis, also experts and facilitators. The key process facilitators are also the creators of the learning space and sometimes content experts. All in all, we distinguish four roles:

- Learner/participant
- Expert
- Process facilitator
- Creator of the learning space

The learner formulates learning goals and learning strategies and participates actively (sometimes by consciously doing nothing) in the learning space. The expert provides subject-matter knowledge and know-how, skills, and attitudes. She supports the transfer of these and helps the learners in obtaining them and developing the relevant skills and attitudes. She provides solicited and unsolicited input to aid the learning. She is also engaged in the design of the program and making the necessary resources available.

A crucial observation here is that the distinction between learner and expert is never absolute and never permanent. The expert is never done learning, and each learner has important, relevant knowledge and/or experience that will make him an expert at times. The distinction is real, but also contingent on the questions investigated. The expert becomes a participant of the learning space only when intentionally taking on a learning mode as well. Some experts might figure as resource without actively engaging herself in learning as well. The absence of the learning intention will then place her outside the learning space.

The process facilitator looks after the mental and physical well-being of all participants (though they have an obligation in this respect as well). They also help in monitoring the progress of the

LEAN EDUCATION CASE: CROSSING EDUCATIONAL BORDERS—TEACHING FROM THE STUDENTS' PERSPECTIVE (Continued)

participants and the group. When progress is halting the group or an individual is not able to remove the barrier he will intervene.

The creators of the learning space are the initiators who conceive the idea, bring together relevant stakeholders, and keep the initiative running, mentally, physically, administratively, and financially. They will share over time more and more of these responsibilities with the participants and strive to make the group owner of the learning space.

HOW

The experiment is designed using the Vision Backcasting method[10] and high impact learning that lasts by Philip Dochy et al.[11] It is group-based learning in which the participants learn by developing a solution to a real problem. This approach to learning is already innovative. We applied it stretching the idea further by engaging a very heterogenous group of students. We started creating the learning space by engaging schools. The teachers helped recruit students. With the teachers, we discussed the framework and restrictions. This proved a challenge in itself since the content was still far from fixed—remember it is designed with the students (which includes the workers from the factory and the teachers as well as the "regular" students) together. So, the schools and teachers had to sign up for something of which the process was clear, but the content not. By engaging them from day one, and taking time, we gradually built the trust and understanding to work in this new concept.

---

[10] The Vision Backcasting method has been designed by Simon Kavanagh at the KaosPilot. More information about the Vision Backcasting method can be found at https://shop.kaospilot.dk/images/shopdownloadfiles/A&CFLS%20-%20Vision%20backcasting%20framework%20INSTRUCTIONS.pdf

[11] Dochy and Segers, *Creating Impact Through Future Learning: The High Impact Learning That Lasts (HILL) Model.*

LEAN EDUCATION CASE: CROSSING
EDUCATIONAL BORDERS—TEACHING FROM
THE STUDENTS' PERSPECTIVE (Continued)

We also provide a bit more structure in both process and content to bridge the divide in approaches. Another important step with regard to engaging the students and schools is relating to the existing educational system. So, by participating in this experiment, students could earn credits for their study. Since the schools work in different systems, this proved quite a puzzle. The teachers helped a lot by creating local solutions. Simultaneously, we started looking for an industry-based challenge. We looked for a company with a real and urgent problem that is open to learning, i.e., a company with a strategic HR agenda. This was relatively easy. Companies turn out to be open, proud, and willing to support schools. And, they are open to learning themselves.

Once students and the company were on board, they all came together to design the program. Using the Vision Backcasting (VBC) method, employees, staff, and teachers determined what the future would probably require from them in terms of knowledge and skills, and what they wanted to learn themselves, also in terms of developing relevant attitudes. They were in charge of the design. The company challenge provided the backdrop. Being in charge and having a live challenge to solve proved both energizing and uncomfortable at first. The idea of having this amount of freedom took some time getting used to.

Using a pressure cooker VBC, the group delivered a blueprint for a program of several days of learning. We worked using brown paper, scissors, post-its, magazines, etc., but no PowerPoints. The process is well-structured in small steps. The participants are rewarded by having visual, tangible results from each step. They are displayed on a large wall wide poster (see Figure 7.1). The design sessions are active, hands-on, and interactive. That contributes toward building group cohesion, which in turn is key in creating a safe learning space.

LEAN EDUCATION CASE: CROSSING EDUCATIONAL BORDERS—TEACHING FROM THE STUDENTS' PERSPECTIVE (Continued)

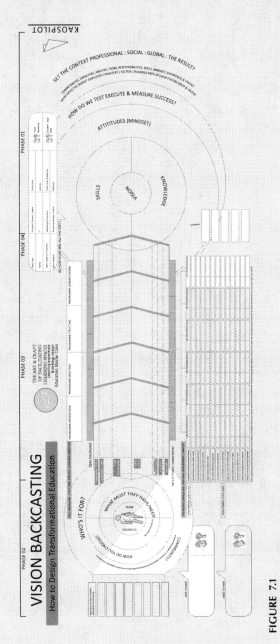

FIGURE 7.1
Vision backcasting framework.

LEAN EDUCATION CASE: CROSSING EDUCATIONAL BORDERS—TEACHING FROM THE STUDENTS' PERSPECTIVE (Continued)

In the next step, we designed the actual program as we would execute it. The materials were put together by the experts and process facilitators. The latter also designed the lesson formats. We scouted for suitable physical and digital learning environments. These are not the traditional four walls and a roof and rooms, but places where knowledge, inspiration, and challenges meet. We found two: a robotics lab at AWL and one in the factory of EBM Beton.

The execution itself was as tantalizing as a roller coaster. There are many things happening at the same moment: different groups of students working on the things they want to learn and develop, group dynamics, parallel content related activities (robotics and business), working on the challenge, learning, meta-cognitive processes, and organizational activities. Some of these had to do with the fact we ran an experiment. But something tells us that each next one will be different and to some extent an experiment again. Which is one of the attractions and consequences of this approach.[12] For us as process facilitators and educators the adagium is: be over prepared and under-structured. After having thoroughly prepared for what we know will probably happen, what might happen, there is category of events you cannot foresee. You have to let it happen. And by under-structuring, provide the chances of unforeseen things happening. This is called serendipity,[13] and it is something we as educators are not well prepared for generally speaking. The freedom created an energetic and dynamic atmosphere that one as a teacher dreams of. It was a special occasion in which we experienced intrinsic drive,

---

[12] When it comes to learning, one learns most when the outcome is uncertain. If you know an experiment is going to fail, you do not need to run it—you know the outcome already. The same goes for success. So, your learning benefits from a real chance of success and failure!

[13] Philip Dochy et al. make this point very well arguing for flexibility in education and less controlled learning settings to allow for spontaneous learning to happen.

**LEAN EDUCATION CASE: CROSSING
EDUCATIONAL BORDERS—TEACHING FROM
THE STUDENTS' PERSPECTIVE (Continued)**

eagerness, and openness, but also safety on part of all involved. The sheer joy of learning!

A key learning for us is that all participants are involved in the ongoing reflection of the learning and cooperation processes. This allows the steering of the process and content offered. It also makes everyone aware of the actual learning. It is meta-cognition at work.

At the end, the group presented their ideas to the board of the company. The board members were triggered by some of the ideas presented. They in turn questioned and challenged the students. This unusual setting put an edge to the presentation and discussion for the students. Not only were they challenged on their knowledge, they had to apply their skills of persuasion, dialogue, and presentation. Engaging in a presentation with board members at the age of 16 is a good experience in itself.

LEARNINGS

The experiment provided rich learnings for all involved. A few of the most important ones are the following.

- Joint development via VBC creates ownership, intrinsic motivation, and connects various groups before the formal learning has started. The informal learning starts at the very start of the design
- The physical learning space, the factory and the FieldLab Industrial Robotics provided an inspiring setting for learning. Many of them had never seen an operational factory inside. They learned what it is to work in an industrial plant, which was not in the curriculum, but one of the many felicitous, serendipitous learnings. The experience in itself was mesmerizing for most of the students
- Everyone learned a lot. It proves hard for most of the participants to express what exactly they have learned. As facilitators,

**LEAN EDUCATION CASE: CROSSING
EDUCATIONAL BORDERS—TEACHING FROM
THE STUDENTS' PERSPECTIVE (Continued)**

we observed small and big steps being made by the participants.
Participating and reflecting is hard. The meta-cognitive aspects
of learning are essential

- We addressed informally several of the twenty-first skills
  that are key to successful cooperation and preconditional for
  boundary crossing
- For the participating teachers, it was challenging to participant
  at multiple levels: as teacher, as learner, and as designers of their
  own education. They learned how to create a new type of learning space
- The mixture of practice with its real live challenges and school
  provides its own challenges. In the experiment, a concrete
  result was one of the objectives. The case is not theoretical,
  there is something at stake. This increases an edge in learning and makes it even more relevant. It provides us also with
  a dilemma: pausing to reflect or continue to get the results in
  time? We need to strike a balance between available time, the
  scope, and intended results, and the (meta-cognitive) learning
  activities. In hindsight, the ambition was too big for the limited
  time available. Crafting a proper balance is a challenge for the
  designers of the learning space.

REFLECTION

Crossing Educational Border (CEB) was an experiment in itself.
As such, it is an example of the Lean Education way of innovating. We
tested at little cost, a small, but radical new form of teaching. Instead
of long talks we went out and did. We had an idea and a problem, we
came up with a plan, executed it, and directly evaluated it. As it was
conducted, the experiment cannot be implemented directly in regular schemes of schools. It provides a proof of concept, it energizes and
creates many learnings that are valuable to the schools. The learnings
help improve the more traditional ways of teaching, and inform the

LEAN EDUCATION CASE: CROSSING EDUCATIONAL BORDERS—TEACHING FROM THE STUDENTS' PERSPECTIVE (Continued)

policy making of the schools. It is clear that other types of learning and teaching require teachers to develop new/other skills and attitudes. Not just in teaching, but also in innovating.

Teachers and administrators will need to discuss their vision on learning and dare to dream beyond what is common practice now. Then shore up the courage to go and do. Be open to an experiment, do not be afraid of failure. You will make many mistakes as did we, but learn even more. And rediscover the joy of learning and teaching!

José Cuperus
Vincent Wiegel

Section III

In Support of Lean Education

8

Strategy, Continuous Improvement, and Innovation

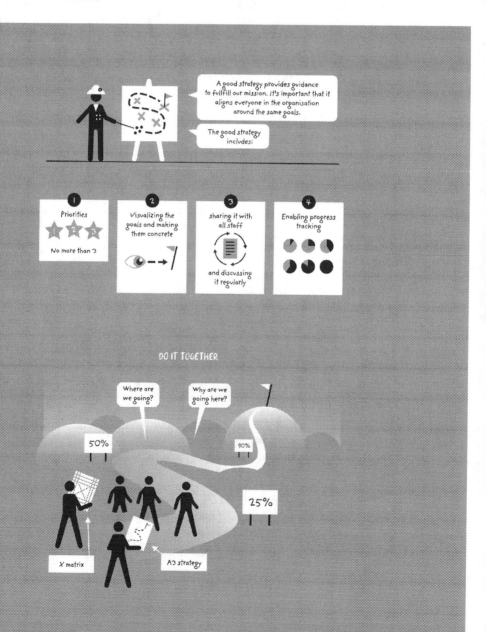

INTRODUCTION

The main focus of your strategy is determining which activities you need to undertake to realize your vision and mission. Aligning all the necessary activities into one direction is the tenet of strategy deployment. Formulating a good strategy is always a challenge. Making sure that every process then works in concert to implement the strategy is hard work, especially in smaller organizations that do not have the staff to support strategy development and deployment, and in ones where the message gets easily diluted. In this chapter, we describe the three steps of: (1) formulating the strategy, (2) breaking it down into smaller components, and (3) synchronizing the components. Communication is vitally important in each of these steps. We introduce some simple yet powerful tools to visualize and share the strategy across the organization. Continuous improvement and innovation is a key component in the strategy. In the fast-changing world there is no time to sit down and let things run unaltered for years. Smaller improvements free up scarce resources to engage in continuous innovation.

BACKDROP

Over the past years, I have visited several schools, primary schools, high schools, and universities. What strikes me is how hard it is to formulate the strategy in a concise and easily transferrable way. When talking to staff, I have seldomly heard it expressed twice in roughly the same way. Often people have an idea of the focus areas or themes of the strategy or of some specific elements that feature in the strategy. The question to explain to me the strategy often raised a frown of concentration. That makes it harder for employees to determine how they contribute toward the implementation of the strategy and to identify with the strategy. This means running the risk of divergent activities that at best do not hamper each other. Ideally, they should reinforce each other. Of course, most schools function at least OK. They open each day, and students are being taught. But they do not make the most of the scarce resources we invest in education and of the many talented people working in education. This is particularly evident in the three divisions that make up a school: teaching and research, professional services, and administration. There can be a divide between teaching and research on the one hand and professional services on the other.

A "we" and "them" divide in which each leaves the others alone as much as possible at best and at worst a situation in which there are recriminations going back and forth ("arrogant," "ignorant"). These divides are obviously not helpful. Instead, what we hope to achieve is active mutual engagement to improve the organization and create more value for students and society. This requires a clear and shared view and understanding of:

- Where the organization is going
- What value to students and society is
- The value streams and how each of the divisions contribute to the creation of value
- How they interface with each other
- What is required to strengthen the other divisions.

This clearly is a tall order, but one that can be accomplished using some of the Lean tools and methods.

For a strategy to work it is tantamount that:

- It is focused on a few things
- All elemelnts from the strategy are tangible
- Everyone understands the strategy and can repeat it
- Everyone can translate the strategy to her own situation.

This is important because you want consistency across the organization and throughout processes that touch upon multiple departments or teams. You want a strategy that is actionable in a way in which the contribution of each action can be validated and progress can be tracked.

This is important for both small and large educational institutions. And it is equally challenging for both, though sometimes for different reasons. There are various obstacles facing administrators that want to formulate and deploy their strategy. Some of the obstacles are:

- Objectifying goals is difficult
- Means often become goals (because they are easier to objectify, e.g., budgets, head count)
- The day to day running of the organization gets in the way of the strategic activities, including the formulation of the strategy itself
- A culture of autonomy that makes it harder to subsume teams and staff under a unifying strategy and the choices that strategy implies.

FORMULATING THE STRATEGY

I have seen schools and universities with over 30 strategic focus points or strategy items. They read like a shopping list or wish list. Of course, schools are complex organizations that often find themselves at the cross roads of society, a place where politics, economics, education, family life, and street life meet. That, however, makes it more important that the strategy provides guidance. For a strategy to be meaningful to staff members, it must be translated to something an individual can both understand/make sense of and act upon. For example, a school might have as a strategic item to further the career opportunities of its students. Now, what does that mean for the math teacher, the team leader in finance, the IT specialist, etc. The finance team leader might have nothing to contribute to this item, the math teachers contribute by teaching data science, the IT specialist by providing access to the latest apps, etc. Now imagine this shopping list of say 22 strategic items that need translating! Everyone will have something that she likes, there will be little coherence, and sometimes even conflicting translations. Translating three strategic focus points across the organization is already a daunting task.

One of the consequences of the unfocused or broad focused strategy is a long list of projects that are initiated. This happens because for each item of the shopping list there will be a senior or mid-level manager who has a stake in it, and by the presence on the strategy list, has a tacit approval to work on it. This long list of projects can never be processed by the existing staff who also have their everyday work to do. Shortage of resources (staff, budget, other) will mean that projects get put on hold, are restarted, delayed, compromised, etc. Of some projects at some point, no one will even remember why they were started, by whom, and what will happen if we stop them. This all means a lot of wasted time and effort, a sense of being overwhelmed, yet getting nothing done. Of course, this is perhaps a somewhat bleak picture, but one that I have seen often being reality.

So, the most important task of management is setting priorities. That is a difficult, painful task. There are so many things that need to be done! Still, the reality is that we cannot do it all. The good news is that choosing makes it also easier to achieve things and show real progress. This progress will mean that resources are freed up to do other things in turn. And then the virtuous cycle of continuous improvement kicks off. Kick starting this virtuous cycle by choosing and persevering is the management's job.

There are a few simple steps that management can take to focus the strategy, to set priorities, and follow up on them. These steps are supported by simple tools that are easy to understand, but difficult to execute. They are difficult because they require a deeper understanding of the strategy and its implications, of the concepts involved, e.g., what does "more efficient professional services" actually mean? They are also difficult because they entail painful choices. But that is what a senior manager is paid to do.

CREATING THE STRATEGY

A school is not a business. Even though education is big business and getting more commercial, there is something that sets it apart from regular commercial businesses. By far, most people working in education do so out of a passion to help people, especially young people, as they grow. They know they have a profound impact on people, some of which will be remembered throughout their life. It is not for commercial gain or fat salaries that they work in education. Which is why I prefer to talk about the purpose of a school as a starting point for strategy development and deployment. The purpose of an organization is why it exists and what sets it apart. It defines to whom it matters.[1] My favorite question is: If your school would cease to exist tomorrow, who would miss it and why? It is important to note that it is not only about to whom it matters, and why, but also what it as a school brings, what sets it apart.[2]

---

[1] Cynthia Montgomery, *The Strategist: Be the Leader Your Business Needs* (New York: HarperCollins, 2012), 46.

[2] Setting a school apart from other schools might sound beside the point since we want all children in our city, region, or country to receive the same education. I argue that this, though plausible, is at the core of many of today's educational problems. We want all our children to have equal opportunities to learn and develop and to achieve certain minimal standards. But children, cities, and regions are different with their own culture and needs. Restraining schools to fit the same muster confuses means and goals. Let us set the same basic goals for all, but leave students, teachers, parents, and local organizations free to set additional goals and choose their own means.

That is a question on the vision on education of your school, its teaching practices, its relationship with the community, etc. A good purpose has four characteristics.[3]

- It ennobles. Doing something that is meaningful is important to people. It inspires us to go to work
- It sets the school apart. It chooses what the school stands for, what it does, and does not. In other words, it guides hard choices
- It differentiates. It makes clear what makes your school different from others. Being different is not about necessarily being better or worse. It gives you a clear identity
- It provides the basis for adding value for our students. Based on the purpose, it is clearer how and where you help students grow.

Breaking down the strategy is one of the key elements of strategy deployment. Skinner and Pitzer, cited in Bodily et al.[4] distinguish four levels: (1) institutional, (2) school level, (3) classroom level, and (4) activity level. The aim of breaking down a strategy means translating the strategic goals to each level of the organization so that at each level it is clear what needs to be achieved. A school determines the needs of its students, the community it is a part of, and the broader regional or national requirements. Based on its convictions, its mission, the school then determines what it wants to achieve and when. To fulfill its purpose, it derives its needs in terms of resources and capabilities. For each function in the organization, the contribution to the realization of the strategy is defined. By a function I mean, for example, teaching, communication, human resources (HR) facility management, and pedagogy. Every function contributes its bit to the school as a whole. Communication ensures the students and parents get the right information at the right time with the proper tone of voice; HR makes sure that the teachers have the necessary skills, knowledge for the teaching tasks; and pedagogy ensures that the teaching approach fits the needs of the students and the learning goals.

---

[3] Montgomery, *The Strategist: Be the Leader Your Business Needs*, 49–52.

[4] Michael Bush Robert bodily, Charles Graham, "Online Learner Engagement: Opportunities and Challenges with Using Data Analytics," *Educational Technology*, Vol. 57, No. 1 (January–February 2017) (2017): 10–18, http://www.jstor.org/stable/44430535.

Let us consider the following example. A federation of high schools adopts as one of its strategic goals to develop and maintain high levels of student engagement. Student engagement is defined as the intrinsic commitment of students to learning, i.e., pride and joy in learning beyond the formal aspects of making the grades. It can be measured in different ways, e.g., by drop-out rates, self-reports by students, extra-curricular activities, and student happiness. Averaging these rates across the schools is not very informative, the improvement rates, however, might be. Individual schools can then, based on the base rate and improvements, target their own goals. These, in turn, can be translated to the classroom level. At that level, they are supplemented by other goals to help direct the improvement efforts, e.g., behavioral and emotional commitment and time spent on assignments and study. These latter are meaningful at the activity-level. Two warnings apply in this breakdown. One, not everything is and should be measurable. The discussion about the goals, and how to find evidence, is as important as the measuring itself. Two, the measuring is not a goal in itself, and the time spent should be limited. Here, both new pedagogies and technologies are supportive. Ultimately, what is done and measured at the activity-level should be related back to the purpose of the school.

The strategic wheel as defined by Cynthia Montgomery provides a powerful yet simple way to depict the relationship between the school's purpose and its functions. She calls it "…a system of value creation, a set of mutually reinforcing parts."[5] It makes clear for which students you provide education how, where, and when. Resources are limited, so it is important that they are deployed in a way that contributes to the purpose. And, in a way that strengthen other functions. Many organizations have functional silos. Each does his thing, only loosely connected and, unfortunately all too often, in conflict with other functions. The strategic wheel places all key functions alongside each other and around the purpose.

A good strategy makes clear what each function should and should not do and how they work together. For the school and each function, you want to able to express the goals that go with the purpose. Goals are multi-faceted and reflect the rich fabric of a school. They might include learning objectives, student and staff satisfaction, impact on the

---

[5] Montgomery, *The Strategist: Be the Leader Your Business Needs.*

community, or financial constraints. Be careful, constraints and means are often confused with goals proper. The goal is to have students that have certain skills and knowledge. That goal needs to be achieved within a certain budget, with certain fixed facilities. Staying within these constraints is required, but it is not why the school exists. They often become dominant because they figure largely in discussions and because they can be quantified more easily (Figure 8.1).

Schools need to be thoughtful about the goals and the way they break them down. No one staff member or team can achieve the school's goals by themselves. Each contributes his own bit, which might be different from other contributions. A concierge contributes by creating a safe yet disciplined environment, a teacher by personalized learning strategies, and the administrator by leadership, rich external relationships, and motivation. Breaking down the strategy to individual contributions of functions and teams, with the associated goals, is the task of the owner of the strategy. The strategy is usually owned by the head master, principal, rector, or vice-chancellor. She is responsible for formulating the strategy. She seeks input and broad support from stakeholders. A strategy is, however, not a democratic process by which everyone gets a say and a vote. The owner of the strategy listens careful, decides, and can explain how the various

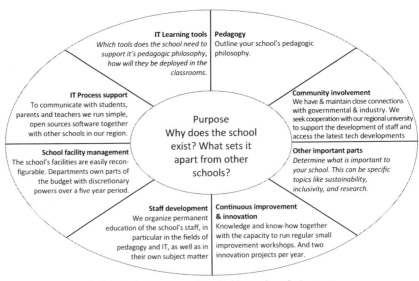

A set of mutually reinforcing part of the school that together realize its purpose.
The parts or functions listed here are just an example. There can be more and different ones depending on the school's need.

FIGURE 8.1
Strategic wheel.

contributions have found their way into the strategy or not as the case may be. Involving staff and other stakeholders is crucial. In Lean, we call this playing catch ball. The process of sharing and soliciting input is made easier by visualizing the strategy.

VISUALIZING STRATEGY & TRACKING PROGRESS

Images are richer than words. By capturing a strategy not just in words, but also in an image, it gains more depth. Visualizing involves the search for images, answering questions like why this picture, what is it that appeals in this image and reflects what we want to achieve. By finding words to go with the images, one explores the strategy. It is also helpful in the communication with and involvement of stakeholders. I find that the conversation with colleagues, students, and companies, gets richer as we have images to guide the conversation. It becomes less abstract. The image invites other images, the narrative other narratives. By listening carefully as the discussion evolves around the images, the owner of the strategy gets a clearer picture of the strategy. As stakeholders present their own image or discuss that of the strategy owner, keywords are used. These keywords are noted and fed back into the strategy when appropriate.[6]

Rolling out strategy and tracking progress often takes the form of lengthy, verbose documents and reports that are hard to digest, not very concise, and hard work to create. The plans do provide direction. Their verbose and roundabout nature, however, makes it harder to translate it to individual departmental and team plans. The annual planning cycle therefore focuses primarily on budget allocation, the reporting on budget utilization, and a few other metrics such as student and staff satisfaction, number of publications, and student scores on exams. In this yearly cycle, intermediate reports are few, mostly financially focused or accident driven (budget overruns, complaints). Once made, they are not revisited until

---

[6] This approach is used by the KaosPilot when they design new curricula (see also Chapter 7). Participants in the development of the course collect and collate images based on a narrative about the future of the students of that specific course. The narrative follows the golden circle of Simon Sinek. Other participants listen to key words that are used as one describes the images, and the narrative unfolds. These keywords are fed back into the curriculum design.

the annual report is due. The reporting is backward looking. Most of the time is spent on clarification and justification of last year's results. The forward-looking aspect is mainly the addition or reduction of the budget with some percent points. Added to this are major one-off activities such as new building projects, new labs, etc.

What we want the strategy to be like is something altogether different. It is not that budgets are not important, but they are the reflection of strategic choices made. The reporting itself should be focused on the tracking of goals around a wider set of themes. The main aim should be learning. What is working, and what is not? Why is it (not) working? Which corrective actions should be taken? How can we share learnings and best practices across the organization? The visualization is helpful again. It helps in staying focused on where the school is going rather than what has transpired. It is the image after all that we are discussing. The image can be adapted to allow the tracking of the progress. Like an outline drawing of a building in which the building parts get colored as they are delivered. As an example, imagine a school that provides vocational training. Its purpose is "to help our students develop themselves into valued craftsmen and educate industry's future staff with the skills and know-how. It does so through education in which theories and practices are seamlessly connected, and its teachers have all made their mark in industry." The image is of a craftsman that is made up of hundreds of pictures of its students that have found a job after graduation. The students that have not yet found a job in the industry leave white spots. For everyone, it is clear in one glance how the school is doing.

I am, personally, time and again surprised by the enormous strength of visuals. Recently, I conducted a masterclass on strategy for Lean master blackbelts for a major international bank. As part of the masterclass, the participants were asked to draw their projects in relation to the bank's strategy. Though initially somewhat hesitant, they did so. And then they went on to redraw it for the whole group on a flip chart and explain both the strategy and the projects they are running while drawing. For the group, but also for themselves, it made things a lot clearer. Some of the unconsciously made assumptions were drawn out, white spots became clear, and the main message stuck better. These drawing are not pieces of art, they are not meant to be. As a means of thinking aloud and conveying messages, they are very effective. For the group of participants, it was one of the top three take-aways of the masterclass.

CONTINUOUS IMPROVEMENT

If change is a given and change is fast, you need to organize for change. Schools in their current set up are the opposite of change. Schools are set up to deliver predictable, uniform, and standardized education in large numbers. Curricula, statutes, and lessons are prepared well ahead and seldomly changed. Schedules are laid for the whole year and courses fixed for several years. Change is required, however.[7] Change does not always have to be big. And big changes do not always have to be made in one big leap. If you improve something every day, you will have made major impact over the course of a year. This continuous improvement is the hallmark of a Lean organization. It is a simple, low cost, and low risk way of changing. Like a marathon, it is one step at the time. Of course, sometimes bigger changes are required, such as the introduction of new IT systems, a new course, or a new teaching method. These changes, run as big projects, tend to absorb all the energy, resources, management attention and money. They are risky and often leave staff feeling left behind. "The reality is that most schools have been inundated with change. The problem is that many of the changes have not brought the desired positive effects or have not been sustained. [...] most of the basic features of schooling remain largely unaltered even over a century."[8]

Nothing beats a habit when it comes to driving behavior. That can make change hard except when change is the habit. The key for successful change in education is making it a habit by ingraining change into the culture of the school, into "the way we do things around here." For change as part of the culture, it needs to be sustainable. There are three key elements in initiating and sustaining change. One, it is part of the routines of the school. That means running a relatively small change at a time, often. An obvious way to proceed is to make it a part of regular meetings the teams of teachers and the management team have.[9] Having their own performance board with

---

[7] Michael Fullan, *Stratosphere: Integrating Technology, Pedagogy, and Change Knowledge* (Don Mills, ON: Pearson Education, 2013).

[8] Ben Levin, *How to Change 5000 Schools: A Practical and Positive Approach for Leading Change at Every Level* (Cambridge, MA: Harvard Education Press, 2008), 64.

[9] I had the honor to attend team meetings at several primary schools. The team of lecturers meet on a weekly basis for 15 minutes. This meeting takes place at the team board which lists the school's objectives and major initiatives. It connects these to weekly actions. The team discusses the progresses, the successes they achieved, and obstacles they came across.

the focus point for the semester or the school year is a powerful element. Two, sustaining change is also furthered by having a clear sequence of steps to be taken.[10] The Lean Kaizen, continuous improvement cycle, is an ideal method. The change process consists of six simple steps that can be used for both small and big changes. Three, all staff is trained in the improvement methods. A common mistake made in education is that because we have a convincing case that is understood by all, we assume everyone also knows how to do it. But seeing sense is not the same as being able (yet).

Experience over of the years has taught me that habits need fostering. Combining training with some light coaching over an extended period will bring the desired results. It needs stamina! It works best if teams are given a goal that is understood and agreed like, for example, increasing literacy to level x. Involve the team in the goal selection, but make sure that it fits within the wider goals of the school. Leave the team the freedom to devise their own strategies to achieve the goals. They are after all professionals with a strong commitment to their students. This ownership will enhance the chances of success. It needs to fit within a structure that tracks progress regularly.

The steps of Kaizen themselves are easy to understand. They follow the well-known pattern of scientific thinking. There is a phenomenon we observe that we want to explain and influence. We form a hypothesis that explains the working of the pattern and how we might influence it. Next, we devise and execute a plan to test the hypothesis. Observing the results from the executed plan, we establish whether we were right, and if not, what we misunderstood. In Lean Education the steps are the following.

1. Determine where you would want the students to be and where they currently are. For example, "the attention of substantial groups wane after x time resulting in unrest in the group which disturbs the learning efforts of other students," or "the retention of particular topics after 6 weeks is low"
2. Investigate the underlying mechanisms and causes of the observed gap. What are the root causes of the observed behaviors and outcomes?
3. Devise alternative learning and teaching strategies that address the root causes

---

[10] The interested reader will find some powerful and practical pointers to change in the following books.
Chip Heath and Dan Heath, *Switch: How to Change Things When Change Is Hard* (Waterville, ME: Crown Publishing Group, 2010); C Duhigg, *The Power of Habit: Why We Do What We Do, and How to Change* (London, UK: Random House, 2012).

4. Plan how to implement the alternative learning and teaching strategies. Include the steps to design materials, instruct students, train other colleagues
5. Execute the plan
6. Track the progress as the plan is implemented. Do this on a regular basis, preferably on a weekly basis, using the performance boards.

CONTINUOUS INNOVATION

Even big changes are done in small steps. But sometimes the scope of the change and the number of steps require a larger, concerted effort. Ideally, these changes are innovations that help schools make a large step and adept to large scale changes in society. The disappearance of a whole economic sector can affect a region deeply. These changes can happen rather fast and require a refocusing of schooling (in addition to many other things). An interesting case is the disappearance of ship building in Odense, Denmark. With the demise of the shipyards, new economic activities had to be developed. In the case of Odense, they focused on robotics. This required a major overhaul of the existing education as one can well imagine. This is an innovation of the curriculum that cannot be realized by small step changes of continuous improvement. But rather than disaster driven, step change by schools should be part of the forces that drive the change. By continuous innovation schools can be the partner in change. So, how to affect step changes in schools? How to implement continuous innovation in schools?

The first question to address is what constitutes innovation in education.[11] Innovation is the introduction of something novel, an idea that did not exist before, meeting needs in ways that did not exist before. The idea is embedded in a product or service otherwise it is nothing but that "a new idea." The performance of that product or service is better. It often involves elimination of a trade-off, e.g., either higher quality or lower cost, but now we provide higher quality at lower cost.

---

[11] Innovation is a large and contentious subject with a very large body of literature. There are literally dozens of definitions of innovation and many methods. This chapter is not a chapter on innovation. I will use an informal description that is operable in relatively small organizations that schools often are. Even large educational institutes will find it useful. Often innovation in schools is rather serendipitous. The infusion of some structure will already affect large impact. A Osterwalder et al., *Value Proposition Design: How to Create Products and Services Customers Want*, Strategyzer Series (New York: Wiley, 2015), have written a usable, practical book that can be used as a guide in innovating.

> Innovation is: production or adoption, assimilation, and exploitation of a value-added novelty in economic and social spheres; renewal and enlargement of products, services, and markets; development of new methods of production; and establishment of new management systems. It is both a process and an outcome.[12]

An innovation often takes a new look at things that allows us to move beyond "the way things are always done." The current way of doing allows for improvements. And that is good. But, it also keeps us from stepping back to take a new, hard look. There have been several innovations in education. For some countries where education used to be a public affair, the introduction of commercial education is innovative. The same goes for the introduction of student-centered learning.

The steps involved in innovation are the following.

1. Having a need for a step change arising from the strategy
2. Exploring the challenge
3. Generating ideas
4. Critical evaluation and testing
5. Designing the new product or service
6. Implementing the new product or service.

Serendipity is not an innovation strategy. The school needs a strategy that spells out the areas that need innovative change and why. As previously described, the school has someone who owns the strategy and whose job it is to signal out these areas. Next, since innovation requires the ability and freedom to look beyond the way we do things, it is a good idea to have one or two colleagues who own the innovation process. This mean designating innovation as one of the school's functions. They have the task to investigate the current situation and the desired outcome. The generation of ideas which relates to both the "what" and the "how" is best done in an open setting in which students, colleagues, and outside organizations get together. Various methods are available to support the idea generation. Design thinking is a good approach to use to support this process. Experimentation is an integral part of innovation, which means that various colleagues need to be open to test ideas and provide feedback based on the experiments they have run in the classroom.

---

[12] Using Evaluation and Improve Teaching, "Teachers for the 21st Century," 2013, doi:10.1787/9789264193864-en.

HANDS ON!

One of the powerful Lean tools that can help you in deploying the school's strategy is the x-matrix (Figures 8.2 and 8.3). It helps in creating an overview of initiatives and forms the basis of tracking the progress. The x-matrix connects five elements of the strategy: the purpose, the strategic goals, goals for the coming year, the improvement initiatives, and the success measures. The purpose is at the heart, as a compass. Each of the other elements are extensions to the north, west, south, and east. Each element is connected to two of the others through the corners.

1. List the mid-term goals (south quadrant)—restrict yourself to five goals maximum
2. Translate the goals to short-term goals (west quadrant)—which goals do you need to achieve the coming year to make enough progress toward the mid-term goals

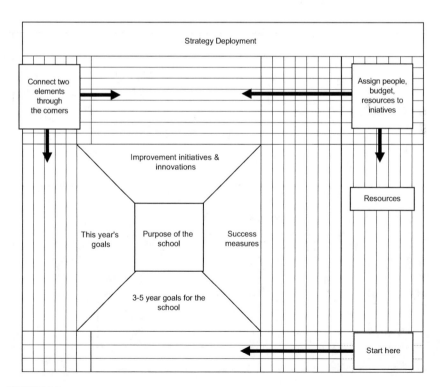

FIGURE 8.2
X-matrix.

3. List the running and new initiatives for continuous improvement and innovation that will help you achieve the goals (north quadrant)
4. Define the success measures that will show you whether you have achieved your goals (east quadrant)
5. Connect each element through the corners. This way you indicate which initiative, for example, contributes to the short-term goals. You need to have a plan which outlines how the initiative will help achieve one or more goals. Every element needs to be connected to at least on other element. Try to limit the number of connections per element though! An initiative to help achieving all goals is probably too big and complex to manage well
6. Consider who of your colleagues, what part of the budget, and which other resources will be needed to execute the initiative well. Often, we have too many projects relying on a few critical resources that are soon overburdened.

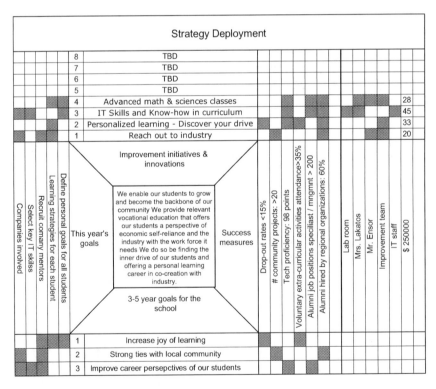

FIGURE 8.3
X-matrix example.

LEAN EDUCATION CASE: REDESIGN OF A COURSE

BACKGROUND (STUDY)

Once a year, the faculties of Technology and of Economics organize an open course on Lean and process management. The course consists of 10 days, over a period of 20 weeks. On a course day students attend class for about 7 hours. In between the course days, they work on their own projects in industry. Over the course period, they are coached by the lecturers. Over the years, we witnessed a drop in enrollment. We took a hard look and tried to make some observations on what was happening.

1. The students did not use the theoretical concept we taught or did not share them with colleagues. As a consequence, their improvement projects had little sustainable, bottom line impact
2. Their project work would soon lag the theory. As a consequence, the theory discussed did not match the practical needs of the students
3. The drop-out rate of students not pursuing the final exam for the certificate was relatively high

This was clearly not a sustainable course, nor professionally satisfactory. The causes of the problems were not obvious at first consideration. Therefore, the lecturers that were involved did a root-cause analysis. This resulted in the following root-causes.

1. The students enrolled with a personal goal in mind. This goal was not made explicit, nor was there a group goal. The lecturers did not share the underlying goals, beyond what was communicated in the course description
2. There was no active tracking and management of the goals, the course work, and student projects. The focus during the teaching days was mostly on the theory
3. Teaching was mostly one-way, slide based theory. Student were mostly listening with little room for exercising. There was little development of practical skills and know-how

**LEAN EDUCATION CASE: REDESIGN
OF A COURSE (Continued)**

4. The change management part of the course was positioned at the very end of the course. Which made is practically impossible to use and apply it on the projects

5. The course was oriented toward the transfer of knowledge. The students were, however, also being trained as facilitators. Important aspects of facilitation relating to attitude and skills were not addressed.

KEY CHANGES (ACT)

To address the causes, we designed several counter measures. For each cause, there was a counter measure.

1. Set the student a joint goal that also indicates when the course is done and what needs to be delivered

2. Active tracking of student progress relating to their goals and projects through performance management. This allows mid-course addressing of issues

3. Short blocks of theory without the use of slides, interlaced with practical, hands-on assignments applying the theory

4. Interlacing the change management component from the very start of the course and throughout the course. This would allow the students to counter issues in implementing their projects

5. Have students actively engaged in the running of hands-on workshops. This allows us to focus on skills and attitudes as well as theory.

DESIGNING THE CHANGES (PLAN)

We considered how to best implement the changes for each teaching plan for a course day.

1. We set out as teacher to add a joint goal for the group in addition to the individual goals of the students. On date x, we have all finished our project work and completed the exam with a passing mark. In addition, each student will have run a workshop

LEAN EDUCATION CASE: REDESIGN
OF A COURSE (Continued)

and facilitated a performance board session. The underlying goal for us as lecturers was to grow a team rather than a group of individuals. Motivation and urgency, we assumed, would be greater if success is a joint effort and responsibility

2. We will start performance board sessions from the very start. The above listed goals will be given, and students will have to design the performance board themselves based on the theory provided by us. The assignment is: "Devise a way to monitor your progress as a group toward the goal." The goal is on the center stage of the performance board. Every course day students will be given 30 minutes for a performance meeting in which to measure progress. The session will be facilitated by one of the students. He will receive feedback on his skills from one of the lecturers

3. We devise teaching plans for each day in which blocks of theory of 20 minutes are interspersed with practice. We agreed to only use flip charts and felt pens to graphically draw while explaining concepts. In addition, we sought games that would illustrate the concepts and theories. The underlying assumptions is that graphical depictions, hands-on experience, and games would make the knowledge stick better, keep the attention of the students better, and allow us to address different perception and communication preferences

4. Various change management themes are integrated throughout the program in each teaching day related to the concepts and theories. One of the red threads, the project A3, would serve as a frame of reference of the change management aspects. Since the students plan their projects using the project A3 format, the change management would align more naturally with the project

5. Also related to the A3 project, we plan to introduce a workshop format that fits the needs of the A3 at a particular stage. The workshop format will be introduced at the end of the teaching day that precedes the day in which the workshop is applicable. A student will be asked to prepare the workshop and execute it during the next teaching day. He will receive feedback both on the mastery of the topic and the skills used in running the workshop.

LEAN EDUCATION CASE: REDESIGN
OF A COURSE (Continued)

EXECUTING THE PLAN (DO)

All counter measures were carefully considered and detailed further in our teaching plans. Then we executed the plan.

1. During the first trial run of the performance board we provided the goals. Then the students discussed, adjusted, and adapted the goals. The goals feature prominently on the board
2. We then asked the students to show how they would execute the progress monitoring. We guided the discussions mainly through asking questions. Our frame of reference was the project A3. "How do you monitor progress? What is your starting position? How do you notice a deviation from the plan?" The students themselves proposed to organize a performance board session every course day
3. For each lesson, we drafted and shared the plan with timing indicators for each topic. Theory was explained drafting graphs on the white board of flip chart. This kept all students hooked, even in cases where we overran the set time. A theory session was always followed by a practice session in which the theory was linked to existing knowledge
4. In preparation for each lesson, we checked which elements of change management could be incorporated. We matched it to the project A3. In the project background description on the A3, for example, we taught the students about stakeholder management. This, the students could apply directly to their own project
5. Each lesson, one of the students executed a workshop. Both peers and lecturers provided feedback on skills and attitudes. This way, we could address common pitfalls in applying a concept, e.g., letting off-topic discussions run too long and engaging in discussions about the content instead of managing the process. If, and when needed, as lecturers, we would steer or correct the discussion to prevent students from missing crucial points or making big mistakes.

**LEAN EDUCATION CASE: REDESIGN
OF A COURSE (Continued)**

THE EFFECT OF THE CHANGES (CHECK)

At the end of the course, we reflected on the changes we designed and implemented. These are our findings.

1. Setting the goals made it very clear when they would be done. The students worked as a team. In particular, during the performance board sessions, they helped each other whenever possible. At the end of the course, the whole class felt bad since one of the students had failed to reach all his goals. Even though this was for private reasons. It wasn't a complete surprise since the progress meetings had brought some problems to light already. Worries and problems were shared, which was good in itself

2. The performance board sessions were active meetings in which all participated and addressed each other's issues. Feedback was not always structured which hampered discussions. Some of the issues addressed were not described clearly enough which lead to unnecessary repeat discussions. It took a while for the students to understand how to facilitate a workshop

3. We overran allotted time for the 20 minutes theory lessons at least once each course day. Despite this, students were positive. The drawing of concepts while explaining them ensured discussions could take place. With the old PowerPoint driving lessons, students would be overwhelmed with info which kept them from considering the offered information. Now they had ample time and could ask questions to deepen their understanding. Following up each theory lesson with a game or assignment theory was translated to practice. This made it easier to grasp and see the relevance of concepts. Students indicated the format worked well for them. Days passed almost too fast

4. The students formed teams at their workplace to work on the project. Together they discussed the project A3. In between the course days, students posted pictures of their project work as it progressed. The atmosphere in the teams was clearly energetic and enthused. They worked on Brown Paper sessions together, mapping out processes for improvement

**LEAN EDUCATION CASE: REDESIGN
OF A COURSE (Continued)**

5. Every student facilitated a workshop. This worked fairly well. They were in need of more structure and clear instructions regarding timing. A further point for improvement is the organization of the feedback. From one to the next workshop, there was relatively little sharing of insights and lessons learned.

RESULTS

Looking back and assessing the results with regard to our goals, it worked out well. We have learned a lot, made substantial improvements, and have several points for improvement in the next year. Listed per issue as outlined at the beginning of this case:

1. The students did not use the theoretical concept we taught or did not share them with colleagues. As a consequence, their improvement projects had little sustainable, bottom line impact
   - During the course students shared pictures of themselves working with colleagues on their project. Every one of the students did so
   - Five months later, the Whatsapp group is still alive, and we receive photos of the students working on new projects.

2. Their project work would soon lag the theory. As a consequence, the theory discussed did not match the practical needs of the students
   - Almost 80% of the students had finished their project work by the end of the course.
3. The drop-out rate of student not pursuing the final exam for the certificate was relatively high.
   - 90% of the students concluded the course successfully. One student dropped out for private reasons beyond our control
   - 10% did not finished the project work.

LEAN EDUCATION CASE: REDESIGN
OF A COURSE (Continued)

At the end of the course, we asked the students how likely it was they would recommend the course to others on a scale of 1 (highly unlikely) to 5 (highly likely). The course received a score of 5.

REFLECTION ON THE CASE

In this case, we see multiple elements of Lean Education featuring prominently both in the organization of the course, but also in the course materials. The focus of the course was on value for students, which consisted of applicable knowledge and know-how together with an ability to perform.

The lecturers organized the evaluation using the Kaizen philosophy of continuous improvement based on the plan-do-check-act cycle. They made bigger upfront and kept a series of smaller changes flowing throughout the course. They shared the end goals with the students. This functioned as a shared reference and ideal state. As the students progressed, their performance was tracked. This provided the impetus for a stream of smaller changes when and for whom needed. The attainment of the overall goals was tracked as well. This completed the full improvement cycle. That is a challenge for many educational projects which are started full of energy, but do not finish the last step: checking whether the goals have been met. The final step is in turn input for the next improvement cycle for the following course year.

Maarten de Groot
Arian Hofland
Vincent Wiegel

9

On the Importance of Professional Services

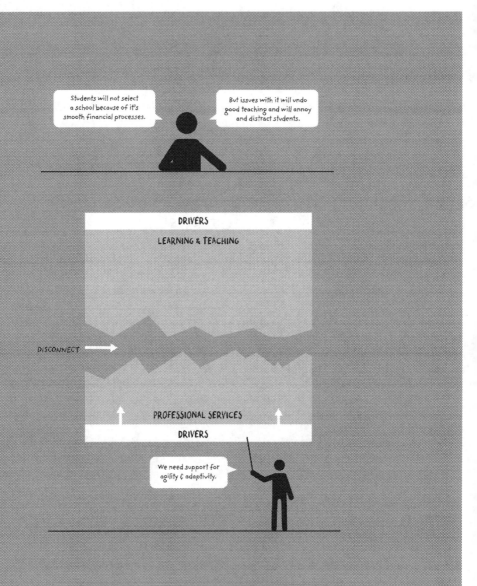

INTRODUCTION

Big and small quality are equally important in the success of a school. The big quality refers to the quality of the education itself, small quality to all surrounding aspects, like the quality of the building, hygiene, schedules, etc. If organized well, small quality provides a winning backdrop for good education. If not enough attention is paid to small quality, it becomes a major distractor that can undo all the good of education. Small quality is big! It is mostly organized in the professional services and support departments. There are three key points of attention regarding small quality and support processes. One, they do not get enough attention in the wider scheme of things. Two, management attention is focused on traditional efficiency thinking that hampers rather than helps educators. Three, they absorb more and more budget.

LEAN EDUCATION THINKING ON PRIMARY AND SECONDARY PROCESSES

There are many excellent case studies and articles on how to organize professional services in schools in a Lean way.[1] Lean can and does help eliminate waste in professional services without a doubt. In this chapter, I want to focus on a more fundamental view on professional services: the integral approach rather than the local improvements of teams or parts of a value stream. Lean Education thinking starts with the student. From the concept of value for the student, we organize the processes of learning and teaching. These processes in turn define what they need and pull what they need and when they need the required support from professional services. Based on the needs of both the primary processes of learning and teaching, and of the secondary processes of professional services, the staff is organized. It is important to understand this ideal of one in service of the other, the client-server relationship as it were. When organized this way, the notion of value suffuses the whole organization. All functions in the organization are aligned. It focuses on the student

---

[1] Any reader interested in how Lean improvements of professional support are processed is referred to a book on Lean Higher Education edited by Steve Yorkstone 2019, forthcoming.

experience, the student journey from the first step of gathering information about schools to help decide which school to attend until graduation. Everything in a school should be organized around the student journey. It is how the value flows. On that journey, the student will touch various parts of the organization. The perspective of the student is on that journey (even if only subconsciously) rather than on the specific part of the organization.

This is, of course, an idealized description. It serves as a north star for the organization of the education. In practice, there can be big discrepancies, e.g., when a student goes to the library to get a book, her key aim is to find the information needed to enhance her understanding of a specific topic. The search may start with an assignment. The completion of that assignment is not the goal, however. The goal is learning, the assignment is a way to help the learning and/or a way to assess the understanding. Getting the loan of a book is likewise not the goal either. It is to obtain information needed to complete the assignment. The library systems serve the purpose to determine relevant literature that contain the relevant information. This way, it continues down to the decisions on stocking the library and the purchase of books. Nowhere in this process is the student interested in how lecturers interact with libraries to check availability of relevant literature, nor in how the library is organized and the fact that the purchasing department is located within the finance division rather than the library, which resides within academic services. To the student and what constitutes value to her, this is all utterly irrelevant. In practice, however, the lecturer might give an assignment that requires other sources than are available in the library. The system will have functionality the helps in searching for sources, but might be outdated because it was designed in the age in which books were the dominant sources of information, whereas now some online videos might be more relevant. Note that in the notion of value, books do not figure! It is the information that counts. Information that is available in many different formats. The library is working on a budget. When turning to the purchase department, it might run into guidelines on what can be purchased from whom under what conditions. These guidelines have been drafted with the whole organization in mind and might not always be conducive to the aims of the library. In this small example, one can already see how notions of value, student journey, professional services processes, and organization lead to situations where the organization is not aligned, and the delivery of value is hampered by the organization.

THE IMPACT OF SMALL QUALITY

It is hard to overstate the importance of small quality and the professional services staff that delivers this small quality. If schedules are well laid, if information is timely and correct, if the building is clean, and all systems work as meant to, no one will notice. It enables the flow of value in seamless ways, and it does not distract attention and energy. If done properly, it provides a sound and strong fundament for learning and teaching, as depicted in the house of Lean Education. So, the impact is twofold, as distractor and dissatisfier on the one hand, and as an enabler on the other hand.

Professional services as enabler means that it is closely aligned with the educational processes. It is intimately aware of its needs and workings. This might strike one as odd, one would assume this already to be the case. But especially in larger institutions there often is quite a distance between professional services and teaching staff. The learning and teaching processes as described in this book are characterized by agility and adaptability. This has clear implications for professional services. It must organize for agility and adaptability. This has an effect on all domains of the organization: buildings, furniture, invoicing, scheduling, and so on. Literally, all functions of the school will be affected. Furniture will need to be such that, for example, it is moved around easily, reconfigurable to smaller and larger groups of tables that support small and large group activities. When a new topic arises during teaching, it should be possible to obtain non-standard materials such as books, tablets, brown paper roles, and post-its on short notice. Nowadays, the purchase process can be long winded and restrictive. Teachers can often not order materials themselves. The process is formal, and restricts items that can be ordered, and can take many weeks to complete. A factory hall or a hospital might be the classroom for a couple of days. This might involve the transport of students and materials. This obviously requires a flexible and supportive organization capable of such logistics.

It is easy to dismiss these ideas out of hand as too expensive and not realistic. But that would be missing the point. The cost of the current system is learning outcomes that fall short of what is needed and of what could be achieved. These costs are much higher. In addition, the current way of organizing incurs a lot of hidden cost in terms of teaching staff involvement in non-teaching work and in terms of under-utilized facilities and materials. As in the processes of learning and teaching, Lean Education requires a paradigm shift in professional services. A paradigm shift, a concept introduced by philosopher of science Thomas Kuhn, indicates another way of looking at the world, a shift in assumptions that underlie our thinking. Through this other perspective things are seen in a new light, new possibilities arise. Under the current paradigm, assumptions about costs, distribution of responsibility, and specialization inhibit our ways of thinking that are required in Lean Education. What we need for professional services is an approach that starts radically from the needs of students and teachers. It means getting closer in understanding what is needed, tailoring what is offered ever more finely. I will address this later in this chapter.

In the current way of thinking, professional services can be a major distractor. It pains me to say this because I've met so many dedicated, hard-working professionals that give their best efforts every day to service their students and teachers. So, let me empathically state that this is not a reproach to them. In the words of Deming, the problem is in the system and not the people. To give just an example of how the system gets out of hand: a school, and there many similar ones, decides to streamline purchasing. Teachers now can order items they need through a service desk. This desk is located at a centralized spot on campus. An item ordered needs to be collected at the desk requiring the teacher a walk up and down. The desk of course is serving multiple staff so there is a waiting line. On collecting the item, the teacher finds the ordered item has been substituted with another, similar item because the ordered one is not on the standard list in the contract with the supplier. The new item does not work because it does not fit the specifications for connecting with other devices. As it turned out, the request for the item is passed on to the purchasing team. The list of authorized items is drafted by yet another team. That the item wouldn't work, the service desk could not know, but they did not ask either. A new one must be ordered. The cost is weeks of missed functionality, walking up and down, waiting time, etc. The cost of the transaction is outweighing the savings several times over.[2] All academic staff and teachers will recognize anecdotes like this. They are not the exception. These are minor irritants that become

---

[2] The counter argument runs that staff could also easily order items that can be gotten cheaper or that are over specified for the need. That argument has some merit. The solution is, however, not the bureaucratic approach.

major distractors when happening too often. Missing materials and non-functioning equipment are major distractors in themselves already. Combined, these factors will substantially reduce the effectiveness of learning and teaching. Again, these observations can be dismissed easily as war stories of disgruntled staff. They are not. But as with customers, most of the complaints will never be voiced. It will affect the atmosphere in a negative way.[3] I heard one teacher say, "my organization will do anything to make our lives harder." This is a hard-working, dedicated teacher with a passion for teaching.

THE BIG ROLE AND SIZE OF PROFESSIONAL SERVICES DEPARTMENTS

There is a wide variance between countries and between individual schools as to how the budget is allocated. Overall, the current expenditure (as opposed to capital spending) accounts for roughly 70%–80% of the budget. Most of this is salaries. Staff is divided in teaching staff and non-teaching staff. This can be janitors, teacher support staff, IT staff, HR staff, administrative staff, etc. Non-teaching staff can account for up to 50% of the total staff[4] and up to a third of the salary share. Again, numbers vary widely across countries and across primary, secondary, and tertiary education. Whatever the exact number, they are substantial. In a search for cost savings, schools have looked to streamline their processes, get better deals from suppliers, and gain efficiency. This has, inversely, led to more professional services staff to organize the purchasing, the IT, etc., which needed policy and management staff to organize them. There is also an indirect effect on available teaching time. The basic idea is that having dedicated staff looking at specific things such as purchasing saves time. As is apparent from the anecdote above, this saving is not so obvious, especially in the age of the Internet.

[3] James R Evans, *Quality and Performance Excellence: Management, Organization, and Strategy* (Mason, OH: Thomson Business and Economics, 2008).

[4] https://edexcellence.net/publications/the-hidden-half accessed January 3rd, 2019. The number of non-teaching staff has risen in the US according to a study by Matthew Richmond, "The Hidden Half: School Employees Who Don't Teach.," *Thomas B. Fordham Institute*, August (2014), https://eric.ed.gov/?id=ED560006 accessed February 2nd, 2019.

TRADITIONAL DRIVERS FOR THE ORGANIZATION OF SUPPORT PROCESSES

The growth of professional services is worrying given the misalignment between the processes of learning and teaching on the one hand and professional services processes on the other. This misalignment stems from two key causes. One, the fact that the drivers, the objectives of each are not the same. They are treated as different realms with differing principles. Two, they are often quite literally disconnected, even though they ultimately are part of one organization. They are organized in different departments or teams that all too often do not meet regularly, do not share one view on the student journey, and are separated by physical and mental barriers.

Let us look at each of these in turn. Drivers, objectives, and guiding principles, refer to what an organization wants to achieve and by what means. The "actual" objective of many professional services is to provide necessary services at low cost. The operative words here are *necessary* and *cost*. Financial reports must be submitted to such and so, compliances with laws and regulations must be ensured, building must be heated, etc. All very true and proper. The key problem here is that they tend to take precedence over all other supporting activities that are either not cost driven or not formally necessary, though they are essential from the view of learning and teaching. An example mentioned earlier is to get specific learning materials within a short time frame. Another would be student progress reports that are required by the regulator and have to undergo an additional internal approval and collection process that eats away the time of teachers and seldom lead to substantive action. The guiding principles are standardization and economies of scale. The underlying drivers are cost reduction and control. Through standardization (and the limitation that ensues), one can process larger volumes. Larger volumes lead to lower cost through lower prices and lower costs of processing, so the assumption goes. To execute the support processes, professional services staff and IT-systems are needed. Systems are purchased to support the process. As the system has, understandably, some limitations, the process is adjusted to fit the system. A system is then configured by IT specialists, who talk with professional services staff, none of whom are intimately familiar with learning and teaching. Of course, teaching staff is consulted, and with the best intentions. These consultations take place in workshops of a couple of hours as teaching staff time is already crammed with teaching obligations. Teachers often do not understand the ramifications of particular system choices, and probably do not have a shared view on the matter to begin with, have IT and professional services interpret their input. So, we have an initiative for standardization and automation not driven by the people towards whom it is intended, that provides input based on a disjointed view of what is needed, without thorough understanding of the implications of the decisions, and whose input is translated through a chain of Chinese whispers to people who do not really understand the processes they are meant to support. What results is a convoluted configuration of standards, IT systems, and processes. This is the tragedy of schools: everyone working very hard and with dedication on something that will make no one happy and proud. This focus on the objective of cost leads away from the underlying objective of good education. Arguments focus on the standard products that can be purchased and on the forms that need filling out for the purchase. Standard and process become the objective. Whereas not even the product that needs to be purchased is the objective. It is a means toward better learning and teaching. But neither learning and teaching, nor the product are any longer the focus of the discussion. Everyone is concerned with the standard list and the forms, how to comply, or how to circumvent them. Exhausted by the system, teachers give up and adjust their teaching to fit the products that are on the standards list. Schools thus end up with large, inflexible systems and fixed processes.

Some people might counter that the picture I paint is too bleak. And there are certainly good examples of support processes and systems that work like hand in glove with learning and teaching. I would invite everyone doubting my view to go to the classroom and actually observe and follow the teachers as they work. Do so over an extended period of time for longer timeslots, so not a quick visit or a short interview, but over several days for many hours. Follow the whole process from end toward the beginning. Try to trace all steps, and with each and every step ask how that step contributes to better learning. Avoid interpreting activities from the standard framework of "how we do things around here," "what we think makes sense."

From the Lean Education point of view, there is nothing wrong with standards and processes. Quite to the contrary, Lean Education promotes process thinking and advocates standards. But there are a few key conditions regarding processes and standards.

1. They always derive from the definition of value
2. They take a holistic view on the process from start until the very end to determine what is effective and efficient
3. They are owned by the people in the process and can be changed by them according to need.

The staff working in the process owns the standards. They are responsible to achieve the goals set for the process and will be held accountable. With this responsibility also comes the ownership. All too often the standards are owned by someone else and focused on a local goal rather than the overarching value delivered by the process. The various parts of the process and the staff working on it are disconnected.

DISCONNECTION

The disconnection mentioned above follows from a siloed organization that starts in large institutions at the very top of the organization with a rector for academic affairs and a director for all professional services. These are each further sub-divided into departments and teams based on expertise (finance, HR, IT, etc.) and scientific domains (social sciences, life sciences, engineering, etc.). This disconnection is quite literal in the sense that they are physically located in different locations and academic staff might not know how to reach out to professional services colleagues. They are separated by contact information that can be hard to find, by service desks that mediate requests and formal procedures.

One of the things that strikes me in every Lean initiative we run is the lack of understanding of what colleagues elsewhere in the process are doing. "I never knew you did this,"; "If only I had known that you needed this information, I could have easily helped," are exclamations that are often heard. This is not to blame people. In Lean, the focus of improvement is the process. If people cannot do their job properly, there is probably something wrong in the process. In this case, support processes, and learning and teaching are "hidden" from each other. The student journey goes across departments and teams, but is not made visible to all, let alone "owned" by someone who has the task to connect all staff involved. The disconnection is in part driven by principles of economies-of-scale and standardization that drive the professional services departments.

This leads to specialization and grouping of similar functions in dedicated teams. As the members of these teams work together more often than with the teaching staff, the atmosphere gets self-referential. The means, that is the materials, procedures, and the standards become the goals.

An excellent way to connect the different realms is by drawing together the customer journey. The student journey refers to all activities a student and his parents undertake, from the start of looking for information to decide in which school to enroll until graduation and all activities in between. It indicates when students, their parents, and others reach out to the school, what they ask and need, which information is exchanged, in what format, etc. The counterpart of the student journey is the organization journey. It depicts the steps the school undertakes to meet the needs of students and other stakeholders. The teachers and concierges are the "frontline" staff with whom students and parents mostly interact. But they in turn rely on their colleagues from professional services. They execute the work "behind the stages" to make everything run smoothly. It will show an intricate, complex web of activities, products, and services. It is an extremely rich picture that provides both an overview and the details of the process. This exercise highlights what the school is for, creates understanding of where value is added, and where time is wasted. But it also helps teams to connect again if this picture is drawn together. Also in smaller schools, where the disconnection is possibly less pronounced, the process will still be complex. And, if the disconnection is not in the organizational chart, it is a definitively a mental one.

SUPPORT PROCESSES IN SUPPORT OF EDUCATION

"No distractions!" This should be the focus of professional services. The director of one of the educational institutions I worked with once said that professional services should be like water from the tap: you turn it on when you need it, doing so without thinking, in the certainty that water will pour out, clean and clear. Professional services should be unobtrusive, distracting no energy, allowing students and teachers to focus on learning and teaching. This is a tall order, and if done well at times an ungrateful one, for few people will notice. Yet it is also a rewarding and indispensable job. Without it, no teaching, however good, can come to full potential. Professional services nurture students and teachers so they can reach their full potential. They are the soil and water, to stick with the metaphor, in which talents of our students can come to full blossom.

CLASS(?)ROOMS THAT STIMULATE LEARNING

Throughout history, thinking and learning have too often been framed as activities done by individuals, on their own. When people think about thinking, they often think of Rodin's famous sculpture *The Thinker*, which shows a lone individual, sitting by himself, in deep contemplation. Of course, some thinking happens this way, but most doesn't. Most of the time, thinking is integrated with doing: We think in the context of interacting with things, playing with things, and creating things. And most thinking is done in connection with other people: We share ideas, get reaction from other people, build upon one another's ideas.[5]

When learning strategies differ, when the type of learning activities changes throughout a day of teaching and learning, even sometimes at the same time, then we need rooms, buildings, and environments that can be changed easily: spaces that are owned by the people that are using them for the time being, spaces that allow things to happen that might not have been anticipated let alone intended, spaces that challenge and facilitate, and spaces that invite different behaviors and stimulate curiosity. Most physical spaces where learning is happening have fixed perimeters, equipment that is hard to adapt except for some tables and chairs that can be moved around. They either have been over-designed to such an extent that there's little freedom for the users or constrained by economic considerations of costs to such an extent that there are few options, but the ones for which they have been economically optimized.

What do they look like, these more inviting, stimulating rooms? The first key element is ownership. The occupants of the room should be able to put the room to use in a way they see fit. By having overly strict structures like a dais, like fixed walls and furniture, students and teachers alike are not invited to take that ownership. When they do, they are restricted by these fixtures. So, the next key element is objects, equipment, etc. that allow the division and joining of spaces to smaller and larger ones. This includes elements

---

[5] Mitchel Resnick, *Lifelong Kindergarten: Cultivating Creativity Through Projects, Passion, Peers, and Play* (Cambridge, MA: MIT Press, 2017), 91.

CLASS(?)ROOMS THAT STIMULATE
LEARNING (Continued)

that reduce or magnify sound, control light, and routes movement of people. Storage cabinets on wheels with sides that can be used as white boards are an example. Third key element is the presence of sets of instruments, tools, and materials that have multiple, not clearly delineated applications. This might include high tech materials like screens that are easily movable, high capacity connection to hook on external experts via video connection, and sensors, programmable machines like Raspberry Pi. It should also include low tech materials and tools like scissors, felt pens, papers, magazines, wires, etc.

It is often feared that these more adaptable rooms are expensive. When some rooms are organized more inviting and flexible, they are the exception and for showcase purposes. They are considered too expensive for wholesale adoption. This is an illustration of separation of different functions (purchasing and teaching) within the school. The requirements for classrooms are a watered-down compromise based on an old view of teaching paired with misguided economic thinking and a lack of creativity. The aim should be to foster learning.

The fear that such rooms are too expensive is based on old economic thinking. If a room is more expensive (and I argue that they need not be), but generates better learning that should be worthwhile. Rooms are based on a few standards so that the purchasing department can order large numbers of items such as screens, chairs, tables, etc. The unit price is lower. But as a consequence that actual usage is lower, occupancy rates are lower, and the overall costs are higher.[6] Room occupation rates are often dramatically

---

[6] A good illustration of this thinking happened when I discussed the New Engineers approach which has such elaborate rooms. The dean of a university objected that such an approach would be too expensive. Later, when we walked through the school building—it was a regular week day at 15:00—on one floor of a wing there were already ten classrooms that were not occupied. The costs of having to build that wing, of not using those rooms, would easily outweigh the costs of five new style classrooms that would have a higher occupancy rate. And more importantly, facilitate better, more effective learning.

CLASS(?)ROOMS THAT STIMULATE
LEARNING (Continued)

low (easily as low as 20%–30%). This mean that a lot of times the rooms are empty. This is due to unfitness for some teaching purposes, e.g., a computer room not useable for regular classroom teaching, by limited teaching hours, by complicated scheduling that leads to over claiming of rooms just to make sure that you have a room, etc. By investing a little more in the classroom, they could be rented out during outside school hours, during exam period in which there is no teaching, etc. Thus, different uses would generate additional income that covers the costs of extra equipment or facilities. If learning and teaching are more effective, the number of teaching hours might be reduced, or we can generate extra value by teaching more. We need new economic thinking to make sure we do not waste scarce budget on ill-fitted buildings and classrooms.

For our minor course with 120 students at the HAN, we claimed and got a large auditorium-like room that was only irregularly used (thinking of cost!). It was stacked with moveable furniture. Some of the furniture was cumbersome, and we got it stuffed away with the help of some concierges. The room was somewhat noisy, and teachers found it hard to be heard, so we installed some simple audio equipment that was on hand for conferences. Students (help) reconfigure the room during class. The class size is 60, so we sometimes split the group. Which makes the interactive, changing teaching formats over the course of a single class easier. Actually, 60 students is a challenging, but manageable size. We do traditional classroom teaching interlaced with small group activity, playing games, and presentations. Walls are used to put up presentations, larger tables facilitate meetings of smaller groups, small tables and chairs are arranged for note taking during lecturing intervals, and put aside or rearranged when reverting to games or small group activities. This change from the traditional room with fixed, immovable furniture did cost us nothing except some time and good relationships with the concierges and the improvisation skills and a fearless jump of our colleagues into an unknown format and room lay-out.

**CLASS(?)ROOMS THAT STIMULATE
LEARNING (Continued)**

A last word on terminology. The word "classroom" is associated with a rigid way of teaching and learning, "a room where school lessons are taught." The room itself is limited, a part of a larger construct or building, separated by walls, floor, and ceiling. It should be a permeable space where learning takes place, a space that is open to the world. This is why I find the term learning space so much more appealing.

10

Lean Education Case: New Engineers—Enterprising Engineers with a Creative Mind-Set

Lejla Brouwer-Hadzialic, Hilde van der Geld, and Vincent Wiegel

INTRODUCTION

This chapter describes how at New Engineers Lean Education is being applied. At New Engineers, new pedagogical approaches, new technologies, and Lean Education are combined to provide a new way of learning and teaching. It is the integral statement of the New Engineers vision and approach as we actually use and share it with everyone involved in New Engineers. It has been integrated as a case in this book to illustrate how the ideas that are discussed can be applied. Of course, there are many different ways in which that can be done. Many of these ideas will have made, in part, their way into the classroom already. It is far from a claim to novelty. What is novel is the radical and integral approach. That will work for some, and not for others. We hope readers will draw inspiration from it and use what they need.

New Engineers is a post-bachelor study. It is accredited by industry, but not formally by the ministry of education in the Netherlands. We didn't seek accreditation in the early stages because that is prohibitively expensive for a small private institution. Moreover, in the early stages, we wanted the freedom to experiment without restrictions or the fear of losing the accreditation. The set-up is such that in the current practice accreditation would have been very unlikely.

New Engineers aims to help engineers of all ages to grow as "Enterprising engineers with a creative mind-set." The fast-paced changes in technology require continuous updating of knowledge and know-how, but also the development of new skills and the honing of certain attitudes. When done right, our engineers will not only be good engineers, but also very effective engineers.

The curriculum focuses on five knowledge domains of which technology is the foremost. The other four are business development, leadership, innovation management, and change management. These are supplemented by a skill set of five skills.

- Learning—ability to define to needs, formulate learning strategies, initiate own learning
- Enterprising—seeing and seizing opportunities in face of uncertainty and odds
- Leading—being aware of own motives and those of others and take action with and/or despite others to achieve intended goals
- Creating—seeing opportunities and connections where others see none
- Communicating—ability to convey and receive intentions and information to and from others in a way that is conducive to goals.

The curriculum is complemented by five core attitudes.

- Boundless—not accepting boundaries till tested
- Curious—drive to know and understand
- Disciplined—restraint toward own passions in light of intended goals
- Eager—intense desire and impatience to act toward intended goal
- Social—awareness of and belonging to groups and dynamics, understanding of self in relation to group.

At New Engineers, we deliver a learning space where students have the opportunity to grow in ways that fit their personal needs best. Everything is organized around this objective. We have pursued the idea to its extreme consequences. Since each student and each new cohort has their own needs and ambitions, we cannot and do not want to fix the program in advance. This means that subject-matters, lesson formats, etc. are not fixed. Therefore, we do not know who the best teacher will be and what will be the best location. Hence, New Engineers has no fixed premises nor any teachers. Based on the group of students, we determine what expertise is needed. We then hire locations and invite experts based on what is required. Our students will also work at a host company where they can apply what they have learned and determine what they would like and need to learn.

In this chapter, we describe in seven sections both the philosophy of New Engineers and the design principles we use when organizing for learning.

VISION—TO OUR STUDENTS, STAFF, AND OTHER STAKEHOLDERS

New Engineers: New Engineers and its students are shamelessly ambitious and committed to discovering new ways of creating products and services, in ways that serve the organizations we work for and the community we are a part of.

We have a joyful way of looking at the world, and technology in particular. Curious and driven, we explore the possibilities it offers and share those generously with the people around us. The New Engineers is a challenging, but also a safe place for people to work, learn, and teach.

The students: New Engineers students are the owners of their learning process. Through critical self-reflection and strong internal drive, they push themselves to the limit and beyond.

They enjoy technology and learning, applying theory to solve practical problems. Curious, enterprising, and investigative, they develop into game changers in the domain of technology and business.

They look beyond the obvious and will not accept "impossible." They are eager and have a strong sense of dedication and discipline.

The staff: The staff of the New Engineers support the students in two separate capacities. They are international experts in their domain and contribute specific knowledge. As coaches, they support the students in their learning process, integrating all and applying it.

Our staff are also students. They keep on learning as domain experts, and as teachers. Moreover, they learn from the students. They share the students' joy in learning and their drive to explore new ways of learning.

Student home company: The companies students work for play an important role in their studies. It offers trust and a position in which students can learn, apply, and practice what they have learned. A place to experiment and innovate.

Our View on Learning

We strive to create a rich learning environment. A rich learning environment is a comprehensive instructional system that:

- Promotes study and investigation within authentic (i.e., realistic, meaningful, relevant, complex, and information-rich) contexts
- Encourages the growth of student responsibility, initiative, decision making, and intentional learning

- Cultivates an atmosphere of cooperative learning among students and teachers
- Utilizes dynamic, generative teaming activities that promote high-level thinking processes (i.e., analysis, synthesis, problem solving, experimentation, creativity, and examination of topics from multiple perspectives) to help students integrate new knowledge with old knowledge and thereby create rich and complex knowledge structures
- Assesses student progress in content and learning to learn through realistic tasks and performances.

LEARNING AND TEACHING AT THE NEW ENGINEERS IS BASED ON THE FOLLOWING SIX PRINCIPLES

1. *Learning in a rich learning environment*: Learning doesn't only happen in an academic environment. Learning becomes meaningful when the student is able to learn while working and directly in contact with the work field. We believe that in order to create a rich learning environment for our students and teachers, we have to connect different ways of learning and create different places where students learn. We combine learning in and by: (a) working in an engineering organization, (b) learning new knowledge and skills during the New Engineers' academic program, and (c) learning by creating new products and processes

2. *We learn from theory and in practice*: The curriculum provides deep theoretical materials that take our students to the actual forefront of knowledge in their fields. These insights allow them a different view on the practice in which they work. They apply what they have learned developing products and services, finding new business segments, and creating alliances with suppliers and customers. All in such a way that they deliver value to the customer and contribute to the organization they are working for

3. *Learning is an individual and a social activity*: We recognize that each student has his own preferred learning strategies and his own special strengths and weaknesses. We believe that the learning and teaching processes should allow and build upon these differences. That can mean facilitating preferred learning strategies, but also the contrary. But whatever it is, it is a considered choice. Students work and study together with other students, colleagues, and teachers inside and outside their network.

They are always part of a team and often of multiple teams. Molding dissimilar people into effective groups is an important part of the learning environment. Teaching is developed to specifically address the learning process in individual, small group, and large group settings

4. *Learning is motion*: While learning, our students develop themselves as a person, developing their qualities and talents. Students absorb new knowledge on selected domains of expertise, their organization, and the economic domain in which they work. Innovation sets things in motion. Sometimes it requires guts to get moving and move people. Students will meet resistance as part of the changing and growing. It requires mental and physical strength. Physical exercise is good for learning and for developing mental and physical perseverance; it activates their brains and provides them with the necessary energy. We challenge them to move, to accelerate, and slowdown in time to recuperate

5. *Learning is an active process directed by the student*: New Engineers offers its students an inspiring and challenging environment in which they are the director of the way in which they learn, what they need to learn, and how to organize their learning. With their active and enterprising mind-sets, they determine, supported by us, what knowledge and expertise they need. Our students share their experience with others and contribute to the learning of all

6. *Learning requires critical self-reflection*: Students develop best when critically and constructively reflecting on their actions. We support them questioning themselves and their fellow students on the situation in which they work and learn. Reflection becomes second nature. Together with other students they analyze and evaluate learning experiences and theory.

PEDAGOGY AND ORGANIZATION

The way we teach and learn, and the way we organize teaching and learning, is ultimately a reflection of technological and economic developments. It should reflect the changing needs of society, companies, their employees and hence our students. Learning and teaching must also separately reflect and fulfill the needs of the students and employees as autonomous human beings with their aspirations that might and might not be related to the direct needs of businesses and society. The curriculum, the subject matters, and methods are derived from the developments in society and industry. ...learning as such grows more important, especially the strategic importance of learning for an organization and content matter addressed.[i]

Table 10.1 shows how we derive both subject matters taught and the skills, attitudes, and knowledge that need to be developed and acquired.

Our pedagogical vision is based on the work of several, current thought leaders on education:

- Filip Dochy and co-workers, *High impact learning*[2]—overall vision teaching and learning and teaching methods
- John Hattie, *Visible learning*[3]—overall teaching, organization
- Dylan Wiliam—*Formative assessment*[4]—role and importance of assessments in learning
- Manon Ruijters—*Liefde voor leren*[5]—overall teaching, business context
- Simon Kavanagh/KaosPilot, *Vision Backcasting*[6,7]—Vision Backcasting method to educational development
- Vincent Wiegel, Lejla Brouwer-Hadzialic[8]—*Lean Education.*

These are not arbitrarily chosen approaches, but approaches that are complementary and relevant to the New Engineers philosophy, the students, the workplace, and the companies.

Teaching is about (1) defining and finding out where students want to go in their learning, (2) finding out where they currently are, (3) finding out how to progress from 2 to 1.[9]

---

[1] John Hattie, *Visible Learning for Teachers: Maximizing Impact on Learning* (New York: Taylor & Francis Group, 2012), 29.

[2] Filip Dochy and Mien Segers, *Creating Impact Through Future Learning: The High Impact Learning That Lasts (HILL) Model* (London, UK: Taylor & Francis Group, 2018).

[3] Hattie, *Visible Learning for Teachers: Maximizing Impact on Learning*.

[4] Dylan Wiliam, *Embedded Formative Assessment* (Bloomington, IN: Solution Tree Press, 2011).

[5] Manon Ruijters, *Liefde Voor Leren: Over Diversiteit van Leren En Ontwikkelen in En van Organisaties* (Deventer the Netherlands: Vakmedianet, 2006).

[6] Christer Windeløv-Lidzélius and Kirstine Bauning, *The Kaospilots 20/20* (Aarhus Denmark: KaosPilots, 2011).

[7] www.KaosPilot.dk accessed May 17th, 2019.

[8] Vincent Wiegel and Lejla Brouwer Hadzialic, "Lessons from Higher Education: Adapting Lean Six Sigma to Account for Structural Differences in Application Domains," *International Journal of Six Sigma and Competitive Advantage* 9, no. 1 (2015): 72, doi: 10.1504/IJSSCA.2015.070104; Vincent Wiegel and Lejla Brouwer-Hadzialic, "Lean Education," in *The Routledge Companion to Lean Management*, ed. T H Netland and D J Powell, Routledge Companions in Business, Management and Accounting (New York: Routledge, 2017), 422–434.

[9] Wiliam, *Embedded Formative Assessment* (Solution Tree Press, 2011), 45.

TABLE 10.1

Drivers for Education

Trends (why)	Requires (why)	Characteristics/Demands (what)	Method (how)
1. Developments in technology, economy, and society, *Influence 2)*	Communications technologies with large numbers of distributes devices generating enormous amounts of data; allowing fast reconfiguration of business networks and economic transactions;...	Growing complexity Distributed activities across organizations, inter-organization cooperation, and decision-making	Only for study and educational organization
2. The position and capabilities of companies, which in turn *drives 3)*	Companies are more networked, need to be agile and adaptive	Less hierarchical New modes of leading/managing	Only for study and educational organization
3. The things employees are required to known, execute, and master, which they are taught to some extent	Apply known technologies in new contexts; formulate and design products and services with new partners in unknown market segments Functional job-flexibility Professional as director of job Working in multi-disciplinary teams Interpersonal effectiveness	Overview over changing constellations—relating self and colleagues and context Ability to see trends Connect to different (corporate) cultures fast—social Flexibility Ability to apply acquired know-how, skills, and attitudes in varying situations Leadership Meta-cognitive abilities Self-efficacy	Only for study and educational organization

(Continued)

TABLE 10.1 (Continued)

Drivers for Education

Trends (why)	Requires (why)	Characteristics/Demands (what)	Method (how)
4. In studies that need to address these changing needs, provided within and supported by 5)	Study that provides a theoretical and practical approach toward building, maintaining, and changing relationships in business context Learning how to learn what is required in new situations Working and learning in teams Communications skills Problem solving abilities Acquiring and selecting relevant information	Models of companies and networks Study starts from real problem, challenge that students relate to Learner agency Relates to student drivers and interests Social interaction Practice relevant practicing	To be determined—input for curriculum
5. An educational organization that facilitates this study through knowledge, settings that stimulate the acquisition of new knowledge, abilities	Reflects and supports similar fast moving and reconfiguring networks of knowledge providers Different teaching-learning models Business model based on new learning teaching requirements	Agility—provide content based on need just-in-time Adaptivity Personalized education Value-based pricing Entry selection Participation of companies in core of education High(er) demands on knowledge and skills of teachers Varying modes of learning (from individual to teams to large group)	To be determined—input for curriculum

Most, if not all, people will subscribe to this definition. The key question is whether we really live this and how we put it into everyday practice. To guide and operationalize this view at New Engineers, we use Lean Education as a method to organize our educational system.

The important first step starts before admission, namely, establishing, clarifying, sharing learning intentions, and criteria for success. Without this step, learning and teaching will be ineffective. The set-up of the learning environment and the teaching-forms and subject-matters will be based on this shared understanding by all stakeholders.

In teaching and learning, the focus is on finding learning strategies that work for the student. This requires a conscious effort on the part of both student and teacher in experimenting with what works and what doesn't. The student becomes the owner of her learning. Being conscious of her learning, the student will work on various learning strategies. This includes enlisting peers as instructional sources as well as being an instructor to other students. The teacher plays an important role in this learning to learn, as well as in providing feedback and monitoring, together with the students progress. Particularly important is finding evidence of learning. Ultimately, an important task of a teacher at New Engineers is the creation of an effective learning environment that engages students and teacher alike and that progresses the learning toward the intended outcomes.

At New Engineers, formative assessments are part and parcel of the ongoing teaching and learning. Students are actively involved in assessing their own work as well as that of others. The focus is not on attaining a grade, but on understanding what makes a good work good. And from that understanding, progress further. Summative assessments are used sparingly. As part of the formative assessments, giving and receiving feedback is key. This is an ability and attitude that will receive full attention at the beginning of the study, as it is a necessary condition for ownership and progress of learning. Feedback must adhere to a few key requirements: (1) enforcing a view of ability as progressive instead of fixed, (2) relate to the learning goals, and (3) provide a recipe for action going forward.[10] All students regardless of their achievements at any time should keep learning.

Roles and Responsibilities

New Engineers engages experts in two capacities: as subject matter expert and as coach. Coaches at New Engineers work with groups of students. Their

---

[10] Wiliam, 119–121.

main responsibility is to support students in their learning. This includes, but is not limited to establishing learning goals, evaluating learning strategies, and integrating all materials taught and learned. Subject-matter experts are recognized international experts on their specific domain. They might come from academia and industry alike. Their primary responsibility is to bring the recent views, theories, and methods to the students. With guidance from New Engineers, they will present their knowledge in ways compatible with the pedagogical views of New Engineers. They will be open to and actively seek cooperation with the students.

DESIGN OF CURRICULUM AND LESSONS: THE GUIDING PRINCIPLES

The curriculum has been designed in close co-operation with companies, former students, and students. Thus, it reflects the needs of the intended beneficiaries of the study. It uses the concepts as described in the art & craft of learning spaces. At New Engineers, the curriculum and lessons follow the six principles described in Section 2. For each principle, we have devised a couple of guiding questions that our educational designers and experts can use when working on a new module.

Principles and guiding questions to the learning designers and teachers:

Principle 1 Learning in a rich learning environment
Questions:
- How does the module promote study and investigation within authentic contexts?
- How does the module encourage the growth of students' responsibility, initiative, decision making, and intentional learning?
- How do you cultivate an atmosphere of cooperative learning among students and teachers?
- What learning activities does the module offer to help students integrate new knowledge, skills, and attitude?
- How can you build in realistic tasks and performances to assess student progress in content and learning to learn?

Principle 2 Learning from theory and in practice
Questions:
- What theory does the student need to master?
- What knowledge sources can you use and provide?

- How can you involve the students working context in the module?
- What assignments can the student do at school and on the job to apply this theory?
- How can you use the learning experience of the student?

Principle 3 Learning as an individual and a social activity
Questions:

- How can you make a balanced mix of working/learning individually, in small groups, and in large groups?
- Is the formation of the small group of influence on the learning process (for instance, are students free to choose a group, do you group students with similar background or with different background)?
- Do you manage the formation of groups?

Principle 4 Learning is motion
Questions:

- How do you create motion in thinking and learning?
- How can you monitor the motion in thinking and learning of the student?
- How can you relate to the learning needs of the student?
- How can sport be a metaphor for your program and used as input for the learning (experience)?
- How can you use it to support the learning process?

Principle 5 Learning is an active process directed by the student
Questions:

- How does the program leave space for the learner agency of the student?
- How to do you balance between receiving information, gathering relevant information, and applying this information?

Principle 6 Learning requires critical self-reflection
Questions:

- How and when in the program do you support self-reflection of the students?
- How can you use sports to exercise self-reflection?
- How and when can you use feedback/feedforward to support the learning process of the student?
- How and when do students give each other feedback on their development? And how can you support the students to reflect critically on the feedback they receive?

DESIGN OF CURRICULUM AND LESSONS: THE LEARNING ARCH

We describe the total program and each part/module of the program as a learning arch. Each arch has a beginning (SET), middle part (HOLD), and a completion (LAND). The space that arises underneath the arch is the learning space, that's where the learning takes place. Both teacher and student are creators of that learning space. The teacher facilitates the learning of the students. Therefore, she designs a framework of knowledge, skills, attitudes, and also a variety of possible ways of learning (lecture, discussion, assignments individually or in groups, presentations, excursions, etc.).

The drawing below is a learning arch for 1 week. As you can see, the week has one large arch with a SET, HOLD, and LAND. Also, each day has a small arch with a SET, HOLD, and LAND (Figure 10.1 and Table 10.2).

To support the design of a module we use a simple format (Table 10.3).

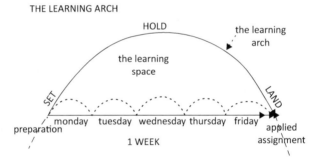

FIGURE 10.1

New Engineers learning arch.

TABLE 10.2

New Engineers Learning Arch

SET	*The start-up of the learning process.* Focus on learning intentions, desired outcomes, program for this week/day, check in, agenda, and time.
HOLD	*The learning process "in action."* This is the part where the students find information, discuss theory, apply theory in assignments, reflect on their learning, cooperate, etc.
LAND	*The completion of the (formal) learning process.* At the end of each arch, we take time to "wrap up." To look back and reflect on the learning process and become aware of what we have learned and how we did this. The learning process will continue also after the week for the student as he/she applies the knowledge, skills, and attitude on the job.

TABLE 10.3

Module Definition Sheet

Module name—

Key topics—

Key questions—

Skills—Knowledge—Attitude

S:

K:

A:

Format

(*for example*)

- Self-study
- Classroom practice and/or real-life practice
- Small group work
- Group and individual exercise
- Reflection
- Intervision

Assignments

(*for example*)

1. Read materials (4 hours)
2. Select a topic for practice (2 hours)
3. Prepare for practice (three times) (3×3 hours)
4. Execute plan and receive feedback (4 hours)
5. Intervision (2 hours)

Sources

Success criteria

(*for example*)

- The student understands the methodology being applied
- The student is able to build an understanding of customer requests and outline a preliminary proposal for the intervention
- The student is able to design sessions and elements of sessions using the methodology
- The student can lead sessions successfully and is able to reflect on his/her own strengths and weaknesses in front of the group.

Grading methods

(*for example*)

- Quality and effect of sessions designed
- Feedback received and self-assessment
- Participants/customer feedback.

Required effort (estimated average)

(*for example*)

Self-study 20 hours

Assignment 34 hours

FOUR STEP APPROACH FOR DESIGNING LEARNING ARCHES[11]

To help you design the learning arch of your module, we describe four steps. We give a short description of "what to do." In some steps, we have specific requirements we use for the New Engineers program, we ask you to use these requirements in the design of the module. At the end of every step, we list the results of the step.

Step 1: learning goals/intentions

The pedagogical experts from which we draw our inspiration all urge us to always begin with the end in mind. Using the learning arches as a design model for education compels you to do the same. First, look at the end of the learning arch: what have the students achieved after finishing this module?

- What is the goal of the module?
- What are the desired outcomes of this module?
- What are the students going to learn?
- What new knowledge, skills, and attitude will they acquire?

It results in a list of learning goals. These learning goals give focus for the *what* (content—knowledge/skills/attitude) and the *how* (learning methods) of the module. It is the fundament you're going to build the program on.

Requirements: Next to the knowledge students learn in the New Engineers program, we focus on developing five key *skills & attitudes* toward a game changer career.

What skills and attitudes do the students acquire in this module?

Select at least one (but preferably more) skill and one attitude that students will actively work on during the module. In the learning goals/intentions, you can describe *how* they will work on these skills and attitudes (Table 10.4).

---

[11] For all experts and teachers involved, we have set-up a guideline to help them design their contributions. This section is an integral reproduction of those instructions.

TABLE 10.4

New Engineers Skills and Attitudes

Skills	Attitudes
Learning: Ability to define needs, formulate learning strategies, initiate own learning	*Boundless*: Not accepting boundaries till tested
Enterprising: Seeing and seizing opportunities in face of uncertainty and odds	*Curious*: Drive to know and understand
Leading: Being aware of own motives and those of others and take action with and/or in spite of others to achieve intended goals	*Disciplined*: Restraint toward own passions in light of intended goals
Creating: Seeing opportunities and connections where others see none	*Eager*: Intense desire and impatience to act toward intended goal
Communicating: Ability to convey and receive intentions and information to and from others in a way that is conducive to goals	*Social*: Awareness of and belonging to groups and dynamics, understanding of self in relation to group

Result of step 1:
- a list of learning goals
- a list of the knowledge, skills, and attitudes students work on in the module.

Step 2: mapping the starting point

In step one, you have set the goals, where we are going. To design how to get there (create a learning space), it's important to know what the starting point is and to proceed to jointly (you and the students) establish the starting point.

- What do students already know about this subject? (knowledge)
- What have they already mastered about the skills and attitudes?
- What have they learned in previous modules and is it possible/ necessary to connect with that knowledge?
- What different backgrounds do the students have/what kind of companies do they work for?

Some of the information might not be available at the moment you start designing your module. For instance, the specific information about the students. In that case, you can describe the assumptions you make on the starting point of the students. As soon as the required information is available, you can check and see if it has consequences for you program. Additional information will be provided by New Engineers.

Results of step 2:
- a short description of the starting point
- information or assumptions you have about the students.

Step 3: designing the learning arch

If we know where we're going (goals) and who is going with us (students), we can start designing the learning arch. In this step, you'll design and develop the program of the week and of each individual day. And before you start designing: also read step 4 about assessment. In that way you can design the program and formative assessment, both at once (Table 10.5).

TABLE 10.5

Sequence of Creating a Module

PREPARATION	Prior to the week/module at New Engineers, students prepare themselves for the module. In that way, students have a shared knowledge base on the subject of the module. Students prepare for example by: • Reading relevant literature/articles • Watching a documentary/TED/movie • Making an assignment • Taking a test • Interviewing people in their company/collecting data in their own company • Following a specific massive open online course (MOOC) • Etc.
Requirement	Max. 8 hours of preparation (reading 5–8 pages per hour appr.) Preferably a mix of (online) sources
To do:	Make a description of the preparation for the students Including (online) sources
SET	At the start of the module (and at the beginning of each day), we take time to make a proper start. We focus on where we come from (for example: previous module, experience, day before), where we stand now, and what is ahead of us. We look at: • (learning) Intentions or goals • Desired outcomes • Agenda • Rules and roles (how do we play the game/work together) • Time. And we take time to Check-in: give each participant a moment to share with the group what's on his/her mind and actively "check in."

(Continued)

TABLE 10.5 (*Continued*)

Sequence of Creating a Module

Requirements	No specific requirements
	SET of the module is planned on Monday afternoon
	(note: there is also a LAND activity on Monday morning, organized by New Engineers. Focus of Monday morning is mainly looking back, collecting learning results of previous period/learning arch).
To do:	Design a SET for the module and a short SET for each day. SET for module and day 1 is one.
HOLD	This is an important and intensive phase of the learning process. In this phase, students do all sorts of activities to learn, gain information and knowledge, experiment, explore, practice, share, reflect, etc.
	Challenge for the designer is to make a balanced mix of learning methods. Including enough space for the students to be in control of their own learning process and to create their own learning experiences and content.
	Questions that can help you design the "HOLD phase":
	• Use the learning goals as your starting point. What knowledge, skills, and attitude will the students work on?
	• In what order will the content/subjects be treated? Or does the student decide the order—in that case, how do you facilitate this process?
	• What information/content is given (by lecture, presentation)?
	• What assignments do students work on to apply the content? Is it an individual, small group, or large group assignment?
	• How do they share the learning results with each other?
	• How can you encourage students to give each other feedback on the results and their development (peer feedback)?
	• Do you want to use sport(s) for self-reflection or to compare the outcomes of a sport exercise with the learning goals and/or the progress?
	• What forms of assessment can you use (see step 4)?
	*Check-out the description about the "Format for a week schedule" below
Requirements	• For lecture/presentation of theory: blocks of max. 1.5 hours with a max of 3 hours a day
	• The mix between passive (listening) and active (applying, working, discussing, creating, playing, sports, etc.) learning is required
	• The program leaves enough space for the students to (partly) design their own learning process
	• About 15% of the time in the module is used for reflection and (peer) feedback on the results and development of the student.

(Continued)

TABLE 10.5 (*Continued*)

Sequence of Creating a Module

To do:	• Completed format/schedule for the program of the week • Presentations/other materials • Short description of assignments used during the week • Overview of supplies/material needed to perform the education.
LAND	At the end of the module (and at the end of each day), we take time to "wrap up." We focus on what we achieved and how we achieved it. We look back at the goals we had when we "SET" off this week or day and evaluate our progress and process. How do you evaluate the learning process and learning results at the end of the day/module? And we take time to Check-out: give each participant a moment to share with the group what's on his/her mind and actively "check out."
Requirements	No specific requirements LAND of the module is planned on Friday end of the morning. (note: there is also a SET activity on Friday afternoon, organized by New Engineers. Focus on Friday afternoon is mainly evaluating and looking forward to the next module).
To do:	Design a LAND for the module and a short LAND for each day. LAND for module and day 5 is one.
ASSIGNMENT	The learning doesn't stop for the students at the end of the week. They take all they have learned with them to their own work at the company they work for. There they will apply, explore, deepen, etc. the knowledge, skills, and attitudes. To give them a focus, we want to give them an assignment to work on. • What result do you expect when the student is back at New Engineers? We reflect on this when we SET the following New Engineers' week • How can the students apply what they have learned during the week in their own work? What assignment could be appropriate? • What literature/articles or other sources can they read or use to learn more about the subject? • How can the students (in any possible way) share their learning process, progress, and results with the other students?
Requirement	Max. 24 hours "off the job" and max. 24 hours "on the job" to make the assignment Students share the results of the assignment. Students give and receive feedback on their progress and result of the assignment by fellow students and teacher
To do:	Make a description of the assignment for the students Including (online) sources

Format for a week schedule

To make the puzzle of all the elements you can put in the module, we made a format you can use. You'll find the format (Excel file) as a separate document. In the format, you'll find a partly empty schedule for 1 week (Figure 10.2).

You can fill in the blanks with the different puzzle parts (underneath the schedule) such as:

- Content/themes
- Assignment
- Sport
- Reflection
- Free (learning) space
- Formative assessment.

In the Excel file you can drag the blocks into the schedule and put them in right place and order. You can also change the length of the blocks (standard time of one block is 1.5 hours, but feel free to make a block shorter or longer except for the lectures and presentations).

The program also has several fixed parts:

- *Breakfast*: each day starts with a collective breakfast. From 8 till 8:45. Program starts at 9.00
- *Lunch*: 1 hour, time depends on the program (can vary each day)
- *Supper*: 1 hour, time depends on the program (can vary each day)
- *Sport*: 1 hour (incl. changing/refreshing), can be scheduled at any time of the day fitting the program
- *SET of the week*: Monday morning: a collective start of the week, looking back at the last period, collecting learning outcomes, sharing insights, etc. This part of the week is organized by New Engineers
- *LAND of the week*: Friday afternoon: a collective ending of the week, looking back at the last week, collecting learning results, making a translation or transfer to the work context, and evaluating the week. This part of the week is organized by New Engineers
- *Inspiration shot*: Wednesday evening: New Engineers organizes an inspirational activity for the students
- *On Tuesday and Thursday evening*: students can work individually or in groups on assignments.

You have 6 clock hours a day except for Monday and Friday on which you have 3 clock hours.

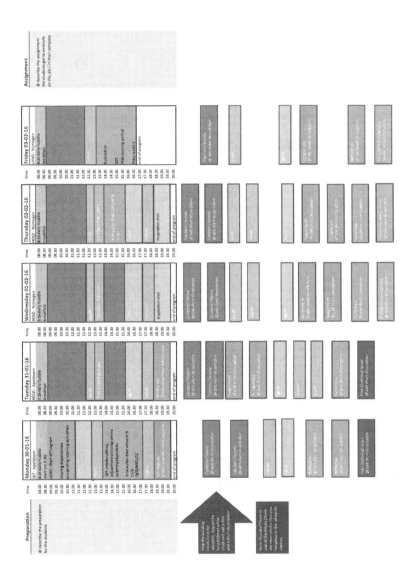

FIGURE 10.2

Building blocks for a week of teaching.

All together, the puzzle parts make the program for 1 week. In the Excel file you'll also find a (fictional) example of a completed schedule. Please use the module description (Table 10.3) to summarize your module program.

It's possible that the framework at some point doesn't fit the ideas or wishes you have for the program you're designing. In that case, let's discuss the plans you have and find a fitting solution. The format is intended as an aid to help you design the program, but should in no way kill creativity of other innovative learning interventions.

Students configure their own program. This means that your module might not be attended by all students and/or only for a specific part. In designing a module, allow for the possibility to attend the morning only. This gives two options: students specializing on your topic attending the morning and afternoon program and students attending the morning program, but doing something else in the afternoon.

Results of step 3:

- Completed schedule for the week (in concept)
- Presentations/other materials
- Description of assignments
- Overview of supplies needed to perform the education.

Step 4: planning and designing moments of formative assessment

Step 3 and 4 are closely related. We think it's important to plan several moments during the week to check whether the offered content helps the student progress toward the intended goals. These moments are formative assessments. Do they comprehend what they have heard, seen, and experienced? Are they able to connect it correctly with other knowledge, etc.

A formative assessment gives the student feedback on their learning process. In a formative assessment, we don't measure the students results by giving them grades, but we create a moment of looking at the development of the student. The feedback the student receives gives him/her the possibility to learn. You can take the learning goals as a starting point and ask the question: how can the student measure if the learning goal is achieved? What form of assignment is suitable?

Several possibilities to apply during the module:

When students make assignments, it often becomes apparent whether they understand the content.

That is a way of formative assessment, giving students (short) assignments in which they can exercise the content and discover if they have mastered it. Fellow students and the teacher can provide the student with feedback on the process, progress, and result.

Another valuable activity is to start with an assessment to measure the starting point/starting knowledge, skills, and attitudes of the student. This can also be part of the preparation of a student. In that way, a student sees what he needs to learn concerning the knowledge, skills, and attitudes of the module.

And you can make a final assessment at the end of the week, an assignment in which the students connect all they have learned in one applied assignment. There are many ways to design a formative assessment, teacher of expert centered ways (expert feedback) and student centered (peer feedback).

Results of step 4:

- Moments of formative assessment are included in the schedule/format
- Short description of the different assessment assignment.

ELEMENTS AND STRUCTURE OF MODULES

At New Engineers, a module has always been the size of a calendar week. This is a size that allows for enough content to be covered and prevent experts from adding too much content to be effectively processed by our students. It is a time horizon that is manageable by students. When including the preparation time preceding the week and the application time succeeding the week, we have a building block of 5 to 7, 5 EC[12]. Each module is designed as a separate learning arch which can contain multiple arches again.

Each week contains a set of elements.

- Content/theme: during this part of the program students get theory, inspiration, information, insights, experiences, innovations, etc. You can divide all the content (knowledge, skills, attitude) of the module into small subject or themes.
- Assignment: to apply the theory students can work on different assignments. This can be short individual assignments or assignments they apply in groups. Take enough time in the schedule to execute and review the outcomes

---

[12] EC or ECTS stands for European Credit Transfer System. 1 EC is 28 hours of study.

- Sport: Sport is a fixed part of the program. It becomes more valuable if there is a link made between the subject of the module (or specific knowledge, skills, or attitude they work on) and the experience the students have when they perform sports. Can you connect the content of (parts of) the module with the sport? Fencing is the default sports activity. It can be replaced by a different sports activity that matches your design better
- Reflection and feedback: reflecting on the (learning) process is important to develop students' learning skills. At least 15% of the time is used for reflection. Students reflect themselves on what and how they have learned. Coach and student will have regular sessions, at least one per module. It's also very useful to have students give peer feedback to their fellow students about their development
- Free (learning) space: students get time to explore, experiment, learn, create, etc. individually or in small groups. They formulate their own assignment or goal based on their learning needs
- Assessment: to check whether the students understand the knowledge, skills, or attitudes, you can use different forms of formative assessment.[13] This can be a small test, an assignment, a presentation, etc. Summative assessments are not a part of a module, but relate to the three main learning arches. They are set by the coaches and cover multiple subject-matters with regard to skills, knowledge, and attitudes
- Maybe we've forgotten a puzzle part that is really suitable and important in your module, please feel free to add it to the format!

Summative assessments are done three times over a 1-year period. Each assessment relates to one of the three main learning arches of the curriculum. The assessment criteria are shared and discussed at the start. The format is semi-fixed. The key condition is that students demonstrate their learning. If they can do so using a different format that is acceptable, even commendable.

---

[13] A formative assessment is defined as follows: "An assessment functions formatively to the extent that evidence about student achievements is elicited, interpreted, and used by teachers, learners, or their peers to make decisions about the next steps in instruction that are likely to be better, or better founded, than the decisions they would have made in the absence of that evidence." Wiliam, *Embedded Formative Assessment*, 43.

REFLECTION ON NEW ENGINEERS FROM A LEAN EDUCATION PERSPECTIVE

The New Engineers way of Lean Education has proven energizing-for students, industry, and lecturers. It is challenging for all. In part, because the program is never the same. It is a puzzle for the coaches annex designers of the program to create a program that satisfies the needs of all participating students and keep them together as a group at the same time. Finding and engaging experts is both challenging and fun. It provides the designers the opportunity to engage with experts that provide the latest insights. On the other hand, the experts are not used to teaching and will need to be supported in designing their contribution. They have developed specific ways of working and teaching over the years which have made them successful, but are not necessarily a good fit with teaching over an extended period of time.

For the students, it is challenging as well. They are stretched beyond what they are used to. This is something they seek and like and at the same time struggle with. You cannot stretch without reaching your panic zone every now and then. Under pressure, they need to develop skills and attitudes that are often new to them. As they succeed, the feeling of achievement is great, which is one of the greatest drivers for later success: having struggled and ultimately succeeded.

Vincent Wiegel

Bibliography

Alp, Neslihan. "The Lean Transformation Model for the Education System." *International Conference of Computers and Industrial Engineering*, 2001, pp. 82–87. www.umoncton.ca/cie/conferences/29thconf/29thICCIE/Papers/paper006.PDF.

Anaya, Antonio R., Manuel Luque, and Manuel Peinado. "A Visual Recommender Tool in a Collaborative Learning Experience." *Expert Systems with Applications* 45 (2016): 248–259. doi:10.1016/j.eswa.2015.01.071.

Antony, Jiju, Netasha Krishan, Donna Cullen, and Maneesh Kumar. "Lean Six Sigma for Higher Education Institutions (HEIs): Challenges, Barriers, Success Factors, Tools/Techniques." *International Journal of Productivity and Performance Management* 61(8) (2012): 940–948. doi:10.1108/17410401211277165.

Balzer, William K. *Lean Higher Education: Increasing the Value and Performance of University Processes*. CRC Press, Boca Raton, FL, 2010.

Balzer, William K. "What Is Lean Higher Education? Presentation." *Lean Higher Education Seminar, ODHE Efficiency Advisory Committee Meeting*, 2016, 1–38.

Barroso, Ingrid P M, Sandra M F Santos, and Maria Antónia Carravilla. "Beyond Classroom Boundaries: How Higher Education Institutions Apply LEAN." *1st Braziliar Symposium on Services Science*, no. 1990 (2010).

Behringer, Reinhold. "Interoperability Standards for MicroLearning." *MicroLearning Conference 7.0* (2013): 10.

Bejlegaard, Mads, Thomas Ditlev Brunoe, and Kjeld Nielsen. "Application of Module Drivers Creating Modular Manufacturing Equipment Enabling Changeability." *Procedia CIRP* 52 (2016): 134–138. doi:10.1016/j.procir.2016.07.059.

Benassi, Victor A, Catherine E Overson, and Christopher M Hakala. "Applying Science of Learning in Education: Infusing Psychological Science into the Curriculum." *Annals of Anthropological Practice* 37(1) (2014): 303. doi:10.1111/napa.12013.

Bennett, Sue, Shirley Agostinho, and Lori Lockyer. "The Process of Designing for Learning: Understanding University Teachers' Design Work." *Educational Technology Research and Development* 65(1) (2017): 125–145. doi:10.1007/s11423-016-9469-y.

Bertholey, F, P Bourniquel, E Rivery, N Coudurier, and G Follea. "Work Organisation Improvement Methods Applied to Activities of Blood Transfusion Establishments (BTE): Lean Manufacturing, VSM, 5S." *Transfusion Clinique et Biologique: Journal de La Societe Francaise de Transfusion Sanguine* 16(2) (2009): 93–100. doi:10.1016/j.tracli.2009.04.007.

Bicheno, John, and Matthias Holweg. *The Lean Toolbox 5th Edition*. Picsie Books, Buckingham, UK, 2017.

Bitner, Mary Jo, Amy L. Ostrom, and Felicia N. Morgan. "Service Blueprinting: A Practical Technique for Service Innovation." *California Management Review* 50(3) (2008): 66–94. doi:10.2307/41166446.

Brooks, Michael, and Bob Holmes. "Equinox Blueprint," A report on the outcomes of the equinox summit: Learning 2030. Convened by the Waterloo global science initiative, Waterloo, Ontario, Canada, (2014).

Brynjolfsson, Erik, and Andrew McAfee. *Race Against the Machine: How the Digital Revolution Is Accelerating Innovation, Driving Productivity, and Irreversibly Transforming Employment and the Economy.* Digital Frontier Press, Lexington, UK, 2012.

Comm, Clare L., and Dennis F.X. Mathaisel. "Less Is More: A Framework for a Sustainable University." *International Journal of Sustainability in Higher Education* 4(4) (2003): 314–323. doi:10.1108/14676370310497543.

Comm, Clare L., and Dennis F.X. Mathaisel. "A Case Study in Applying Lean Sustainability Concepts to Universities." *International Journal of Sustainability in Higher Education* 6(2) (2005): 134–146. doi:10.1108/14676370510589855.

Conde, Miguel, and Ángel Hernández-García. "Learning Analytics: Expanding the Frontier." In *Proceedings of the 5th International Conference on Technological Ecosystems for Enhancing Multiculturality*, 36:1–36:5. TEEM 2017. ACM, New York, 2017. doi:10.1145/3144826.3145386.

Darrell M. West. "Future of Work." In *From The Future of Work: Robots, AI, and Automation*, 2018. doi:10.7864/j.ctt1vjqp2g.7.

Dochy, Filip, Mien Segers, Inneke Berghmans, and Anne-Ka Koenen. *Creating Impact Through Future Learning: The High Impact Learning That Lasts (HILL) Model.* Taylor & Francis Group, London, UK, 2018.

Duhigg, Charles. *The Power of Habit: Why We Do What We Do, and How to Change.* Random House, New York, 2012.

Emiliani, M. L. "Improving Business School Courses by Applying Lean Principles and Practices." *Quality Assurance in Education* 12(4) (2004): 175–187. doi:10.1108/09684880410561596.

Emiliani, M. L. "Special Issue: Lean Six Sigma for Higher Education Evolution in Lean Teaching," (2016): 1–17.

Erixon, Gunnar. Modular function deployment: A method for product modularisation. PhD. Thesis, KTH, Department of Manufacturing Systems, Stockholm, 1998.

Ertmer, Peggy A. "Teacher Pedagogical Beliefs: The Final Frontier in Our Quest for Technology Integration?" *Educational Technology Research and Development* 53(4) (2005): 25–39. doi:10.1007/BF02504683.

Evaluation, Using, and Improve Teaching. "Teachers for the 21st Century," 2013. doi:10.1787/9789264193864-en.

Evans, James R. *Quality and Performance Excellence: Management, Organization, and Strategy.* Thomson Business and Economics, Mason, OH, 2008.

Fink, Dr. L. Dee. "Creating Significant Learning Experiences (Review)." *Journal of College Student Development* 45(1) (2003): 105–106. doi:10.1353/csd.2004.0016.

Fisher, Ron, Kaoru Kobayashi, and Rod Gapp. "Implementing 5S within a Japanese Context: An Integrated Management System." *Management Decision*, 2008. doi:10.1108/00251740810865067.

Flumerfelt, Shannon, and Greg Green. "Using Lean in the Flipped Classroom for At-Risk Students." *Educational Technology and Society* 16(1) (2013): 356–366.

Francis, David E. "Lean and the Learning Organization in Higher Education." *Canadian Journal of Educational Administration and Policy* (157) (2014): 1–23.

Fullan, Michael. *Stratosphere: Integrating Technology, Pedagogy, and Change Knowledge.* Pearson Education, Don Mills, ON, 2013.

Fullan, Michael, and Katelyn Donnelly. "Alive in the Swamp: Assessing Digital Innovations in Education," Impact Plus - a white paper Collaborative Impact SPC, Seattle, Washington, 2013.

Fullan, Michael, and Geoff Scott. "Education Plus," 2014.

Goldberg, D E, M Somerville, and C Whitney. *A Whole New Engineer: The Coming Revolution in Engineering Education*. ThreeJoy Associates, Incorporated, Douglas, MI, 2014.

Goleman, Daniel. "Rethinking Mainstream Education," 2014, 31–35.

Goodyear, Peter. "Teaching as Design." *HERDSA Review of Higher Education* 2 (2015): 27–50.

Gray, Dave, S Brown, and J Macanufo. *Gamestorming: A Playbook for Innovators, Rulebreakers, and Changemakers*. O'Reilly Media, Newton, MA, 2010.

Gray, Dave, and Thomas Vander Wal. *The Connected Company*. Oreilly and Associate Series. O'Reilly Media, Incorporated, Sebastopol, CA, 2012.

Guerriero, Sonia. "Teachers' Pedagogical Knowledge and the Teaching Profession: Background Report and Project Objectives." *Better Policies for Better Lives*, 2013, 1–7. http://www.oecd.org/edu/ceri/Background_document_to_Symposium_ITEL-FINAL.pdf.

Hattie, John. *Visible Learning for Teachers: Maximizing Impact on Learning*. Taylor & Francis Group, Hoboken, NJ, 2012.

Heath, Chip, and Dan Heath. *Switch: How to Change Things When Change Is Hard*. Crown Publishing Group, New York, 2010.

Hendriks, Lotte, Rianne A. de Kleine, Theo G. Broekman, Gert-Jan Hendriks, and Agnes van Minnen. "Intensive Prolonged Exposure Therapy for Chronic PTSD Patients Following Multiple Trauma and Multiple Treatment Attempts." *European Journal of Psychotraumatology*, 2018. doi:10.1080/20008198.2018.1425574.

Hines, Peter, and Sarah Lethbridge. "New Development: Creating a Lean University." *Public Money and Management* 28(1) (2008): 53–56. doi:10.1111/j.1467-9302.2008.00619.x.

Hood, Nina, and Allison Littlejohn. "Knowledge Typologies for Professional Learning: Educators' (Re)Generation of Knowledge When Learning Open Educational Practice." *Educational Technology Research and Development* 65(6) (2017): 1583–1604. doi:10.1007/s11423-017-9536-z.

Illeris, Knud. *Contemporary Theories of Learning: Learning Theorists... In Their Own Words*. Taylor & Francis Group, New York, 2018.

Indicators, Oecd. *Education at a Glance 2018*, 2018. doi:10.1787/eag-2018-en.

Ito, Hiroshi. "Is a Rubric Worth the Time and Effort? Conditions for Its Success." *International Journal of Learning* 10(2) (2015): 32–45.

Langworthy, Maria, and Michael Fullan. *A Rich Seam: How New Pedagogies Find Deep Learning*. Paerson, 2014. doi:10.1016/j.jbmt.2011.01.017.

Lee, Eunbae, and Michael J. Hannafin. "A Design Framework for Enhancing Engagement in Student-Centered Learning: Own It, Learn It, and Share It." *Educational Technology Research and Development* 64(4) (2016): 707–734. doi:10.1007/s11423-015-9422-5.

Levin, Ben. *How to Change 5000 Schools: A Practical and Positive Approach for Leading Change at Every Level*. Harvard Education Press, Cambridge, MA, 2008.

Liker, Jeffrey K. *The Toyota Way: 14 Management Principles from the World's Greatest Manufacturer*. McGraw-Hill Education, New York, 2004.

Luckin, R, B Bligh, A Manches, C Crook, and R Noss. "Decoding Learning." *The Proof, Promise and Potential of Digital Education*, 2012.

Macfadyen, L. P., S. Dawson, A. Pardo, and D. Gasevic. "Embracing Big Data in Complex Educational Systems: The Learning Analytics Imperative and the Policy Challenge." *Research & Practice in Assessment* 9(2) (2014): 17–28. doi:10.1017/CBO9781107415324.004.

Macleod, Flora, and Michael Golby. "Theories of Learning and Pedagogy: Issues for Teacher Development." *Teacher Development* 7(3) (2003): 345–361. doi:10.1080/13664530300200204.

Maguad, Ben A. "Lean Strategies for Education: Overcoming the Waste Factor." *Education* (2007): 248–256.

Maharjan, Shyam K. "Implementing the 5S Methodology for the Graphic Communications Management Laboratory of University of Wisconsin-Stout." *American Psychological Association* 6th edition (2011): 1–52.

Mankins, Michael, Karen Harris, and David Harding. "Strategy in the Age of Superabundant Capital." *Harvard Business Review* (2017): 66–75.

Manning, Christopher D., and Prabhakar Raghavan. *An Introduction to Information Retrieval*. Edited by A Cannon-Bowers and E Salas. Cambridge University Press, issued 2009. doi:10.1109/LPT.2009.2020494.

Markovitz, Dan. "Information 5S." *Management Services* 56(1) (2012): 8–11.

Mayer-Schönberger, Viktor, and Kenneth. Cukier. *Lernen Mit Big Data: Die Zukunft Der Bildung*. REDLINE-Verl, München, Germany, 2014.

Mike Serena, Ed. D. "Progressive 5S: We' Re Not Talking Trash." *TBM LeanSigma*, 2010, 5. www.tbmcg.com.

MIT. "Institute-Wide Task Force on the Future of MIT Education Final Report." *Institute-Wide Task Force on the Future of MIT Education*, 2014. http://web.mit.edu/future-report/TaskForceFinal_July28.pdf.

Montgomery, Cynthia. *The Strategist: Be the Leader Your Business Needs*. Collins, London, UK, 2012.

OECD. Education at a Glance 2017: OECD Indicators. OECD Publisher, 2017. doi:10.1787/eag-2017-en.

Osterwalder, A, Y Pigneur, G Bernarda, A Smith, and T Papadakos. *Value Proposition Design: How to Create Products and Services Customers Want*. Strategyzer Series. Wiley, New York, 2015.

Ott, Claudia, Anthony Robins, Patricia Haden, and Kerry Shephard. "Illustrating Performance Indicators and Course Characteristics to Support Students' Self-Regulated Learning in CS1." *Computer Science Education* 25(2) (2015): 174–198. doi:10.1080/08993408.2015.1033129.

Partnership for 21st Century Learning. "P21 Partnership for 21st Century Learning." 2015, 9. http://www.p21.org/documents/P21_Framework_Definitions.pdf.

PISA (Programme for International Student Assessment). "Pisa 2015," 2015, 2015–2016.

Redecker, Christine, Miriam Leis, Matthijs Leendertse, Yves Punie, Govert Gijsbers, Paul Kirschner, Slavi Stoyanov, and Bert Hoogveld. *The Future of Learning: Preparing for Change-Publication*. Publications Office of the European Union, 2011. doi:10.2791/64117.

Resnick, Mitchel. *Lifelong Kindergarten: Cultivating Creativity Through Projects, Passion, Peers, and Play*. MIT Press, Cambridge, MA, 2017.

Richmond, Matthew. "The Hidden Half: School Employees Who Don't Teach." *Thomas B. Fordham Institute*, August, 2014. https://eric.ed.gov/?id=ED560006.

Riezebos, Jan. "Lean Schools." In *The Routledge Companion to Lean Management*. Edited by Daryl Powell and Torbjorn Netland, pp. 435–448. Routledge, New York, 2017.

Rizvi, Saad (IPPR), Katelyn (IPPR) Donnelly, and Michael (IPPR) Barber. "An Avalanche Is Coming," 2013. https://www.ippr.org/files/images/media/files/publication/2013/04/avalanche-is-coming_Mar2013_10432.pdf.

Robert Bodily, Charles Graham, Michael Bush. "Online Learner Engagement: Opportunities and Challenges with Using Data Analytics." *Educational Technology* 57(1) (2017): 10–18. http://www.jstor.org/stable/44430535.

Robinson, Mark, and Steve Yorkstone. "Becoming a Lean University: The Case of the University of St Andrews." *Leadership and Governance in Higher Education* 1 (2014): 42–71.

Rother, Mike. *Toyota Kata: Managing People for Improvement, Adaptiveness and Superior Results*. McGraw-Hill Education, New York, 2009.

Ruijters, Manon. *Liefde Voor Leren: Over Diversiteit van Leren En Ontwikkelen in En van Organisaties*. Vakmedianet, Deventer, the Netherlands 2006.

Scheer, Andrea, and Hasso Plattner. "Transforming Constructivist Learning Into Action," 2011, 8–19.

Shook, John. Managing to Learn: Using the A3 Management Process to Solve Problems, Gain Agreement, Mentor and Lead. Lean Enterprise Institute Series. Lean Enterprise Institute, 2008. https://books.google.nl/books?id=0BbxadIjK6sC.

Spector, Jonathan Michael. "Reflections on Educational Technology Research and Development." *Educational Technology Research and Development* 65(6) (2017): 1415–1423. doi:10.1007/s11423-017-9545-y.

Sullivan, H J, A R Igoe, J D Klein, E E Jones, and W C Savanye. "15–Perspectives on the Future of Educational Technology." *Educational Technology Research and Development* 41(2) (1993): 97–110.

Susskind, Richard, and Daniel Susskind. *The Future of the Professions: How Technology Will Transform the Work of Human Experts*. OUP Oxford, Oxford, UK, 2015.

Tondeur, Jo, Johan van Braak, Peggy A. Ertmer, and Anne Ottenbreit-Leftwich. "Understanding the Relationship between Teachers' Pedagogical Beliefs and Technology Use in Education: A Systematic Review of Qualitative Evidence." *Educational Technology Research and Development* 65(3) (2017): 555–575. doi:10.1007/s11423-016-9481-2.

Wiegel, Vincent, and Lejla Brouwer-Hadzialic. "Lean Education." In *The Routledge Companion to Lean Management*. Edited by T H Netland and D J Powell, pp. 422–434. Routledge Companions in Business, Management and Accounting. Routledge, New York, 2017.

Wiegel, Vincent, and L. Brouwer Hadzialic. "Lessons from Higher Education: Adapting Lean Six Sigma to Account for Structural Differences in Application Domains." *International Journal of Six Sigma and Competitive Advantage* 9(1) (2015): 72. doi:10.1504/IJSSCA.2015.070104.

Wiegel, Vincent, and John Maes. *Succesvol Lean*. Pearson, Amsterdam, the Netherlands, 2013.

Wiliam, Dylan. *Embedded Formative Assessment*. Solution Tree Press, Bloomington, IN, 2011.

Windeløv-Lidzélius, C, and K Bauning. *The Kaospilots 20/20*. KaosPilots, Aarhus, 2011.

Winick, Erin. "Lawyer-Bots Are Shaking Up Jobs." *MIT Technology Review* 12 (2017). https://www.technologyreview.com/s/609556/lawyer-bots-are-shaking-up-jobs/.

Womack, Jim, and Dan Jones. *Lean Solutions: How Companies and Customers Can Create Value and Wealth Together*. Free Press, New York, 2015.

World Bank. "Learning To Realize Education's Promise." *World Development Report* 26, 2018. doi:10.1016/S0305-750X(98)90001-8.

Yorkstone, Steve. "Lean Universities." In *The Routledge Companion to Lean Management2*. Edited by Daryl Powell and Torbjorn Netland, pp. 449–462. Routledge, New York, 2017.

Ziskovsky, Betty. "Applying Lean Thinking To Improve K-12 Education In The Classroom," Lean Education Enterprises, Inc., 2012.

Index